CHILDREN, ETHICS, AND THE LAW

Children, Ethics, & the Law

Professional Issues and Cases

•

GERALD P. KOOCHER

&

PATRICIA C. KEITH-SPIEGEL

University of Nebraska Press

Lincoln & London

Copyright © 1990 by the University of Nebraska Press

All rights reserved

Manufactured in the United States of America

The paper in this book meets the minimum requirements of
American National Standard for Information Sciences –
Permanence of Paper for Printed Library Materials,
ANSI Z39.48-1984.

Library of Congress Cataloging-in-Publication Data

Koocher, Gerald P.

Children, ethics, and the law: professional issues and cases

Gerald P. Koocher and Patricia C. Keith-Spiegel.

p. cm. – (Children and the law)

ISBN 0-8032-4731-1 (alk. paper)

1. Child mental health services – Moral and ethical aspects.

2. Child psychotherapy – Moral

and ethical aspects.

3. Children – Counseling of – Moral

and ethical aspects.

4. Mentally ill children – Legal status, laws, etc.

I. Keith-Spiegel, Patricia.

II. Title. III. Series.

RJ499.K64 1990

174'.2 – dc20

89-78514

CIP

We dedicate this volume to our children,
Abby Greenwald Koocher and Gary Brian Spiegel

Contents

Preface

The intended readership of this volume is the full range of behavioral scientists, mental health professionals, and students aspiring to such roles who work with children. This includes psychologists (applied, clinical, counseling, developmental, school, including academics, researchers, and practitioners), family counselors, psychiatrists, social workers, psychiatric nurses, child protection workers, and any other mental health professionals who work with children, adolescents, and their families.

Working with children is both rewarding and demanding. The work is fraught with more acceptance of responsibility, confusions, intrusions, and potential ambiguity among the various players in the system than is working with any other clinical population. Although it is unfortunate, it is perhaps no wonder that many mental health professionals attempt to avoid working with children altogether, often citing concern about potential legal and ethical dilemmas. It is not that such professionals dislike or are unsympathetic toward children. Rather, they are concerned about what people who are legally defined as minors bring along, and not usually by their own choice, into a professional relationship.

Those who work with children cannot always count on dealing with loving and cooperative parents who will make appropriate sacrifices for their children or give mental health professionals appropriate latitude to do their work according to their own best judgment. Professionals cannot rely on local, state, or federal laws and policies related to children to say what they mean in easily interpretable language or never to contradict or preempt one another. Nor can we assume that community agencies and the courts will provide prompt, highly competent, compassionate, and well-orchestrated services. We cannot even rely on our own professional associations to have ethics codes or other information that delivers clear guidance as to how a member of the profession should proceed in a given circumstance related to children. All these factors combine with continuing disagreements about the meaning and desirability of increasing children's rights to self-determination. Although there is a growing recognition of the autonomy of children and respect for their input to matters affecting them, there remains a general lack of consensus as to when and how children's input should be considered, even in *everyday* matters.

Despite the risks and uncertainties that surround professional work with children, the need for such professionals is greater than ever before. Demand for such services is increasing, even as the number of individuals in training as child specialists declines.

This book introduces the reader to a variety of ethical and legal dilemmas that may arise for mental health professionals in the course of their everyday work with children, adolescents, and their families. Although we are not always able to offer a definitive action that can be successfully applied in every similar instance, we aspire to give sound general advice, to aid the reader in identifying the key factors to take into account, and to help with the formulation of decision-making strategies. We have attempted to cover a broad spectrum of professional functions and work-setting contexts such as counseling in the schools, psychotherapy in private practice, research in the university laboratory, and serving as an expert witness in court. We have also attempted to cover a wide range of ethical-legal dilemmas reflecting the peculiar twists that unavoidably occur when children are involved. These include special considerations related to confidentiality and record keeping, consent to treatment and research, and psychological assessment of children. It was, of course, impossible to cover every conceivable topic in a single volume, so no inference about the lesser importance of uncovered materials should be made.

We make frequent use of case vignettes to illustrate the ethical and legal dilemmas under discussion. Many of these incidents are based on ethics files of professional associations or public domain sources, usually litigated cases. Our own consultation experiences provide another major source of case material. In instances in which the sources are confidential, we have used a variety of techniques to disguise the incident and the identity of the actual people involved. We are also grateful to our students and to the large number of colleagues (whose names follow) who contributed ethical dilemmas or problems to us via the ethics casebook project of the Section of Clinical Child Psychology (of the American Psychological Association's Division of Clinical Psychology): Kristi Alexander, Russell Bauer, Frank H. Boring, Emily Bronfman, Debra Carmichael, Robert Cornnoyer, Sheila M. Eyberg, Edward D. Farber, Eileen Fennell, Peter Goldenthal, Jacqueline Goldman, Nancy Grace, Linda J. Gudas, David Hayes, Kenneth D. Herman, William F. Hodges, Jane Irion, Grace R. Kalfus, Sophie L. Lovinger, Ramasamy Manikam, S. J. McKenzie, D. Louise Mebane, Michael D. Miller, Linda L. Reed, Audrey Ricker, Elizabeth C. Rickitt, Lois J. Rifner, Michael C. Roberts, Gloria M. Roque, Lanning S. Schiller, Audrey Sistler, F. Beth Stone, Elaine Sweeney, R.S.M., June M. Tuma, Margaret Witecki, Deborah Young-Hyman, and Virginia Youngren.

The routine methods of designating the principals in disguised case materials (e.g., "Dr. B." or "the child") were avoided in favor of contrived names. We have found this technique useful in teaching and improving the readability of the text. We do not in any way intend to trivialize the importance of the issues at hand, yet we also wanted to assure that the names of our characters were unlikely to correspond to the names of real people. Any similarities that remain, despite our efforts, are purely coincidental and in no instance resemble the actual names of the principals. The exception to this rule is that when citing public domain cases we use the real names of the parties and cite the relevant case law or public source. As a convenience to readers, we have also included a glossary of important cases described in this volume.

Finally, we wish to extend our special thanks to our colleagues Gary B. Melton, Michael C. Roberts, and Dee Shepard for their thoughtful review of the manuscript and detailed suggestions for improving it. The manuscript is significantly improved as a result of their efforts.

CHAPTER ONE

•

Introduction and
Basic Concepts

THE LAW VERSUS ETHICS: RAMBO MEETS BAMBI

Most moviegoers will have little difficulty grasping the contrasts between
Rambo and Bambi. This cinematic analogy provides a context for quickly
absorbing some of the important differences between legal and ethical
standards as applied to psychological interventions with children and
families. These differences chiefly include the origins, purposes, and
manner of enforcement of the standards. Before addressing these in
detail, the reader without much legal background will need some con-
textual information.

Legal standards addressed to family issues often originate in common
law, which has its roots in legal traditions inherited from America's early
European ancestry. *Common law* generally refers to legal principles that
derive from sources other than formal legislative enactment. The second
cluster of legal standards most commonly encountered by mental health
professionals are statutory law and case law. *Statutes* are those laws

enacted by legislative bodies at the local, state, or federal level, and *case law* refers to precedent-setting decisions handed down by courts. Finally, one occasionally encounters *administrative laws* that bear on family functioning. These are often termed *regulations* and originate in the executive branch of government, as opposed to legislative or judicial branches, and usually deal with policy implementation (e.g., rules governing the treatment of participants in research using federal funds or rules governing the administration of the social security benefits system). Federal regulations are published in the *Federal Register*, and state regulations are usually available through the offices of the various secretaries of state.

Ethical codes generally refer to basic philosophical notions and professional norms about the morality of human conduct (Weithorn & McCabe, 1987). Such codes are often promulgated by professional organizations (e.g., the American Psychological Association [APA], the American Psychiatric Association, and the Society for Research in Child Development [SRCD]). In addition, groups charged with policy-making (e.g., the President's Commission for the Study of Ethical Problems in Medicine and Biomedical and Behavioral Research) also occasionally undertake explication of ethical guidelines. Beauchamp and Childress (1983) have underscored key principles that guide codes of ethics. These principles include *autonomy* (i.e., respect for the right of self-determination), *beneficence* (i.e., the obligation of members of the profession to help others), *confidentiality* (i.e., preventing disclosure of information received in the context of a professional relationship), *fidelity* (i.e., keeping one's promises), *justice* (i.e., offering fair and equal treatment to all), *nonmaleficence* (i.e., the obligation to "do no harm"), *privacy* (i.e., respecting people's personal decisions about when and what information to provide about themselves), and *veracity* (i.e., truthfulness).

The value of professional associations' ethics codes as applied to everyday practice is limited. Except for the code of the SRCD, which is focused on children, professional association ethics codes say little or nothing about children. In addition, the SRCD ethics code is now so outdated that parts of it actually conflict with some federal regulations on the protection of children in research projects. Many groups with ethics codes, including the SRCD, have no monitoring or enforcement capability (e.g., ethics committees with investigatory and disciplinary authority). In these instances, the ethics codes are essentially educational and consciousness-raising documents for the members of the organization or statements for public relations purposes. Thus, some ethics codes ignore the special interests and needs of children, and others are totally toothless. Most professional groups with a focus on children have no written ethics code at all.

Although morals and laws often have the same goals and suggest similar underlying social values, the vigor with which they are enforced and the adequacy of the protection that they afford society are highly variable. Despite its failings, the government has, through the legal system, a complex array of personnel and procedures available to enforce laws (e.g., Rambo, the well-armed enforcer) by comparison with the more limited and relatively toothless resources available to those who attempt to enforce professional ethical codes (e.g., Bambi, being guided chiefly by conscience or fear of embarrassment). Although ethical codes may well be enforced on members of professional organizations, the ultimate sanction available is generally limited to expulsion from the group. This is not an entirely benign sanction since it may include dissemination of the "guilty" finding to licensing boards and members of professional associations (Keith-Spiegel & Koocher, 1985). In addition, such findings can lead to termination of professional liability (i.e., malpractice) insurance coverage.

Clouser (1973) noted that, despite the apparent overlap, morality is external to law and that laws frequently deal with matters that are not moral concerns at all. Likewise, many matters of morality or ethics cannot be sanctioned by law because of inconvenience or the impossibility of enforcement. Frequently, a lack of congruence exists between what is legal and what is considered ethical in terms of professional standards. For example, a psychologist who is convicted of shoplifting has broken the law but may still be an ethical practitioner of her or his profession. Likewise, a practitioner may behave in ways that are unethical or potentially harmful to clients while at the same time violating no actual statutes. The following case is illustrative:

CASE 1-1: It is not unusual for Brian Brash, Ph.D., to invite discussions of specific problems on his radio call-in show, "The Children's Hour with Dr. Brian Brash, Child Psychologist." A parent called in and described her 8-year-old child's behavior, which included temper tantrums, argumentativeness, constant challenges to parental authority, and refusal to respond to requests that he clean up his room. In response, Dr. Brash stated that a diagnosis of "oppositional disorder of childhood" seemed likely.

In this case, no law is violated, although the APA ethics code (American Psychological Association, 1981, principle 4k) admonishes psychologists to refrain from offering a diagnosis in a context other than a traditional professional relationship.

When working with children in clinical, institutional, or research settings, the distinctions between legal and ethical obligations become even more complex. Society's laws are generally framed with adults in mind. As such, the law often treats children as "exceptions to the rule," which may be either beneficial or insidious, depending on the precise context. The purpose of this volume is to highlight and discuss the special ethical and legal considerations required when studying children and their families or when delivering psychological services to them. To use the analogy with which we began this chapter, this volume is generally focused on educating Bambi rather than on calling in Rambo.

LEGAL BACKGROUND
Historical Considerations

Children have long been treated by the courts as valuable property of their parents. In many societies, children have represented a means of establishing a labor force or providing parental support during old age. In our own legal system, parents have been held to possess a "right of control" over their children (see *Meyer v. Nebraska*, 1923; *Pierce v. Society of Sisters*, 1925; brief summaries of these and other important cases cited in this volume appear in the case glossary). Although parents' rights of control over their children are limited by a prohibition against making "martyrs of their children" (*Prince v. Massachusetts*, 1944, p. 170), this restriction was advanced, not because of an enlightened view of children's rights, but rather as an assertion of society's interest in the socialization of children. It was actually not clear until the mid-1960s that children were deemed "persons" within the meaning of the Fourteenth Amendment, which applies the Bill of Rights to all the states.

Under common law, children up to the age of seven were considered *doli incapax* (i.e., the defense of infancy) and therefore could not be held responsible for their actions. Older children under the age of majority were also considered incompetent unless the state could prove them *doli capax* (Melton, 1983a, 1983b). Although one can easily question the validity of this doctrine and the age levels used, such questions were irrelevant until the Supreme Court's decision in the case *In re Gault* (1967). Prior to that decision, juvenile courts were deemed to be acting in the best interests of the children before them under the doctrine of *parens patriae* (i.e., the principle of the state performing parental functions for those deemed incompetent under law). In the *Gault* decision, the Supreme Court concluded that "neither the Fourteenth Amendment nor the Bill of Rights is for adults alone" (p. 28).

This decision and others that followed, combined with the increasing recognition of the prevalence of social problems such as child neglect and abuse, runaway youths, and changing child custody practices, contribute to an increasing involvement of children in the legal system. Similarly, the involvement and roles of mental health professionals who work with children have changed. We are increasingly called on to advise or testify on such matters and in so doing expose ourselves to new duties and responsibilities with special obligations for which we may not be fully prepared.

CHILDREN'S ABILITY TO MAKE
COMPETENT DECISIONS

Much of this volume will revolve around questions of decision making by and for children. The ability of children to make well-informed decisions about their lives and their exercise of that ability, directly or through proxies, is a core issue that cuts across many ethical problems. The law, society, and many mental health professionals generally presume that children are not able to make major life decisions on their own. This presumption is often correct, and the rules that exist to deny children independent decision-making authority generally serve to protect them in the long run. At the same time, the relative dependency, vulnerability, and immaturity of children often interact with complex family roles to create complicated conflicts of interest. By the nature of their work, human service professionals frequently encounter such conflicts in work with families, and ethical dilemmas often result.

Assessment of specific competency (in the case of children) or incompetency (in the case of adults) revolves around four basic elements (Leikin, 1983; Weithorn, 1983b; Weithorn & Campbell, 1982). These include (1) the person's ability to understand information that is offered about the nature and potential consequences of the decision to be made, (2) the ability to manifest a decision, (3) the manner in which the decision is made, and (4) the nature of the resulting decision.

These elements involve psychological aspects of comprehension, assertiveness and autonomy, rational reasoning, anticipation of future events, and judgments in the face of uncertainty or contingencies. In the following pages, relevant developmental trends will be discussed in relation to these basic elements of competency. The points discussed here represent an overview of the various approaches to determining competence. The matter of whether any single circumstance represents a valid exercise of competence is obviously linked closely to context and subjective interpretation.

There are five key elements in fully informed decision making: information, understanding, competency, voluntariness, and decision-making ability (i.e., reasoning). In this context, *information* refers to access to all data that might reasonably be expected to influence a person's willingness to participate. Information includes only what is offered or made available to the person. *Competency* includes the capacity to *understand*, the ability to weigh potential outcomes, and also the foresight to anticipate the future consequences of the decision. *Voluntariness* is the freedom to choose to participate or to refuse. *Decision-making ability* refers to the ability to render a reasoned choice and express it clearly (Lidz et al., 1984).

6

Although the concepts of competency and informed consent are different, it is clear that there are many overlapping elements between them. Competency is a prerequisite for informed consent. An offer to provide a person with informed consent is simply not meaningful unless the individual in question is fully competent to make use of it. Across the developmental trajectory between infancy and adulthood, there are many aspects of human development that act to inhibit or enhance competency and the ability to give consent.

HOW ARE CHILDREN SPECIAL IN THIS REGARD?
Socialization

It is no secret that we begin life as egocentric beings, largely unaware of our own capabilities and without verbally based interpersonal relationships. We progress through developmental stages that involve a focus on interaction in the family, in the peer group, and ultimately in society as a whole. Along the way, we are "socialized" or taught about various interpersonal and societal roles by our parents and social institutions (chiefly our schools). As children, we are taught to do what older and bigger people (i.e., authority figures) tell us.

There is a substantial body of data to suggest that, even after children become capable of understanding that they have certain rights or societal entitlements, their exercise or assertion of those rights is often a function of their social ecology (Melton, Koocher, & Saks, 1983). Many children regard their rights literally, as those entitlements that adults permit them to exercise (Melton, 1980, 1983c). Although a parent may say to a child, "Please pick up your toys," children as young as 3 are well aware that adverse consequences will follow a failure to respond. Adults' interactions with children are often framed as requests, yet children are seldom fooled into thinking that they have a real option to decline.

The "terrible twos" and the "rebellious adolescent years" are well-known societal concepts that present the adult perspective that it is difficult to deal with children who challenge or question authority. The point to be made here is that the process of socialization presents considerable pressure for children to conform to or acquiesce in adults' wishes.

As a result of these pressures, it is quite likely that offers to exercise various rights will not be recognized or acted on by many children. Likewise, oppositional responses may sometimes occur more as a function of developmental stage than reasoned choice.

Time Perspective

"Do you want a little candy bar today or a big one next week?" To the young child for whom next week may seem a decade away, immediate gratification is the obvious choice. Psychologists have conducted a considerable amount of research investigating children's time perspective, including a now classic body of social learning theory (Mischel, 1971). The ability to go beyond the present and conceptualize the future, including hypothetical or potential outcomes, is closely linked to stages of cognitive development. We must be mindful of this when asking children to participate in decisions or to give consent involving long-term consequences of future outcomes.

Time perspective becomes critically important whenever a decision involves being able to weigh its short- versus long-term consequences. It is also an important consideration when developmental level predisposes children to choose immediate gratification while ignoring or failing to weigh their longer-term best interests. The effect of developmental level has been especially well documented as an issue in health-related decision making, with respect to both pregnancy decisions (C. C. Lewis, 1981) and more general health attitudes (Jessor, 1984; Roberts, Maddux, & Wright, 1984). The classic paradigm, of course, is the adult patient facing major surgery who says, "Well Doc, what are the odds?" The ability to weigh probabilities and to make some kind of long-term cost-benefit analysis is crucial to an informed decision.

Concept Manipulation

The ability to manipulate concepts using a developmental model of consent has been well described in a previous volume (Melton et al., 1983) as well as in many subsequent studies (e.g., Belter & Grisso,

1984). Considering the Piagetian model in simplistic form, for example, one can examine the basic reasoning shifts that occur between preoperational, concrete-operational, and formal-operational stages (Phillips, 1975).

In the preoperational stage, children are limited to their own experiences as a primary data base for decision making. Fantasy and magical thinking are also very powerful at this stage and may carry equal weight with more valid or reality-based data in a child's reasoning. While children at this stage are very interested in their environment and interpersonal relations, their perspective is self-centered. They understand others' behavior and their own experiences chiefly in terms of how these affect them personally. When they ask questions or observe events happening to others, preoperational children interpret the events chiefly via projection and identification.

During the concrete-operational stage, the child for the first time becomes capable of truly taking the perspective of another person and using that data in decision making. While observational learning and asking questions are obvious in much younger children, the concrete-operational child is able to integrate and reason with these data in a more logical and effective manner than was possible at an earlier developmental level. In addition, this is the stage at which children first become able to explore their motivation from the standpoint of another person (Phillips, 1975).

With the arrival of formal operations, the child becomes able to use hypothetical reasoning. For the first time, the way things are now is recognized as a subset of the way things might be. Cause-and-effect reasoning becomes generalized in a manner that permits the child to extrapolate and theorize about future events and outcomes. Likewise, the ability to understand contingencies and consider probabilities (e.g., "There is a 50% chance that you will get well without treatment") will generally require cognitive talents that do not arrive prior to formal-operational thought. Such thinking is obviously critical if a child is to make a decision regarding his or her long-term best interests.

Consent, Permission, and Assent

Among those writing on the interaction of developmental stages with competence to consent, a clear distinction is often made among the terms *consent, permission,* and *assent.* To give consent, a person should be able to understand the facts and consequences relative to a decision and manifest that decision voluntarily. We usually like to see the adjective *informed* precede *consent,* implying that all the data needed to reach a reasoned decision have been offered in a manner that can and has been understood. Often the person must meet a legal age requirement, typically age 18, in order for the decision to be considered valid or binding.

More and more often, consent is being defined as a decision that one can make only for oneself. Thus, the term *proxy consent* is decreasingly used in favor of the term *permission.* Parents are usually those from whom permission *must* be sought as both a legal and an ethical requirement prior to intervening in the lives of their minor children. Assent, a relatively new concept in this context, recognizes that minors may not, as a function of their developmental level, be capable of giving fully reasoned consent but may still be capable of reaching and expressing a preference. Assent recognizes the involvement of the child in the decision-making process while also indicating that the child's level of participation is less than fully competent.

Granting assent power is essentially the same as providing a veto power. What can be done to respect the rights of a child or some other "incompetent" when the consequences of a poorly exercised veto could be disastrous to the individual in question? This is often the case when some high-risk medical procedure offers the only hope of long-term survival or when the person in question is preverbal, mute on the matter, or comatose. In such situations, a substitute or proxy is needed.

The degree to which children ought to be permitted to make binding decisions on matters involving their own welfare is a matter of much controversy (Wadlington, 1983). The point of this volume is not to argue a position so much as to clarify the issues with respect to the psychological capacities of children to make such decisions and the ethical obligations of professionals who work with them. Although the law has seldom been guided by psychological principles, a growing body of psychological studies is shedding new light on how children's decision-making capacities, as a function of development, interact with legal concepts. Mental health professionals are increasingly being asked to come into court as experts with respect to children's needs and capacities. With this expanded visibility comes added risk. Those who do come forward as experts are more likely to be held accountable for their professional behavior. Unfortunately, ethical guidelines that apply particularly to work with children and families are all too rare.

Use of the term *competence* as a legal concept in this chapter is no accident. In many ways, the concept of competence provides a paradigm for the manner in which the legal system deals with children. Adults are presumed competent, and children (i.e., minors) are presumed incompetent in virtually all legal contexts. Although children may be "heard" on behalf of themselves or may be treated as adults in a variety of special circumstances, these situations are generally preceded by a qualifying process. Some examples of statutory and common law exemptions are discussed below. At times, the basic elements of the process may be quite specific under statute, as in the matter of whether a juvenile defendant is to be tried as an adult. On most occasions, however, the process by which a minor is deemed competent for any given purpose is open to determination by the broadest judgment of the court. The process of determination of competence and the reasoning applied vary widely as a function of both the case context and the willingness of the court to consider psychological input. In at least one context (i.e, decisions about admitting a minor to a psychiatric facility for inpatient treatment), the Supreme Court gave approval to considering a mental health professional as an administrative or "neutral fact finder" who acts in place of a judicial one (*Parham v. J.R.*, 1979).

Competence to consent is generally categorized as either *de facto* or *de jure* in nature. *De jure* competence is competence under law, *de facto* competence the actual or practical capacities of the individual to render a competent decision (or cooperate competently in some ongoing process such as a trial). In most jurisdictions, people over the age of 18 years are presumed to be competent unless proved otherwise before a court. When a determination of incompetence is made under law for adults, it is usually quite precise. That is to say, under law a person's competence is conceptualized as a specific functional ability. In legal parlance, the noun *competence* is usually followed by the preposition *to* rather than presented as a general attribute of the person. An adult who is deemed incompetent to stand trial for a particular offense is still presumed competent to function as a custodial parent or manage his or her financial affairs. For the adult, incompetence must be proved on a case-by-case basis.

Conversely, a minor child is presumed incompetent for most purposes without any concern for whether he or she has the capacity to make the requisite decision in a practical sense. Children who are deemed legally competent for one purpose are likewise still considered generally incompetent in other decision-making contexts. For example, juvenile offenders who have been transferred to adult court for trial and found competent to stand trial are still considered generally incompetent to consent to their own medical treatment or enter into legal contracts.

One class of exceptions to the presumption of incompetence is children who have been specially designated by the courts as "emancipated" or "mature minors" under specific state statutes. Although specific statutes vary widely across jurisdictions, this category would generally include minors who have married or enlisted in the military (presumably with valid parental permission) or who are financially independent and living apart from their parents. If the minor in question is not legally married or military personnel, the status of "emancipation" or "maturity" must generally be conferred by a court hearing. The usual criteria for such court decisions involve whether such minors are financially and by residence independent of their parents. The cognitive or reasoning abilities of the minors need not routinely be addressed in such hearings. Such minors are not granted all the rights of majority (e.g., the right to vote or purchase alcoholic beverages) but can enter into contracts and consent to medical care.

Another context in which minors may be deemed competent to consent involves certain types of medical treatments. These generally include special medical conditions where the individual right to privacy of the minor and/or the public interest is best served by permitting the person to consent directly. These situations are discussed in chapter 4, but they commonly include contraception, venereal disease, abortion, drug and alcohol problems, and, in at least a few jurisdictions, mental health treatment.

PROXY DECISION MAKING

Since the law generally regards children as incompetent per se, who is to speak for them? When a decision is to be made on their behalf, it is usually exercised by a parent, guardian, or some other responsible party acting *in loco parentis* (i.e., meaning "in place of the parents"). The general assumption is that the adult is providing a kind of proxy consent acting in the child's best interests or exercising *substituted judgment*. In this model, the adult is supposed to "stand in the shoes of the child" and make the decision that the child would be expected to make were he or she competent.

Are Parents Always the Best Decision Makers?

The concept of substituted judgment presumes a great deal. Most notably, it assumes that the persons making the decision are willing and able to act in this capacity in the child's best interests (i.e., without a conflict of interests). Even within the loving, intact, two-parent family, not all parental decisions regarding the children are without conflicts of interest (Koocher, 1983; Melton, 1982, 1983c). Although parents often subordinate their needs and preferences to the best interests of their children (or to what they believe are their children's best interests), they do not always do so.

The courts have traditionally respected the sanctity of the family unit and are quite reluctant to become involved without clear evidence of abuse, neglect,, or some similar dramatic turn of events. In the vast majority of situations, such deference to parents is appropriate. Unfortunately, however, the threshold for intervention is often set beyond the level at which psychological problems are precipitated. That is to say, errors or decisions that are not in the child's best interests often do not come to the attention of the law or reach a level at which legal intervention is possible despite the fact that psychological harm may be occurring.

13

CASE 1-2: Harry Skin became increasingly distressed when Harry Jr., age 15, was late returning home on several successive summer evenings. He told Harry Jr. to consider himself "grounded for 6 months!" When Harry Jr. snuck out despite the grounding order, his father dragged him to the barber and ordered his head shaved bald. The father noted, "Now he'll be too embarrassed to go out until his hair grows back!"

CASE 1-3: Mary Bergamasco was distressed when her 6-year-old son showed a sudden spurt of lying and petty stealing. In order to teach him a lesson, she tied him to a chair in front of their house, painted his face blue, put a makeshift pig snout on his nose, and hung a sign around his neck that read, "I am a pig." Photos of the child with tears streaming down his face appeared in the national media, and the local child protection agency placed the boy in emergency foster care. Both criminal charges and civil custody actions were initiated by the state against the mother.

Both Mr. Skin and Ms. Bergamasco came up with plans that they expected would embarrass their children into behaving differently. In both cases, the children were placed under great social pressure and stigmatized. Although far less drastic plans of action would have had a good chance of success, both of these parents had their own ideas. In some states, their actions might be deemed to constitute emotional abuse of the children, although in other states the use of such techniques would be considered their right as parents despite the potential lasting emotional consequences for their children. Ms. Bergamasco was able to obtain the services of Melvin Belli, the renowned San Francisco trial attorney. In a nationally televised broadcast (ABC *Nightline*, August 29, 1988), Ms. Bergamasco reported using the strategy because it had worked when done to her as a child. In the same broadcast, Attorney Belli described her as a caring mother who was being singled out for prosecution because of media sensationalism. He also recounted an episode from his own childhood in which he had been emotionally abused by a governess who locked him in a room with a coffin to "teach him a lesson." As both of these incidents illustrate, emotional abuse of children may lead to emotional abuse of the children's children.

In some cases, courts have recognized parental conflicts of interest and have ruled that the child's rights are to be held paramount when parents' and children's rights conflict (see *Doe v. Doe*, 1979; *In re Pernishek*, 1979; *Matter of Male R.*, 1979). In other cases involving substantive conflicts, courts have been willing to terminate parental rights (see *In re C.M.S.*, 1979; *Jewish Child Care Association v. Elaine S.Y.*, 1979; *Nebraska v. Wedige*, 1980). Such cases, however, are generally extreme exceptions. Recent Supreme Court decisions have belied a rather naive "parents know best" attitude (Rothman & Rothman, 1980).

As an example of psychosocial factors in termination of parental rights, consider the case of Tamela Pernishek (*In re Pernishek*, 1979):

CASE 1-4: Tamela, age 9, was diagnosed as a "psychosocial dwarf." She was approximately half the normal size for a child of her age. Her growth rate improved dramatically whenever she was placed outside her natural home. Each time she was placed in a stressful situation, her growth rate dropped. Because not much is known about the syndrome and because the ability of children to catch up in growth declines after age 10, the court ordered placement of Tamela out of the home.

In this particular case, a Pennsylvania court focused entirely on the best interests of the child with almost no description of the home situation and acted with unusual speed. The situation was ordered reviewed every 3 months, with the intent that Tamela would be returned home should placement in the Home for Crippled Children fail to prove effective. As is evident in this case, however, the circumstances must be unusual or dramatic to provoke such action.

COMPETENCE AND CONFLICTS OF INTEREST

Many of the case examples cited in this volume will raise issues about a child's competence to make a decision and potential conflicts of interest among a variety of parties, including the child, parents, researchers, and mental health professionals. Detailed case examples and discussions of these issues occur under a variety of category headings throughout the book, but it seems appropriate to introduce some here in order to illustrate these concepts:

CASE 1-5: The mother of 6-year-old Pete arrives at a child guidance clinic. She reports that he is making home life unbearable for her and her spouse. Among the complaints are Pete's constant "talking back," his disagreeableness at the dinner table, his penchant for making animal noises and "other crude sounds," his lack of cooperation when asked to help out around the house, and his general "argumentative nature." Further questioning reveals that the parents' expectations are that children "should be seen and not heard." The mother's notion of a normal and healthy young child is one who is always polite and well mannered, obedient, and cooperative in maintaining a "quiet and peaceful" household. She has read a bit about behavior modification and requests that a program be developed to "reshape" Pete into a "normal child."

CASE 1-6: Eleven-year-old Susie is brought to therapy by her exasperated parents, who claim that she is so disruptive and uncooperative at home that they are "at their wit's end." Susie makes it clear that she does not want to "be shrunk" and vigorously protests attempts to sway her to a more cooperative attitude. The parents urge the therapist to give it a try anyway, and they accompany Susie to every session, waiting for her in the reception area. During the initial session, Susie sits straight and rigid in her chair, does not utter a single word, and makes no eye contact or other response to the therapist's best efforts to interact or communicate. Two similar sessions follow, but the parents remain convinced that Susie will "break down soon" and ask the therapist to keep on trying.

Both of these cases raise a number of questions regarding parents' decision making on behalf of their children. In addition, both cases will certainly be somewhat familiar to any child therapist who has been in practice for a few years. Both children have parents who want to define the goals of therapy independently of their child and perhaps independently of the therapist's advice. Both cases also represent a clash between parents' and child's needs and priorities. In Pete's case, we seem to have a normal child whose parents have inordinate expectations given the normal course of human development. In Susie's case, it is not clear whether her behavior is a reflection of the extent of her pathology or simply an assertion of the only power she has in this situation (i.e., the option to refrain from participating). We may need more data about Susie to make a diagnosis; however, the discrepancy between her parents' wishes and her own is evident.

THE PROFESSIONAL'S ROLE

The ethical and responsible professional must strive to obey the law and safeguard the best interests of his or her clients while also delivering competent services (assuming that there are no conflicts among these duties). At the same time, however, those of us who work with children are always in a potential dual-role conflict situation. Since children seldom seek mental health services of their own accord (and are usually not considered legally competent to do so), they are brought to us by parents, guardians, or representatives of social agencies who have some definite agenda in mind. Sometimes the adults' agenda will be highly congruent with the child's. The professional providing services, however, must never simply assume this to be the case.

It is the professional's duty to know and understand the legal obligations and responsibilities that apply when children are the clients. In addition, service providers must be able to perform their own assessment of the clients' needs with a full recognition that any given family member may have different "best interests" from the others. Service plans should be developed with full consideration of all parties' best interests and relative vulnerabilities. This is often a difficult task involving strong mediation skills and recognition of subtle nuances. An understanding of children's evolving capacities to reason and make decisions, coupled with knowledge about emotional and social development, is critical to such work. Examples and discussion throughout this volume will serve as a general guide to practitioners but cannot replace basic didactic and experiential training as preparation for competent service delivery to children, youths, and families.

Much of the material in this chapter makes the point that the "client" in mental health services to children is often best conceptualized as a child in a specific context (i.e., the child in the family). We have illustrated the complexities of the child-parent relationship in this regard, but there are many other people and contexts within which the issue of who the client is becomes blurred. Schools, child-care agencies, and extended family members are good examples:

> CASE 1-7: A psychologist consulting to a day-care center is asked to see Anna Noid, age 3, who is of some concern to the staff by virtue of her antisocial behavior. When the psychologist telephones Anna's parents to recommend treatment, the pair of Noids are outraged and accuse all concerned of violating their privacy.

> CASE 1-8: Frieda Frank, M.S.W., has been treating 6-year-old Billy Bereft for the past 6 months. Billy's mother died about 7 months earlier following a long bout with cancer, and his father sought counseling for Billy to assist him in coping with his grief. One afternoon Ms. Frank received a phone call from Billy's maternal grandparents. They are also concerned about Billy and are upset that they have not been allowed to visit with him in the months since his mother's death. They have many reservations about whether their son-in-law is taking proper care of their grandchild and want to know how he is doing.

Although all the players in both cases seem to have legitimate concerns, the psychologist must be prepared to draw careful distinctions regarding which of the parties are due specific professional obligations. In the case of the Noids, for example, the psychologist is a paid consultant of the day-care center but also takes on certain obligations to Anna and her parents if he agrees to see her. These obligations might include a duty of confidentiality requiring specific waivers before the case could be discussed with others (including the day-care staff). In addition, the psychologist should not undertake delivery of services to any child (including an assessment or "informal screening") without the knowledge and consent of the parents or guardian, except in those cases in which a child is deemed legally competent to consent. In this case, the problem could have been avoided by calling the parents or sending a note home asking their permission to evaluate Anna. In programs in which a consulting psychologist performs such consulting services for all children in the setting, it might be more appropriate to seek a general parental consent for this during the registration period. This practice would make such consultation a routine part of the program that all parents are told about (and for which permission is obtained) from the beginning.

In the case of Billy, the grandparents may well have a legitimate interest in knowing how he is doing, but they may also be meddling, and they are not the legal guardians of the child. In such cases, it is appropriate to thank them for their concern and direct them to their son-in-law. Ms. Frank also should alert the father to the call and ask whether he would authorize a more detailed response to the grandparents.

Another case of interest under the heading of who is the client is that of *Forrest v. Ansbach* (1980), discussed in detail in chapter 3 (case 3-11). It involved a conscientious school psychologist who found herself caught between the demands of her employer (a school system) and the professional obligation to serve the best interests of the children she was to evaluate. These are not easy issues to resolve when the clients are adults. They are made far more complex when children are involved because of the automatic dual relationships involved. As noted at the start of this chapter, every child will have a parent, a set of parents, or a legal guardian. In addition, each will reside in a legal jurisdiction where a variety of laws (e.g., child abuse and neglect reporting, mandatory school attendance, child labor regulations, etc.) and social agencies (e.g., public schools, departments of social service and public welfare, juvenile courts, etc.) may also dictate professional obligations. Children have special developmental needs and limitations that require consideration and sensitivity beyond that needed for successful work with adult clients. Our goal is to begin the process of sensitizing mental health professionals to recognize, analyze, and accept these responsibilities.

•

CHAPTER TWO

Psychotherapy
with Children

Psychotherapy with children and families is quite different from adult work in terms of both developmental and ethical issues. As discussed in chapter 1, nearly every case will raise some degree of role conflict and highlight significant differences in power relationships among the identified patient and other family members. Usually, responsible adults must contract for (i.e., consent to) treatment of the child, including arrangements to pay for the services. Likewise, the decision to seek psychological treatment for a child is usually based on adults' wishes to change some aspect of the child's behavior. The child does not necessarily share the same enthusiasm for such intervention. At various points, the mental health clinician may be deemed an adviser, expert, service vendor, advocate, mediator, or rescuer (not to mention a fool or meddler), with each member of the family taking a different view based on his or her own perspective.

Because there are probably as many different definitions of what psychotherapy is, and what is or is not a psychotherapeutic activity or experience, as there are psychotherapists, it seems wise to state our basic premise from the outset. It is certainly true that some have viewed psychotherapists with a jaundiced eye, claiming that psychotherapy is either not helpful or actually harmful (e.g., Eysenck, 1965, 1966). However, we shall generally assume that, while goals of treatment, strategies, tactics, and theoretical underpinnings may differ, psychotherapists intend their efforts to enhance emotional growth, foster maturity, and promote adaptive functioning in those they treat.

The professional who attempts to negotiate therapeutic intervention for children and families must be sensitive to ethical subtleties and the relative vulnerabilities of all parties. Because children are by definition the least in control and hence most vulnerable, the therapist must keep their best interests paramount. This is no mean feat because it is obviously in a child's best interests to have caring and competent parents. Within any given family, trade-offs must occur between the needs and the preferences of some members over others. Child psychotherapists must also be prepared to confront their own values as they formulate treatment plans in conjunction with their clients. In this context, children and their parents share the client role, and the interests of both must be considered carefully.

CASE 2-1: Fred and Linda Yuppie met in law school and married shortly thereafter. Fred is just on the verge of "making partner" in the firm where he works, and he must put in very long hours. Linda's career has been on a back shelf for the past 3 years while she was pregnant and providing primary parenting to Danny, age 3, and Franny, age 2. Linda is eager to resume her legal career and wants to find a good day-care arrangement for the children. She notes, "I'll be depressed, frustrated, and no good to anyone if I'm stuck at home being a full-time parent." Danny is unyielding in his desire to stay home with Mom.

CASE 2-2: The Bopp family had looked forward to the birth of the new baby, and all had gone well through most of young Jonathan's first year. His parents and two older sisters (ages 4 and 7) doted on him, and family life was just fine. Sometime before his first birthday, however, Jonathan seemed to develop a disinterest in the family. He no longer made eye contact and did not like to be held, his speech development slowed, and he seemed to spend most of his time in perseverative play with one or two toys. Then the bad times really began as Jonathan became increasingly destructive around the home and developed self-injurious behaviors. By the time that the diagnosis of autism was made, the family had changed dramatically. Virtually all the family's life and much of their financial resources revolved around Jonathan's care. By his fourth birthday, Mr. and Mrs. Bopp made the decision to place Jonathan in residential care. "We'd like to keep him at home with us," said Mr. Bopp, "but it just isn't fair to the rest of the family."

Both these cases involve the issue of substitute child care and pit the wish that children may have for continuity of care by parents in their home environment against the needs of other family members. In the case of the Yuppie family, one can argue that the resentment and emotional distress that Linda might feel regarding her interrupted career would compromise her parenting skills and cause her to be less emotionally available to the children. In the Bopp family, Jonathan's best interests must compete with those of his siblings as well as his parents. Life at home with an autistic child requires many compromises, which may have seemed too much to the family.

In cases such as these, there is often no question of a "right" or "wrong" decision. Instead, a weighing of the valid interests of all the people concerned is required. At times, the therapist must be prepared to advocate the interests of the child client while remaining open to the constraints of reality and the rights of other family members. There is no way to anticipate all the possible situations that a therapist might encounter, but one can learn to approach each family with potential problem issues in mind.

DEFINING GOALS

Setting the goals of treatment is probably the most important aspect of undertaking psychotherapy. Ideally, arriving at an agreement on therapeutic goals is one of the first steps in forming a therapeutic alliance or contract (Hare-Mustin, Marecek, Kaplan, & Liss-Levenson, 1979; Keith-Spiegel & Koocher, 1985; Liss-Levenson, Hare-Mustin, Marecek, & Kaplan, 1980). Because the child will often be introduced to psychotherapy at the behest of an adult, the goals of the two may be quite discrepant. The child may view participation in psychotherapy with the same alacrity as an extra homework assignment (or worse!).

Occasionally, parents view psychotherapy as a coercive extension of the socialization process whereby a more powerful adult (i.e., the therapist) will help them get the child to behave in the manner they would prefer. Such goals are often founded in the belief that the adults know what is best for the child. This can be (though it is not necessarily) correct.

> CASE 2-3: The parents of 14-year-old Morris Turbo bring him for psychotherapy at the suggestion of his school guidance counselor. The adults are concerned that Morris is not interested in his academic classwork and seldom turns in his homework. Instead, he spends most of his free time working on friends' cars, reading about cars, and hanging around a local garage. He has considerable skill when it comes to automobile repair and is quite proud of his abilities in that realm. Although his standardized test scores are respectable, his abysmal school grades have earned him the label of "underachiever." Morris gets along well with peers, has a positive view of himself, and reports that he is very happy with his life. He wants to be an auto mechanic and believes that he is taking the right steps to achieve this goal. Meanwhile, his parents express concern that Morris is on his way to "wasting his life" unless he soon shows an interest in attending college.

> CASE 2-4: Paula Pious is an active, attractive, physically healthy 7-year-old. Peter Pious, her father, is a computer systems analyst, and her mother, Pam Pious, teaches at a small Bible college. Both parents are devout members of a fundamentalist religious sect, consider themselves pillars of the community, and abhor secular humanism. They have brought Paula for outpatient evaluation and "therapy" because

she is "overactive." They hope that medication and/or psychotherapy can help her. Specifically, the parents report that Paula has recently begun to contradict them in conversations at home, that she cannot sit still in church, and that she is "hanging around with some very bad influences in the neighborhood" from whom she has learned some "foul language." The parents hope that Paula will soon return to being the "little lady" she was just a year or so ago. On further investigation, the psychiatrist conducting the evaluation learns that Paula is doing quite well in school, with no behavior problems reported. Her parents tend to disregard this data because they view the teacher (who is divorced) as having low standards for acceptable behavior. The evaluation reveals an essentially normal youngster whose social development is reasonably appropriate for her age, although clearly in conflict with parental values.

The Turbos and the school counselor may be correct in their concern about Morris's poor scholastic achievement and failure to turn in homework. He may be unable to relate the immediate relevance of the academic work to the career goal he seems to have set for himself. At the same time, however, the adults in his life may be failing to recognize and value these same goals. Perhaps Morris could do well in college, but he has little interest in that pathway. Although a therapist working with this family can strive to help both parents and child understand each other's positions and perhaps seek compromises, the apparently conflicting goals must be addressed.

The Pious family is a bit different in that Paula's only real problem seems to be the conflict with parental expectations. It would probably not be difficult to engage Paula in treatment, but to what end? Is it appropriate for her to take on the role of the "identified patient," with the potential adverse implications that this might have for her self-esteem? Should therapy be needed for any child who is behaving in a reasonably normal manner for his or her age level? One could rationalize that therapy could help Paula develop values more in congruence with her family, or, conversely, one could argue that she needs help learning to live with rigid and demanding parents. One could try to mediate between parents and child or even confront the parents on the inappropriateness of their expectations. The latter course, however, could well result in a parental decision simply to keep shopping for therapists until one is found who will do the job they are asking to have done.

The basic ethical issue for practitioners working with both Morris and Paula is to involve them in the process of making decisions about therapeutic goals. As a teenager, Morris might well be expected to assert his own views with support and encouragement from the therapist. While Paula may be too young fully to conceptualize the issues and make informed choices, she can and should be made a part of the process. It is likely that even at 7 she has the capacity to participate in the discussion and planning without additional injury to her self-esteem. After all, what Paula and Morris both want is the ability to live in a supportive family with a minimum of stress.

INSTITUTIONALIZATION AND THE RELUCTANT VOLUNTEER

If one concedes that outpatient psychotherapy for children has some coercive potential, then institutionalization or residential treatment certainly represents an extreme end of that continuum. Adults cannot be involuntarily hospitalized for more than a brief emergency interval unless a formal court proceeding finds them dangerous to themselves or to others. Children have no such constitutional protections. Beyer and Wilson (1976) described this situation as the case of the "reluctant volunteer," referring to the legal authority of a parent or guardian to commit a minor child to a psychiatric facility "voluntarily" (i.e., without a formal court hearing).

Consider the following example:

CASE 2-5: Kevin Bartley, age 15, is one of four children in a home with many problems. His mother has been followed in psychotherapy by a social service agency and has been diagnosed as having a "borderline personality." There has been a high level of marital strain and conflict in the family home, with multiple separations over the past few years. At present, the parents are separated and on the verge of divorce. During this recent period of family stress, Kevin's behavior, which was never angelic, has worsened. He has been generally disobedient, staying out late at night, drinking illegally obtained alcoholic beverages, fighting with siblings, and simply beyond his mother's control. His mother has decided to seek residential treatment for Kevin and brings him to the child psychiatry unit of a local hospital. Because Kevin is a minor, she seeks to have him "voluntarily committed" over her signature for treatment. Kevin is angry and unwilling to be hospitalized, asserting, "I'm not crazy . . . you have no right to put me here!"

In simplified form, this case represents the facts in *Bartley v. Kremens* (1975), where a three-judge federal district court ruled that a Pennsylvania statute permitting parents to commit their children "voluntarily" to a state mental hospital violated the due process clause of the Constitution. A similar ruling by a federal tribunal in Georgia (*J.L. v. Parham*, 1976) was subsequently overturned by the Supreme Court (*Parham v. J.R.*, 1979). In writing the majority opinion, Chief Justice Warren Burger noted: "Although we acknowledge the fallibility of medical and psychiatric diagnosis, we do not accept the notion that the shortcomings of specialists can always be avoided by shifting the decision . . . to an untrained judge." The Burger Court assumed somewhat idealistically that the parent will inevitably act to promote the child's welfare. In addition, the Court suggested that the medical officer at the hospital who authorizes the admission is actually providing the child with a kind of due process hearing obviating the need or even the wisdom of additional formal court proceedings.

Although there is general agreement that the "least restrictive alternative" is the most desirable, the questions, How much restriction is necessary? and, Who is best able to provide it? remain difficult to answer. This type of situation has three problematic parts. First is the issue of the circumstances under which parents ought to be able to commit their child to a psychiatric hospital without extrafamilial legal review. Another part involves interpreting the meaning of the phrase "least restrictive alternative" and determining who ought to decide on such issues. The third part of the problem involves potential conflicts of interest when the for-profit sector of the mental health industry is involved.

The issue of hospitalizing children at profit-making facilities has never been examined by the Supreme Court because all the cases brought to its attention have involved public psychiatric facilities. Perhaps the chief justice was correct in suggesting that this is a matter best left to mental health experts. On the other hand, given the diversity of professional opinion that may exist, it is not unreasonable to permit opposing experts to be heard and evaluated when some objections to the hospitalization are raised. This is especially true in the light of the increasing number of proprietary psychiatric facilities opening around the country.

We do not mean to imply that good psychiatric care is not possible at facilities that are operated for a profit. Rather, we suggest that the admitting officer at such facilities may well have a conflict of interest when a potential patient arrives and an empty bed exists. Physicians at such proprietary hospitals are not infrequently stockholders or participants in incentive compensation plans intended to maximize institutional profits and minimize costs. It may well be easier for the admitting officer at one of these hospitals to admit a patient now and worry about the need for hospitalization over the next several days. It is not unusual to find that a public hospital will decline to admit a given patient on clinical grounds, although a private-sector proprietary hospital will admit the same patient so long as he or she has sufficient financial resources to pay the bill. All too often the children's length of stay at a private hospital seems to coincide with the coverage limits of their parents' insurance policy.

The potential adverse side effects of psychiatric hospitalization of children are many. Aside from the stresses of confinement and potential abuses of children that may occur in residential facilities, even a brief inpatient stay can result in lingering problems for patients. The message communicated to the child by the hospitalization itself (e.g., you are too sick or too bad to be cared for in our family) can damage a child's self-esteem. Separation from the family and disruption of the parent-child relationship during a crisis may not be constructive. The psychiatric hospital can also be a place to learn some previously unconsidered behaviors (e.g., suicide attempts). More subtle adverse effects of psychiatric hospital admission are also possible. In a personal communication from Kevin Bartley's attorney, for example, we learned that, subsequent to his release, Kevin was turned down for at least one job on the basis of his "history of psychiatric hospitalization." Labeling and stigmatizing, which may follow children for extensive periods, will be discussed in detail later in this volume (see chap. 3).

THE THERAPIST'S CONFLICTS

As in any client-therapist relationship, a variety of issues that are tied to the therapist's personal attributes may have a bearing on the conduct and progress of a child's treatment. In addition to conflict-of-interest issues, as discussed above, these may include conflicting values, countertransference or personal boundary problems, and burnout.

Conflicting Values

A fundamental dilemma exists when the goals of the client and therapist differ. When the client is a child, matters become more complex because the therapist may have some defined roles representing the interests of the state (i.e., being a mandated child abuse reporter). Another set of goals may enter the picture when the adults involved (i.e., both parents and therapist) all have quite different beliefs regarding what is in the best interests of the child. In adult cases, the therapist is obliged to deal with such differences by discussion and contracting with the client. In the case of child clients, such contracting is also desirable, although in addition the parents must be involved much of the time. There may be circumstances in which the basic values of the family are of such concern that a therapist also feels obligated to take action on behalf of the child against the parents (e.g., in situations in which abuse or neglect is suspected and reporting is mandated under law):

> CASE 2-6: Mr. and Mrs. Private have considerable disdain for the public school system in their community and have decided that they want to "teach and socialize" their 8-year-old son at home rather than send him to the public schools. They have complied with state regula-

tions for such procedures and have been teaching the boy at home for 3 years. They bring him to a psychologist for evaluation because he seems "depressed and lonely," and the evaluation reveals a youngster with few friends and little opportunity to interact with peers outside the home. Schooling or increased social contact with peers would go a long way toward improving the boy's condition, but his parents are opposed to considering such plans.

CASE 2-7: Zelda Schwartz, age 15, is the daughter of white suburban parents who have become distressed that she is dating a black high school classmate from a different religious background. Her parents believe that she is "acting out adolescent rebellion issues" by dating this young man and are pressing for her to enter therapy with the hope that she will essentially be talked out of the relationship. Zelda is distressed by her parents' "racist attitudes" and seems willing to work on reducing family tension, but she refuses to discuss her dating partner in treatment sessions.

CASE 2-8: Ralph Bigot is a 14-year-old high school sophomore who has sought treatment in response to feelings of inadequacy and embarrassment about his lack of athletic ability and late pubertal development. A good therapeutic alliance has been formed, and Ralph is working effectively on these sensitive issues. As he has felt more comfortable in therapy, Ralph has begun to evidence a considerable amount of racial and ethnic prejudice. He often criticizes some of his classmates as "Niggers" or "Jew Bastards." Ralph is unaware that his white therapist is Jewish and is married to a person of color.

In the case of the Privates, parental goals may actually be interfering with their son's development. At the same time, the parents' behavior may be perfectly legal in terms of their right and obligation to exercise their judgment as to what is in their son's best interests. The youngster who is dependent on his parents and has not known different life experiences may not be able to articulate a meaningful personal perspective on these issues. The therapist should identify the problem and the range of potential remedies to the Privates but can do little else if the Privates refuse to accept the proposed goals of treatment. The therapist must be careful to keep the focus on valid and developmentally appropriate therapeutic goals and should be willing to raise for discussion viewpoints that differ with stated preferences of the parties. At the same time, however, the therapist should not go beyond what reasonably can be stated in order to attempt revision of the family's goals. For example, the therapist would be wrong to warn, "Your child is bound to be emotionally disturbed as an adult if you do not start sending him to public school." It would be more appropriate to acknowledge the merits of the values they espouse while asking them to give serious weight to the negative factors associated with this type of an education.

Similarly, the Schwartz family has a basic disagreement about the goals and foci of treatment. If the therapist can forge a common agenda, perhaps some treatment can go forward. Here, as in the case of the Privates, however, the therapist must remain mindful of his or her own values. Issues such as interracial dating and home schooling can be as emotionally loaded for some therapists as they are for the other parties involved, and the therapist must be able to deal with the clients at the level of their concerns. Although this is true in serving both children and adults, children are often less able to articulate or assert their needs than are adults, and the therapist's services are generally sought by the adults, who have considerably more power in the relationship than do the children.

The case of Ralph Bigot focuses more clearly on the clash of client and therapist values. Should the therapist offer self-disclosure in an effort to provoke some enlightened attitude change on Ralph's part? It is clear that Ralph did not seek psychotherapy to improve his race relations. In such cases, the therapist should make every effort to maintain clear personal boundaries and focus treatment on the issues raised by the client. Should Ralph discover that his prejudices apply to the therapist, it would then be appropriate to discuss them as one would any aspect of the therapeutic relationship. Self-disclosure and initiation of such a discussion by the therapist, however, would constitute an inappropriate intrusion into Ralph's ongoing treatment because Ralph does not (at least initially) experience his biases as problems. Attempting to call his attention to these prejudices could place additional emotional stress on Ralph while not addressing the problems that he presented in requesting help.

A more difficult question is whether Ralph's therapist can maintain an adequately empathic relationship or whether negative countertransference and conscious anger will begin to compromise treatment. This is a question that therapists must ask themselves frequently when conflicting values unrelated to foci of treatment are raised by clients. In such circumstances, it is most appropriate for the therapist to seek guidance or perhaps therapeutic consultation from a colleague to assess the legitimate therapeutic needs of the client as distinct from his or her own. The therapist's issues should never become the client's problems.

Sensitive Situations

In psychotherapy with children, the line between fantasy and reality is not always as clear as it is with most adult clients. Sometimes this results in unusual and troubling situations:

> CASE 2-9: Bart Baffle, Psy.D., is treating a 9-year-old girl referred by her father with symptoms of anxiety and depression. After a few sessions, the girl tells her therapist that she is scared of her father because she once saw him dress up as a woman and then beat his wife (the child's mother). She reports being afraid that he will some day do this to her too. Although Dr. Baffle inquires further, the girl says, "Well, I'm not sure. Maybe I saw it, but maybe I only dreamed it."

In cases of suspected child abuse and neglect, there is a relatively low threshold for action by psychologists who have reason to believe that a child is at risk. Such problems are reviewed in detail in chapter 4. In this case, however, the child appears to be in no immediate personal danger. The therapist must consider how credible the story and its recanting are, what meanings it might have as either fantasy or reality, and what risks (if any) exist for the client. In situations in which such presentations occur with a relatively new or unfamiliar client, it is generally best not to act precipitously. One might consider, for example, tactful interviews with each parent separately to elicit their perspectives on their child's concerns without disclosing the specific content of the child's interview. If the problem is genuine or even a persistent fantasy, it will recur as an issue in treatment and can be dealt with thoughtfully over time. Unless specific risk is suspected, however, it is generally unwise to act abruptly in response to such reports by young clients.

Another type of sensitive situation involves the so-called small world phenomenon. Nowhere is this more acute than when one is practicing in a modest-sized or rural community:

CASE 2-10: As the only psychologist practicing in a farming community, Calvin Cramped, M.A., is frequently involved in treating the children of acquaintances: the nephew of a friend, the daughter of the grocery clerk, an altarboy from church, or even his own children's friends.

Although we are taught to eschew such dual role relationships, this is not always possible when one is the only trained clinician in the county. In such situations, it may be impossible to avoid *all* dual role relationships. The therapist should, however, be particularly cautious about confidentiality and professional boundaries. It is wise to discuss the therapist and client roles with each new client at the beginning of the professional relationship. Set clear and comfortable limits, and consider scheduling so as to avoid awkward waiting-room encounters, if possible. Finally, keep in mind that there are often alternatives to initiating a dual role relationship (e.g., referring to a colleague in a neighboring town) and that one should rule out all such alternatives prior to accepting such a client.

Another difficult problem involves relatives, friends, or colleagues who want the clinician to provide treatment or assessment for their child. Such requests for help are by no means rare and often come as emergency requests:

CASE 2-11: Paul and Pam Pal were concerned about their 15-year-old daughter Polly's increasingly secretive and disobedient behavior. Their concern was elevated to panic when the girl did not telephone or return home until 4:00 A.M. one morning. They asked their close friend, Betty Buddy, Ph.D., to come over and help them deal with the situation and to begin seeing Polly professionally.

The potential hazards in a dual role situation such as this one are significant. For example, the Pals may have some expectations of what Dr. Buddy will do that may not be congruent with Buddy's ethical obligations (e.g., "What did Polly tell you about where she was last night?"). They may expect Buddy to effect an unreasonably rapid "cure" of Polly or anticipate that Buddy will be "on their side" of the issues that come up in treatment. In addition, Polly may tell Dr. Buddy some things that will interfere with her friendship with Pam and Paul (e.g., "My parents fight a lot," or, "They think you dress like a bag lady"). A good and knowledgeable friend can be an important help in an emergency such as the one the Pals are facing, but developing a longitudinal professional relationship with Polly is fraught with problems. It would be far better for Dr. Buddy to suggest a referral for ongoing treatment. She could also help locate a good therapist for the family (i.e., another act of friendship).

COUNTERTRANSFERENCE AND PERSONAL BOUNDARY PROBLEMS

All psychotherapists are taught that their own feelings and emotional histories affect their psychotherapeutic work. The most ethical therapists are those who can recognize when their personal concerns impair their abilities to provide intervention based solely on the needs of the client. Unfortunately, there are times when therapists may be blind to their own weak spots. In such circumstances, the therapist may act in a manner dictated by his or her own emotional needs rather than responding to the needs and best interests of the client. With adult clients, it is not at all unusual for feelings of sexual attraction to be a part of the transference or countertransference feelings that come up over the course in treatment (Pope, Keith-Spiegel, & Tabachnik, 1986). With child clients, the unconscious wish to be a protector, rescuer, or ideal parent is more common, from both the transference and the countertransference perspectives:

34

CASE 2-12: Helen Helper, M.S.W., has chosen to work with children and their families because of her often-stated caring about children. In fact, she often tells her colleagues that her clients are *her* children and that she loves each and every one as if they were the children she never had. She is currently treating a young child who lives with her grandparents. The grandparents are trying hard to raise the child well, but they are somewhat old fashioned in their parenting philosophies. Helper suggests to the grandparents that she be allowed to take the child on outings between family sessions, and the grandparents agree. However, after a while, the grandparents complain that the child is becoming distant and unresponsive to them and frequently expresses a wish to be with Helper all the time. She constantly talks about Helper at home and eagerly awaits each excursion as though it were the most important aspect of her life. Helper tells the grandparents that the child's behavior is nothing to be concerned about and that the extra time she spends with the child will encourage emotional growth.

CASE 2-13: Sam Saver, M.D., was treating the severely depressed 10-year-old son of a divorced mother. Saver became outraged when the boy's mother abruptly terminated treatment. Saver believed that he was the "sole emotional lifeline" to this child. After several vigorous attempts to change the mother's mind, Saver contacted her ex-husband (the boy's father) and volunteered to put forth any effort necessary to remove the boy from the mother's custody. Dr. Saver revealed to the father complete information on the boy's mental state as well as a detailed negative evaluation of the mother's parenting skills. Badly shaken by the call, the father contacted the police and demanded that they take the boy into protective custody. The mother filed an ethics charge against the therapist for breach of confidentiality and threatened to sue on account of defamation.

CASE 2-14: Nan Nurture, Ph.D., is treating 15-year-old Nellie Kickout at the request of her parents. Despite Nellie's initial resistance to treatment—because "my parents are the sick ones"—she has come to respect and like Nurture. She continues, however, to have conflicts at home, and her parents have been less than fully cooperative with Nurture's treatment plan. One emotionally stormy evening the Kick-outs have a severe argument at the dinner table and tell Nellie to "get out and never come back!" With only $20 in her purse and nowhere to go, Nellie shows up at Doctor Nurture's office. Deeply concerned about the girl's plight, Nurture invites Nellie into her home with the intent of letting her stay long enough to resolve matters somehow. Two weeks later, the parents learn of Nellie's whereabouts and threaten Nurture with legal action for continuing to treat Nellie without their consent and for kidnapping.

In each of the cases, the therapist had assumed a self-determined role above and beyond what is usual psychotherapeutic practice. In the cases of Dr. Saver and Ms. Helper, the therapists' own belief systems and personal emotional needs led them to assume such roles. In Dr. Nurture's case, an initial act of compassion was complicated by permitting her nocturnal visitor to remain for an extended interval while apparently making no effort to contact the family or involve social agencies better able (and legally mandated) to provide the services her client needed.

Imagine for a moment that Dr. Saver and Dr. Nurture were treating children of the opposite sex rather than the same sex. Such a circumstance could lead to even more intense suspicion and social disapproval and more severe legal action, even if sexual contacts were not explicitly a part of the client-therapist relationship. In all these cases, the therapist's behavior has the net effect of moving the relationship to a different level from that of client and therapist, with a potential of emotional harm to the child client as a result.

A related situation involves particular biases that therapists may hold regarding the treatment needs of their clients:

CASE 2-15: Cindy, age 20 months, contracted a venereal disease, and it was ultimately determined that she had been sexually abused by a male friend of her unmarried mother. The mother sought an assessment of Cindy from Carla Confronto, Ed.D., a psychologist experienced in work with victims of sexual abuse. Dr. Confronto found that

Cindy was a normal 2½-year-old, without symptoms of behavioral disturbance and with no apparent memory of the abuse event. Dr. Confronto nonetheless advised Cindy's mother that therapy was needed to make Cindy aware of what had happened to her so that she could experience "appropriate outrage and release." Without such treatment, Dr. Confronto advised, Cindy would almost certainly have problems later.

Dr. Confronto is presumably basing her advice to Cindy's mother on her clinical experiences with children who had been sexually abused. However, the only research that is well documented in such cases is of a retrospective nature and, in children of Cindy's age, often involves children with significant behavioral symptoms. Is the need to confront Cindy at this time truly in her best interests, or is it an undocumented belief of the therapist?

In other situations, one's conscience and sense of propriety may seem to conflict with one's obligations to an agency or institution. How about the case of a trainee therapist who feels caught between client advocacy and institutional responsibilities?

CASE 2-16: Nellie Novice, M.A., was a graduate student taking a pediatric psychology practicum at a charity hospital. She was assigned to consult with a young black mother from a rural community in order to help the woman accept her 6-month-old daughter's limitations as a result of severe brain damage secondary to meningitis. Just prior to seeing the mother, Ms. Novice was informed by a medical intern that the child's brain damage was the result of negligence on the part of the medical staff, as the usual intervention to reduce intercranial pressure had not been performed.

What are Novice's obligations to her client and to the institution? On the surface, the ethically correct thing to do would be to "blow the whistle" on the negligence. At the same time, Ms. Novice lacks the medical knowledge necessary to assess the accuracy of the medical intern's statement. It would be most appropriate for Novice to review this matter with her supervisors at the field site and at her university. If, after appropriate professional investigation, the intern's statement appears credible, we would hope that Ms. Novice would have the support of other professional staff in assisting the mother to seek appropriate redress. This is one situation in which the university-based faculty at a student's graduate program might be especially helpful. They could assist in getting at the truth and guiding the student without being subject to the same direct pressures that might be exerted on an on-site supervisor who was also the employee of the institution that might be sued.

Burnout

There are times when the stresses of the workplace put unique pressures on a psychotherapist. Such pressures often lead to the syndrome of burnout, which has been compared to a kind of overwhelming emotional exhaustion during which people may become unable to give of themselves any longer. At such times, the therapists may develop an emotional detachment or even disdain for the very clients they have worked for so hard and so long. Freudenberger (1974) and Maslach (1982) have been among the leaders in describing the burnout syndrome among mental health professionals.

Specific papers have discussed the hazards of burnout for many types of mental health professionals who work with children. These include the risk of burnout among institutional child-care workers (Freudenberger, 1977), workers with autistic and severely handicapped children (Foster, 1980), those who work with pediatric cancer patients (Koocher, 1980), child protective services workers (Daley, 1979), school counselors (Boy & Pine, 1980), and day-care workers (Maslach & Pines, 1977). The following cases illustrate the problem in detail:

CASE 2-17: Dotty Dix, M.S.W., has worked for a child protective agency for 9 years. The caseload is quite high, making it impossible for her to give full attention to any one case. Dix is becoming increasingly depressed and frustrated. Despite the high hopes with which she entered the profession, she finds herself believing that the world is going insane and that there is nothing she can do to help. She frequently draws parallels between the horrors of the battlefield and events that she had uncovered inside American homes. She is increasingly absent from her job and perfunctory in her reports and has been overheard to tell colleagues, "These people are garbage and they give birth to more garbage."

CASE 2-18: Carl Care, Psy.D., has spent the last 5 years working on the pediatric oncology service of a large medical center. Much of his time lately has been spent consulting to the bone marrow transplantation service, where children with suppressed immune systems must often live in sterile isolation for several months while waiting to see whether their graft marrow will "take." During the past month, a flu epidemic caused the death of two patients he was working with whose cancer had been "under control." In addition, a favorite patient who had been thought cured recently suffered a relapse that is deemed untreatable. Dr. Care is especially angry because "these are good kids" and "there's nothing I can do to make a difference for them." He is reluctant to take on new referrals and finds ever-increasing reasons to stay away from the ward where his patients are admitted.

Both Ms. Dix and Dr. Care are suffering from burnout caused by the sustained, intense emotional drain associated with their work. Someone has to perform these jobs, but the cost can be quite heavy. In the face of psychological exhaustion, not only have Dix and Care lost their effectiveness, but they may also end up hurting the clients they are supposed to serve. Much of the responsibility for preventing burnout rests with supervisors and administrators who manage human service delivery systems, but individual therapists are also responsible for their own competence, welfare, and professional behavior. Perhaps a vacation or personal psychotherapy will help such people to reorganize their approach to their jobs, but in other cases a change of work to focus on a less stressful client population may be in everyone's best interests. Some institutions make job rotation plans available. Other therapists working in high-stress settings tend to do so only part time while holding a second part-time job in a less stressful environment.

Aversive Therapies

The use of noxious stimuli for psychotherapeutic purposes has sometimes been referred to as aversive conditioning. Such procedures are occasionally advocated as treatments of choice "in efforts to overcome recalcitrant problems" (Davidson & Stuart, 1975, p. 756). Examples might include the work of Lovaas and Simmons (1969), who used electric shocks to the extremities as part of a treatment program aimed at terminating self-mutilative behaviors of some autistic and severely retarded children.

At times, such paradigms are employed with a focus on specific behaviors to the exclusion of the child as a whole person with a multiplicity of needs, abilities, and sensitivities. Often the children who are candidates for such treatment are among the least socially or intellectually capable of making a decision about therapy:

CASE 2-19: Kim Crunch is a 6-year-old severely retarded child who has been institutionalized since shortly after birth. She has a history of pulling out her hair and inflicting superficial scratches and bites on herself. In recent months, she has begun to bang her head against walls and punch herself in the eye with her fist. The institutional staff attempted a variety of interventions, including therapeutic holding and distracting her with music and stroking, and finally fitted her with a protective helmet and face mask. Kim has managed to injure one eye severely and now seems bent on damaging the other eye at every opportunity. The consulting psychologist on the unit where Kim is treated wants to attempt using aversive stimuli in the form of ammonia capsules (held under the nose) or mild electric shocks to the extremities with a cattle prod in an effort to disrupt her self-damaging behavior.

CASE 2-20: Sally Shooter is a 16-year-old with a history of substance abuse who has been confined to a juvenile treatment facility following a conviction for selling "crack" to her classmates. During an angry outburst at a staff member, Sally swallows a handful of pellets from a dish of rat poison set in a corner of the dayroom. The therapist in charge of the program decides to do nothing for the next hour, reasoning, "She'll get good and sick from that stuff and it will teach her a lesson." Sally is subsequently hospitalized with internal bleeding but recovers over a period of several weeks.

In both of these cases, use of "aversive stimuli" is described, although the contexts are markedly different. In the case of Kim Crunch, the use of such techniques is presented as an option only after several less noxious techniques are attempted, and then only to prevent further permanent injury. Presumably, the aversive techniques will be attempted on a controlled, well-supervised, trial basis and will be discontinued if they fail to produce a beneficial result. In addition, the stimuli to be used, while noxious, have no permanent damaging effect. In the case of Sally Shooter, the therapist in charge seems to have some ill-conceptualized notion of "teaching her a lesson." At the same time, however, there is a failure to recognize a potentially fatal suicidal attempt and a degree of sadism implied in the therapist's delayed intervention.

Although Sally's therapist was clearly unethical and negligent in the decision to use an aversive means to "teach her a lesson," the proposed trial of aversives with Kim may be justified. The process of oversight and consent remains a difficult one. Therapy plans of this sort should undergo review and approval by qualified professionals functioning independently of the family (who had left Kim in the institution for many years) and the institution or therapist to administer the techniques (who may have some special agenda that differ from Kim's). It is not always easy to discern whether the treatment goal justifies the means, and few clear templates for making such decisions exist (Koocher, 1976b).

Medical Treatment

Mental health professionals are often called on for advice in assessing the competence or best interests of children with regard to medical procedures or treatments. Because we have studied child development, we may be asked for advice regarding predictions of certain treatment outcomes over a long term or to offer an opinion regarding a child's best interests with respect to a medical decision or quality-of-life issue. Many psychologists will find the legal guide by Morrissey, Hofmann, and

Thrope (1986) useful in thinking about such issues. Although laws are under constant revision, Morrissey and his colleagues provide a relatively recent update on the statutes for consent and confidentiality in the medical care of minors across all 50 states as an appendix to their text.

One type of medical treatment that has evoked considerable emotional and legal reaction is that of abortion for pregnant minors. The Supreme Court has held that the state cannot impose a parental veto on a minor's decision to have an abortion (*Bellotti v. Baird*, 1979) and that the state must provide an alternative procedure whereby a pregnant mother may demonstrate that she is sufficiently mature to make the abortion decision herself or that, despite her immaturity, an abortion would be in her best interests (*City of Akron v. Akron Center for Reproductive Health*, 1983; *H.L. v. Matheson*, 1981; *Thornburgh v. American College of Obstetricians and Gynecologists*, 1986).

The first comprehensive attempt to provide a dispassionate and scholarly application of psychological knowledge to legal assumptions regarding adolescent abortion issues appeared in an earlier volume of this series on children and the law (Melton, 1986). The decision-making process is not always clear, nor is it always helped by a mental health professional's participation:

CASE 2-21: Felicia Fecunda is 16, a high school junior, and 4 weeks pregnant. She has "always wanted a child to love" and is well aware of state regulations that will make her eligible for welfare support in a few months. She plans to move out of her parents' home and care for the child on her own. Her parents have brought her to see a psychologist who can "talk some sense into her." They want her to finish high school and tell her that she is too young to be on her own with a child. They offer to support her in having an abortion or in carrying the child to term and putting it up for adoption. They argue that she is "too psychologically immature" to function as a parent.

There are many ethical issues in this case that involve Felicia's wishes, those of her parents, and the sensitivities of the therapist. While many of the issues are indeed appropriate for therapeutic exploration, a biological clock is ticking. The therapist must decide quickly what role he or she is willing to take in this case. Will it be a role focused on helping Felicia sort through her plans, goals, and options? Should the therapist attempt to function as a mediator between Felicia and her parents? What if Felicia has "her mind made up" and no interest in therapy? What if the therapist is the parent of an adolescent daughter or has strong moral or personal convictions regarding the appropriateness of abortion? We need more data to explore this case from the ethical perspective. However, the complexity of the issues clearly illustrates the scope of one type of "medical" problem in which a mental health professional may become involved.

Other elective medical procedures may result in conflicts in decision making that carry significant psychological impact:

CASE 2-22: Jason Smote, age 14, was injured in an automobile accident at the age of 14 months. A large, highly visible scar remains on his left cheek. Jason is extremely shy and socially isolated. He has developed a habit of holding his left cheek down onto his shoulder in an apparent but unsuccessful and counterproductive attempt to conceal his disfigurement. Medical specialists are certain that the scar could be virtually eliminated. A psychologist who evaluated Jason is convinced that the scar is causing the youngster considerable emotional harm. Jason's parents, however, have refused to seek or allow plastic surgery because of their religious belief that the scar was willed by God. They believe that Jason and the family must endure "what God hath wrought."

There are serious legal questions regarding the degree to which parents may make religious martyrs of their children (see *In re Green*, 1972, and *Prince v. Massachusetts*, 1944, in the case glossary section of this volume). Psychological expertise may be very useful in helping courts formulate decisions serving the best interests of children in such cases. Such cases will occasionally reach the jurisdiction of the court when medical or mental health professionals report suspected child neglect, as was the situation in *In re Phillip B.* (1980) and the successor case *Guardianship of Phillip B.* (1983).

Another type of situation that draws dramatic attention to the involvement of psychologists in medical treatment decision making is the request to terminate life support equipment, as in the well-known case of Karen Ann Quinlan. Another similar case involving a minor was *In re Guardianship of Barry* (1984):

CASE 2-23: Barry was an infant whose parents sought to terminate life support equipment when it was clear that he was "in a permanent vegetative state with more than 90 percent of his brain function gone and without cognitive brain function." The parent's petition was supported by the child's attending physician and a court-appointed guardian *ad litem*. Psychological arguments were raised to attest to the quality of life that he might face in the future. The state objected, arguing that its interest in preserving life outweighed parental assertions of Barry's right to privacy.

Although Barry had minimal brain stem function and therefore did not meet the state's definition of *brain dead*, the court authorized termination of life support equipment, basing its order on the doctrine of substituted judgment. In Barry's case, the court determined that the parents and their medical advisers should make the decisions. The level of proof required was clear and convincing evidence of what Barry's choice would have been were he competent to make it.

Other problematic situations involve so-called no code or DNR (i.e., do not resuscitate) entered in patients' medical records. These are medical decisions or orders to withhold care that could extend a patient's life. Such orders require a balancing of any given patient's right to treatment and right to refuse treatment. Sometimes DNR orders are upheld by courts on the grounds that it is not in the patient's best interest to be resuscitated (Robertson, 1983). The Massachusetts courts upheld such an order in the case of a 5-month-old infant who was abandoned at birth and also suffered from profound congenital heart and lung malformations (*Custody of a Minor*, 1982). The child had no medical hope of survival beyond a year and was admitted to a hospital with a severe bacterial infection.

The child was placed on a respirator, and his physician recommended that the state Department of Social Services, which was his legal guardian, authorize a DNR order in the event that the child suffered a respiratory arrest. When the department refused to consent, the hospital sought authorization from the juvenile court. The juvenile court authorized the DNR order, and this was subsequently upheld by the Massachusetts Supreme Judicial Court, which found that a full code order (i.e., maximum efforts to resuscitate) would involve a substantial degree of bodily invasion, discomfort, and pain and would only prolong the infant's agony and suffering. In substituting its judgment, the court ruled that it would therefore not serve the child's interests to be resuscitated and that the child would reject resuscitation were he competent to decide.

No mental health professional was called on to advise the court in the latter case, though this well could have happened. Would it have been ethical to attempt to offer an expert opinion about what such a child might choose where he or she competent to make such a choice? We doubt it. So many variables interact in such situations as to make meaningful psychological prediction impossible. Any "expert opinion" would almost certainly be based on the philosophical leanings of the witness rather than on clear psychological data, and any witnesses purporting to base their opinions on a body of behavioral science data would almost certainly be misrepresenting or extrapolating to an unreasonable degree. In a significant number of cases, such as that of Jason Smote (case 2-22 above), psychological issues have been important in attesting to the quality of life enjoyed by a child in an effort to secure life-saving or restorative surgery over parental objection (e.g., *In re Green*, 1972; *In re Phillip B.*, 1980; *Guardianship of Phillip B.*, 1983). However, such contexts are quite different from the cognitive gymnastics required to assume the role of the child in order to make substituted judgment to terminate life support or decline resuscitation.

GUIDELINES

1. Consider the needs of both child clients and their families when planning psychotherapeutic interventions. Involve all the relevant parties

in setting constructive goals that respectfully consider the child's needs and wishes.

2. When considering hospitalization or other treatments that would require due process or formal consent procedures by adults, give preference to the least restrictive ones consistent with the needs and best interests of the child.

3. Be aware of the value systems of your clients and the fact that parental values may differ from those of their children. Seek to foster mutual understanding while respecting the personal values of the client.

4. Special dual role relationship problems can occur with child clients and their families. Remain sensitive to these possibilities and seek to avoid them as much as is reasonably possible.

5. Child clients may elicit unique countertransference reactions from psychotherapists. Strive to maintain an awareness of unique personal boundary issues when working with children and their families.

6. Aversive therapeutic techniques should not be used unless less noxious approaches have failed and such techniques are necessary to avoid significant harm to the client. Use of such techniques with children should always be preceded by obtaining proper consent from parents or guardians and should be employed only to the extent needed to address the problems that threaten to harm the child.

7. Mental health professionals who work in medical settings should familiarize themselves with legal standards and case law dealing with the care of children in their jurisdictions. If called on to become involved in such cases, professionals should be aware of the limits of their knowledge.

•

CHAPTER THREE

Ethical Issues
in the Psychological
Assessment of Children

Children were among the first beneficiaries of psychological testing and probably also among the first victims of its misuse. Beginning in 1904, public school administrators in Paris, France, took steps to address the problem of too many "nonlearners" in their system. They sought to transfer such pupils to special schools where they would not be held to the standard curriculum. Well aware of potential teacher biases in making such decisions, they asked Alfred Binet, a prominent French psychologist, to assist them in developing a scientific means of separating out the "dull and feebleminded" children. Out of perceived practical necessity, the original Binet scale was published in 1905, and so began the application of standardized psychological assessment of children.

Crossing the oceans took more time in those days, but by the end of World War I America had fully caught on to the utility of such assessment tools. In the autumn of 1922, a young American reporter named Walter Lippman began a critical commentary on the trends in the application of

"Mr. Binet's test." Long before most psychologists, Mr. Lippman cautioned that "great mischief" might result if society came to believe that such tests "constitute a sort of last judgment on the child's capacity" (Lippman, 1922, p. 297). Difficulties of the sort he envisioned still persist today, although the mental health professions are now considerably more attuned to the potential hazards.

Ethical problems in psychological assessment may arise in a number of ways. There may be difficulties in the basic science underlying the instrument (i.e., the construction, validity, or reliability of the tool), the administration of the test, the competence of the test user, or biases built into the structure of the test. Other problems may relate to professional standards in the use and application of such tools, including the specific purpose to which the data are put, the issue of informed consent by test takers or their parents or guardians, handling of obsolete test data, and the release of raw test data to others. Much of this chapter focuses on school-related issues simply because the educational system has been the most frequent user of psychological assessment techniques with children since Binet began his work for the public schools of Paris. Because tests are frequently used in schools and other agencies serving children, and because of the powerful impact that test results may have in children's lives, limiting the misuse or abuse of these techniques is especially important.

BASIC PSYCHOLOGICAL SCIENCE CONCEPTS
Key Concepts

Although this chapter is not intended as a substitute for formal course work in psychological assessment and test construction, it seems appropriate to summarize briefly—with apologies to those thoroughly familiar with measurement techniques—a few important concepts which are often central to ethical complaints regarding the assessment of children. These key concepts include reliability, validity, sources of error, and the standard error of measurement.

Reliability is that property of the test that assures repeatable results. A reliable instrument measures whatever it measures dependably over time and across populations. Tests of relatively stable attributes should have a high test-retest reliability. For example, if a ninth-grade student earns a certain score on a French vocabulary test on Friday, that same student should earn a similar score on readministration of the same test the following Monday, other things being held equal (e.g., assuming that no special studying or presentation of additional material occurred over the weekend). Likewise, the test should yield similar scores for people of relatively similar French vocabulary ability when tested under similar conditions, whether or not they differ on the basis of other extraneous characteristics such as age, sex, or race. If any given test does not measure something reliably, it is useless since one could never know whether differences in scores were related to the skill or trait being assessed or to the unreliability of the tool.

Validity refers to the concept of whether an otherwise reliable test actually measures what it is supposed to measure. As noted above, a test cannot possibly be valid if it is unreliable. On the other hand, a test may yield highly reliable scores, but those scores may not be a valid assessment of what it purports to measure. For example, we could design a highly reliable means to measure children's foot size, but we could not reasonably claim that this is a valid indicator of childhood depression. Those who develop, publish, and market tests are responsible for demonstrating that a particular instrument is appropriately valid for its recommended uses.

Validity may be considered from several different perspectives. First, *content validity* is the simplest type of validity to conceptualize. It is some-times referred to as *face validity* because the items are deemed valid simply by looking at them (i.e., on their face). A test that samples behavior from the domain that is of interest would be said to have content validity. For example, a sixth-grade math test should contain problems or calculations that are typically taught in the sixth grade. The tasks should be related to the performance ability that we wish to measure.

Second, *construct validity* refers to the degree to which a test's scores may be used to infer individual differences associated with some hypo-thetical construct (Green, 1981; Guion, 1974). Even basic assertions regarding the very existence of some hypothetical constructs can be controversial (e.g., constructs such as ego strength, penis envy, or even intelligence). One result is that tests purporting to measure such constructs are often controversial themselves. A classic example of questionable construct validity in a test designed for administration to children is the Blacky Pictures (Blum, 1950). The test involves displaying a series of cartoon pictures featuring a dog named Blacky and members of his family acting out various Freudian constructs such as oral gratification, auto-eroticism, anal rage, and castration anxiety. Needless to say, the demand characteristics of the stimuli evoke certain types of responses. Freudian psychologists would assert that the responses are proof of the construct's validity and proceed to make personality interpretations. A behaviorally oriented colleague would find such an inference laughable and discount the Freudian constructs as not being directly observable in behavior. The burden of establishing whether a test measures a given construct as claimed falls to the test developer. Clinicians using such tools, however, must also be prepared to defend their choice and application of the instruments.

Third, *criterion-related validity* refers to whether a particular test's outcome is related to other criteria in either predictive or concurrent fashion. For example, do Scholastic Aptitude Test scores obtained during high school predict grades during the freshman year of college? Does a newly developed test of intelligence correlate well with scores of the same children on an existing test of intelligence? These two questions illustrate the points of predictive and concurrent validity, respectively.

Sources of error arise in many different ways to effect test scores. One child may have come to school hungry on the day of the test. Another might be highly motivated to please the examiner, whereas many of her classmates could care less. Still another child might be feeling ill or nervous or be very familiar with some of the tasks on a given test. The significance of any particular source of error depends on the specific use of the test in the context of the specific individual who took it. One of the reasons for studying the reliability of a test is to locate and estimate the magnitude of the errors of measurement that might affect it. Any given test has many sources of *standard error*, and the user is responsible for becoming familiar with these and considering them in the context of the comparisons to be made. A *standard error of measurement* is a score interval or range of scores that, given certain assumptions, has a certain probability of including any individual test taker's true score.

CASE 3-1: Mr. and Mrs. Fret were very concerned about the educational progress of their 8-year-old developmentally delayed daughter, who had been diagnosed as moderately mentally retarded. They sought a reevaluation by Manual Krock, Ed.D., who administered a WISC-R (Wechsler Intelligence Scale for Children—Revised) and obtained Verbal and Performance IQ scores 4–5 points higher than the previous testing results. Krock reported to the Frets that this was a sign that their child "could be making intellectual progress."

CASE 3-2: As part of a child custody evaluation, Cynthia Numb, Ph.D., administered the Rorschach Inkblots to a 12-year-old child. Numb later testified in court that the results of the Rorschach showed that there was a "50% probability the child will suffer a personality disorder if forced to continue residing with the mother."

CASE 3-3: Harry Dud, Psy.D., has developed a new psychological test for children, the Dud School Function Test (DSFT). The DSFT is a collection of test items loosely adapted from several existing instruments. Dud publishes and markets the test as a means of evaluating children's learning skills on the basis of "expected norms" that he has extrapolated from other test manuals. He has not attempted the expensive and time-consuming task of standardizing the DSFT on a representative sample of children.

Each of these cases illustrates a different aspect of ethical violations associated with misapplication of basic testing science. Dr. Krock apparently did not understand the basic concept of standard error. If he had, he would not have misled the Frets by suggesting that their child had made some intellectual gains since the actual score obtained was essentially the same as the prior score when standard score variations are taken into consideration.

Dr. Numb's "expert opinion" is inexcusable and dangerous both from a scientific perspective and in terms of the effect that it may have on the parties involved if a judge were to base a decision on it. To begin with, the Rorschach Inkblots have never been validated for use in child custody decision making. In addition, there is no basis for drawing conclusions about future personality development and the mother's role in it from a single set of test data collected from the child. Finally, the 50% probability asserted by Dr. Numb is essentially the product of her own imagination, although she presents it in a manner that implies that it has some empirical validity.

Dr. Dud may well be violating copyright law in the development of his "new test" since it appears that he may be drawing on copyrighted test material without proper consent. Beyond that, however, he has apparently set up a situation wherein children may be evaluated by a totally bogus set of norms. He has adopted a "quick and dirty" strategy of test development that ignores all basic principles of validity documentation. Because trained psychologists are likely to recognize these problems, one must also question the target audience for Dr. Dud's new test. One suspects that he may hope to market it to pediatricians or other professionals not trained in psychometrics and probably too naive to see the problems. This could make matters worse since the unsophisticated users might then mislead others, and so on.

Revised Standards

Those interested in ethical issues associated with the psychological testing of children will certainly want to become familiar with the revised *Standards for Educational and Psychological Testing* compiled jointly by the American Educational Research Association, the American Psychological Association, and the National Council on Measurement in Education (1985). In addition to reviewing basic technical standards for test construction and professional standards for test use, this book provides detailed guidelines for consideration when assessing children in schools, linguistic minorities, and handicapped persons. Among the other key principles detailed in these *Standards* are assumptions that those who give and interpret the tests are trained to understand and adhere to administration and scoring procedures, interpret test results, and conform to accepted practices with respect to safeguarding confidential materials and timely reporting of the test results.

Standard Operating Procedures

The principal value of psychological tests derives from the fact that they prescribe a means for collecting and analyzing a standardized slice of human behavior. Rules for test administration and scoring must therefore be carefully followed. Reference manuals with detailed instructions and norms must be made available by the publisher.

CASE 3-4: The test manual for the Childhood Reading Achievement Profile, developed by Manfred Dreck, Ed.D., provides information on converting raw scores to age and grade equivalents, but it contains no information on the sample population used in establishing the norms such as geographic distribution, socioeconomic status, ethnic or racial composition, or similar demographic variables.

CASE 3-5: Cindy, age 7, has been having problems in the second grade, and her parents have asked for a conference with the principal. Anxious to collect some data before the parent conference, the principal orders Cindy sent to sit in with a fourth-grade class in which group-administered intelligence tests are being given. When her scores are compared to second-grade norms, they are low, and the principal advises the parents that Cindy has intellectual deficits.

CASE 3-6: When the Waterville Child Guidance Center was flooded, many of the psychological testing supplies were damaged. In order to save money, the executive director tells his staff to photocopy test blanks and cut out pieces of cardboard to replace waterlogged puzzle parts rather than purchasing new supplies.

Dr. Dreck's test manual is simply inadequate. Users have no access to information that is critical to interpreting test scores. The omission of such data effectively voids any potential application of the test, even if it is valid and reliable. As matters stand, there is no basis for test users to conclude that the sample of children to be tested reasonably resembles the population for which norms exist.

In Cindy's case, usual procedures were substantially violated. She was removed from her classroom without warning, placed with a strange group of children (most likely in a desk too large for her), and asked to take a test that was not explained to her in advance. She was probably already feeling badly about not doing well in school and might perceive this treatment as a punishment. She was most likely at a substantial emotional disadvantage in this context. Even if we assume that the test is reliable and that the administration was valid, it would be inappropriate to base a significant conclusion about any child's ability solely on the basis of a paper-and-pencil test. The primary ethical problem in this case was undertaking an assessment in circumstances in which the child's psychosocial environment had been disrupted and not making any effort to assist her to adjust. The best approach would have been to schedule the assessment with sufficient time to provide Cindy with an explanation and then to test her with a group of peers. Alternatively, an assessment could be undertaken by an individual examiner who could take the time to form a rapport with Cindy and make individual behavioral observations. In any case, the test results should be interpreted only in the context of what is otherwise known about Cindy (i.e., her family and school history, health, general behavior, etc.).

One can be sympathetic about the Waterville flood, but that does not justify violation of copyright laws, as would be the case in photocopying official test record booklets. More troubling, however, is the plan to make new test kit pieces from cardboard cutouts. The test norms were developed using certain standard stimuli. Handcrafting new puzzle parts alters the standardized stimuli and will have an unpredictable effect on the test results, invalidating them for direct comparison with scores obtained with a standard set of test materials.

Test Bias

The issue of test bias has been the focus of considerable public attention and debate. The term itself has many complex aspects. It may manifest itself as a function of a skill or trait being measured, a statistical phenomenon, a selection model, a problem with test-item content, a matter of overinterpretation, a use of improper criteria, or even a problem in the environment where the testing took place.

In an overview of the scholarly research on test bias, Cole (1981) argues that the basic issue in the matter of test bias is simply a question of validity. She distinguishes between whether a test is valid for some specific purpose and whether it ought to be used (even if valid). The use of tests per se has served as a lightning rod or focal point of anger related to more broad and difficult social questions. Testing itself will never provide all the answers. Problems that have been associated with psychological testing, such as inappropriate labeling of children and self-fulfilling prophecies linked to teacher expectancy, are more appropriately viewed as the result of poor users rather than poor tests (Hobbs, 1975). Answers to complex problems can rarely be found with a psychological test. The test data may provide clues, suggest directions, or record progress, but the benefits or drawbacks are the products of human interpretation.

In the case of *Larry P. v. Riles* (1979), the federal courts prohibited the use of standardized intelligence tests as a means of identifying educable mentally retarded (EMR) black children or for placing such children in EMR classes. The genesis of this case was the fact that black children were disproportionately overrepresented in such classes and that the primary basis for such placement in California (at that time) was such tests (Lambert, 1981). Attorneys for the children argued that the test items were drawn from white, middle-class culture, that whites had more advantages and opportunities than blacks, and that the language used by black children may not correspond to that used in the test. In addition, they noted that the motivation of the black children to perform on the tests may have been adversely influenced by the race of the examiners, who were mostly white, and that the number of blacks in the standardization sample was very low.

The type of problem demonstrated in this case is essentially a validity issue. That is to say, the test was being used for making a type of discrimination or judgment for which it was neither intended nor validated. Using a single psychometric instrument as the sole or primary criterion in making critical educational or other life decisions fails to consider each individual as a whole being in a specific life context. As such, this use of a test indicates unethical assessment practices.

In the case of *PASE v. Hannon* (1980), a federal court in Illinois reached the opposite decision from its West Coast counterpart in the *Larry P.* case. Continued use of psychological tests in educational decision making was permitted. This contrast is of interest because many of the same psychological experts testified in both cases, both cases were under active judicial review simultaneously, and the outcomes were quite different. One might be tempted to read these cases as a contrast or contradiction in the legal system. We believe the contrasting opinions are best viewed as context specific. That is to say, the court was most likely convinced that use of the psychometric tools in Illinois was more appropriate to the context than was the use of the same instruments by the psychologists in the San Francisco school district. The fact that two different judges and sets of facts were involved, however, makes a definitive conclusion on this point impossible. The point to be made is that the clinician who becomes involved in testing that is to be used for critical decision making bears an especially heavy ethical burden to assure that the data are applied in an appropriate scientific context that does not unfairly discriminate against any individual being assessed.

As an aside, it is somewhat ironic that the judge in the PASE case permitted the questions and keyed answers to standardized IQ tests to become a part of the public record. The court clearly had little concern for the matter of test security.

User Competence

Who is qualified to purchase, administer, and interpret a psychological test to be used with children? This is not a simple question when applied to those who assess adults, but when children are the objects of the evaluation, the matter becomes more complex. At the simplest level, user competence may refer to the ability of an individual examiner to administer and score a particular instrument in a manner that yields a valid test protocol. More important, however, is the ability to interpret the meaning of the test results for the particular individual being tested in the context of that person's life situation.

A wide variety of tests are available for use with infants, toddlers, and older children, but these are not generally taught in graduate programs where most clinical or counseling psychologists are trained. Such programs have traditionally focused the bulk of their psychometrics course work and practica on the testing of adult clients. In addition, the behavior of children has a wider normal range of variation than that of adults. Establishing the proper rapport with children is more time consuming, and understanding the difference between a response that means "I don't know the answer" and one that means "I'm not going to cooperate with you" or "I know, but I won't tell" takes a special awareness of child development and an understanding of children. The pace of the assessment interview and need for the examiner actively to engage the client is often more variable and demanding than with adult clients.

The role of the test publishing companies in the determination of user competence is a "sometimes" issue. Most reputable companies classify their products into usage categories and seek to establish at least minimal user qualifications prior to sale. Such companies are, however, not in the credentialing business and are more concerned about making profits on the sales of their products than on the impossible task of preventing all possible unauthorized uses. Determination of user qualifications usually means requiring that the party placing the order be either a member of the APA or a licensed psychologist. As discussed in detail in chapter 4, not all licensed psychologists and certainly not all APA members are qualified to use psychological tests, let alone test children. In addition, even those test publishers who do specify user qualifications for purchase by individuals may ignore their own stated policy when shipping in response to institutional purchase orders from large hospitals or school systems. We must conclude that there are no assurances that the sale of psychological tests is restricted to qualified users and that, as a result, many individuals who obtain and administer such tests may not be technically qualified to do so.

CASE 3-7: As a supervisor in an APA-approved internship program, Tom Turkey, Ph.D., was assigned to work with Ned Novice, a trainee who had little experience in child work. Ned was assigned to assess a toddler, although he was unfamiliar with the particular test instruments that would be needed to test a child of that age adequately. He mentioned his reservations to Dr. Turkey, who told him, "Read the test manual and practice the items and go to it."

CASE 3-8: Frederick Facile, Psy.D., has a large consulting practice that involves considerable psychological testing. After meeting a child briefly, Dr. Facile usually leaves the youngster in the hands of a psychometrician, who administers the appropriate instruments, scores them, and drafts several descriptive paragraphs. Dr. Facile subsequently edits the materials into a psychological evaluation report to which he signs only his own name.

CASE 3-9: Tabula Data, Ed.D., is head of psychological services for the West Numbskull Regional School District. In an effort to "streamline and economize," she has purchased a variety of psychological testing software packages that can be used on the desktop microcomputers in each of the school buildings. Some of the software packages are intended to administer psychological tests to children who sit at the terminal alone. Other programs generate psychological evaluation reports based on intelligence test subtest scores computed by psychometricians in the school system. The numbers are punched in, and a finished report prints out. Dr. Data is very proud of bringing her department into the "computer age."

Ned Novice has a difficult situation on his hands. He is more sensitive to the ethical problems involved in inadequate test-user competence and more aware of his own limitations than is his supervisor, Dr. Turkey. At the same time, however, Novice wants to be seen as a good trainee by his supervisor and is under some pressure to ignore his sense of what is in the patient's best interests in this particular case. In the ideal circumstance, Novice could approach Dr. Turkey and reframe the concern as an ethical dilemma for him: "Dr. Turkey, I feel uneasy about testing this child without first being checked out more thoroughly on this instrument. I'm afraid that it would be unethical of me to undertake the assessment without some help." This type of approach highlights the problem without attributing blame to Turkey. If Turkey ignores or trivializes this request, Novice may decide to seek counsel from other colleagues on site or from the training director at his university. We would hope that he would not give in to the pressure to undertake an assignment that he cannot adequately complete without additional training or supervisory support.

Dr. Facile's model for conducting child assessments is not entirely ethically appropriate. He is clearly being assisted by a psychometrician in a substantial manner but is producing reports that are signed in a manner that might mislead readers into concluding that he was the sole evaluator of the child in question. Assuming that the assistant is properly trained, supervised, and authorized under state law to perform the functions described, the use of an assistant in this context is not unethical per se. The ethical problem is that of fairly and accurately representing for readers of the report and for the third-party payers (e.g., insurance companies) who actually conducted the evaluation. In addition, Dr. Facile would be expected to review the test data and discuss the child's examination behavior with the assistant in order to grasp the context fully before preparing the report. One would want to know more about these details before rendering final judgment on the propriety of Facile's behavior.

Dr. Data's plans raise a number of significant ethical questions. Although it is not unusual to have adult clients enter responses to test items on a computer keyboard as these are displayed on a monitor screen, it is another matter entirely to leave a child to perform such tasks in an unsupervised manner. Without taking the child's attention span, fine-motor coordination, and reading abilities into consideration, it is not possible to determine how valid or reliable the test data obtained by these means might be. Although there are many software programs that generate reports based on simple data entry, these reports generally fall into two categories: data summaries and interpretive reports. The data summaries present scores, averages, ratios, graphs, and so on. The interpretive reports generally produce narrative or descriptive paragraphs com-posed by mechanical means, but often sounding as though they may have been written by a clinician. When generated by software produced by reputable firms, these reports include a printed warning that the data can be interpreted only by a trained clinician. The difficulty is that this statement may be absent or ignored. Many psychologists believe that interpretive reports should be generated in a manner that precludes their use without reformulation or refinement by a well-trained clinician. Dr. Data's planned use of the new technology does not seem to give adequate consideration to these points. It would be well for her to review the *Guidelines for Computer-based Tests and Interpretations* prepared by the APA's Committee on Professional Standards and Committee on Psycho-logical Tests and Assessment (1986).

SOME CONSEQUENCES OF ADVOCACY AGAINST MISUSE OF TESTS

At times, psychologists have been placed in the unenviable position of having to advocate on behalf of clients in matters involving misuse of psychological test data or techniques. Such advocacy is especially painful because it often involves pointing out problems caused by other col-leagues or their assessment methods. At the same time, however, psy-chologists are better equipped by training and experience to recognize and properly criticize such abuses. Nonetheless, the personal costs of such advocacy can be significant.

CASE 3-10: Sylvia Sharp, Ph.D., a psychologist in private practice, was asked by parents to undertake evaluation of their child, who was experiencing school problems. When the child recognized some of the standardized test items, she inquired and discovered that Dennis Dense, Ph.D., a psychologist within the school system, had begun a similar evaluation a few days earlier without the parents' knowledge. Sharp attempted collegial consultation with Dense and met with lim-ited cooperation. She soon discovered that Dense had made some significant errors in his assessment procedures and the school system, relying in part on his work, was refusing services to which the child seemed entitled under state and federal law. Unable to resolve the matter informally, Dr. Sharp filed complaints against the school psychologist and the municipality with agencies of the state and federal government. A variety of countercharges were then filed by Dr. Dense against Dr. Sharp with licensing and ethics boards, and rumors were spread in the community that she was emotionally unstable.

CASE 3-11: Muriel Forrest was a master's-level school psychologist who had an unblemished record in a dozen years of service as a school psychologist to the Edgemont Union Free School District. In the face of increasing special education costs, she was prohibited by her superiors from conducting full and comprehensive evaluations, discussing the results of her evaluations, denominating specific handicapping conditions of the children she assessed, or making recommendations for appropriate services and programs for handicapped children. When she refused to go along with these prohibitions, her reports were rewritten, and she was chastised for criticizing the school system's policy. Her contract was ultimately terminated in a manner that allowed her only 5 days' notice to prepare rebuttal prior to recommendation of termination (see Bersoff, 1980; *Forrest v. Ansbach*, 1980).

Although both these cases revolve around misguided assessment strategies (one by Dr. Dense and the other dictated by the Edgemont Union Free School District), both also demonstrate some of the hazards of attempting to be a strong child advocate in the public arena. Dr. Sharp was eventually successful in having the proper services provided to her client, but assorted complaints against her before licensing or ethics panels persisted for many months and were not disposed of before incurring considerable legal expenses and great personal aggravation. In addition, she had no real means of addressing the rumors that had been started about her "emotional instability." These unfounded aspersions had a significant adverse effect on her private practice.

Although Dr. Sharp lost some clients, Muriel Forrest lost her job without redress. In an amicus brief filed jointly on Muriel Forrest's behalf by the American, New York, and Westchester County Psychological

Associations, Bersoff (1980) concluded, "The only permissible inference which may be drawn from the failure of [the school system] to renew [Ms. Forrest's] contract in the light of her splendid record of over a dozen years is that they objected to her activities devoted to advocating, supporting, and enforcing the civil rights of handicapped children and their parents" (p. 41). Nevertheless, Ms. Forrest's appeal for reinstatement was ultimately lost some 4 years after her termination on a procedural technicality. Unfortunately, being right and ethically correct does not always assure a desirable outcome.

Consent

Psychological assessment should not be undertaken without the informed consent of the person being evaluated. When the client is a child, a parent or guardian should be asked to consent on behalf of the child. The process of obtaining consent should provide the adults making the decision with all the information that might reasonably be expected to influence their decision on behalf of the child.

> CASE 3-12: All the students in grades 3, 5, and 7 at the North Elementary School were given the Urban Scholastic Achievement Tests to assess their progress midway through the school year. No advance notice was given, nor was specific permission obtained from their families to test the children.

> CASE 3-13: Randy Raucous, age 10, was a behavior problem at the Hillside Memorial School, and he also seemed to be falling behind in his work. In an effort to assess psychological aspects of the situation and provide appropriate interventions, Mr. Hasty, the school principal, asked the psychologist assigned to Hillside to conduct a full assessment of Randy on an urgent basis. Neither Mr. Hasty nor the psychologist sought formal permission from Randy's family before beginning the process.

The testing begun in both these cases seems relatively benign, but that does not excuse the failure to seek permission in Randy's case or to give adequate notice (and the opportunity to express concerns) in the North

Elementary School case. Although routine school achievement testing is relatively noninvasive, parents have the right to be informed both of the testing and of the results. In some school systems with a history of discrimination against people of color or inappropriate use of test data (see, e.g., the case of *Larry P. v. Riles* discussed earlier in this chapter), parents or the psychological consultants may want to monitor the testing and use of results closely. When individualized assessment is recommended for a child, both federal and many state laws combine to dictate parental involvement and consent prior to initiating the assessment. Seeing Randy without his parent's consent could possibly result in formal charges being filed against both the psychologist and the school system. In both situations, however, it is in the best interests of the schools to maintain a cooperative and nonadversarial relationship with parents. It is far wiser to provide abundant information and seek permission routinely rather than to have to undo the damage caused by failure to use a thoughtful approach. Psychologists may be helpful in making this point to school administrators, who may inadvertently overlook it.

Obsolescence of Test Data

Psychologists are obligated to purge obsolete test data from files of their private patients. When psychologists are employees of hospitals, clinics, or other agencies, they are obliged to work with the record-keeping staff at those agencies to see that obsolete materials are not kept on file in a manner that could possibly lead to inappropriate use. This is a particularly important issue with respect to children who may be the objects of psychological assessment early in their development. The data yielded in the assessment will have little relevance many years later.

CASE 3-13: Max Interval was evaluated with a full psychological battery of cognitive and projective tests at the Central City Child Guidance Center when he was 6 years old. More than a decade has passed since that time, and the raw test data remain in the case file on Max in the Guidance Center's record room. At the age of 18, Max enlists in the military. Subsequently, access to his files is sought by official personnel evaluating Max for security clearance.

Although some psychologists might have an intellectual curiosity about Max as an 18-year-old, no one could argue with any form of scientific validity that cognitive, visual-motor, or projective test data collected at age 6 are in any way relevant to his appropriateness for military security clearance. Perhaps if Max had been tested routinely in longitudinal fashion for several years, some useful information might exist. Such compilations of data over time on a single child are rare in clinical practice. If any data on clients such as Max do exist, someone may someday want to come looking for them. Providing obsolete data in Max's case, however, is a double disservice. It is a disservice to Max since it is not valid for any meaningful purpose and could ultimately be used to his disadvantage. For similar reasons, providing such data to other agencies, even with Max's consent, is a disservice because they might be led to believe that they have information with some valid present meaning. The most appropriate course of action would be to cull files of such information routinely (removing, e.g., raw test data or protocols and obsolete reports). The definition of *obsolescence* should be made in consideration of the age of the client at the time, the nature of the problem, and the current context.

Who Owns the Data

Psychologists are frequently asked to release copies of raw test data. The actual test protocols are generally the property of the individual practitioner or agency where the assessment was done, much as case notes or medical records would be. Unlike more general notes or records, however, raw test data and test protocols are specialized information that cannot readily be understood or interpreted by individuals without specialized training. The ethical propriety of supplying copyrighted or limited-circulation material depends on the purposes for which the data are sought and on the qualifications of intended recipients.

CASE 3-14: Mary Quandary, Ed.D., received a telephone call from Izzy Insisto, the father of a child she had tested a few weeks earlier. Mr. Insisto had read her report and disagreed with several of her conclusions and recommendations. He demands that she provide him with copies of the raw data and test protocols. "After all," he notes, "I paid for the testing and I have a right to my child's records."

This parent's demand presents a number of ethical problems. To begin with, some of the test protocols may be copyrighted with distribution to the general public prohibited (e.g., IQ test record blanks). In addition, the raw data collected during assessment sessions will often contain casual observations, marginal comments, or other working notes of a speculative nature that were never intended for public disclosure. Similarly, some data or comments may be elicited from the child that may be confidential in nature or otherwise ought not to be reported directly to individuals not trained to consider it in context (e.g., a response to a projective test stimulus card where the "child in the story" says or does something unpleasant to or about the "parent in the story"). The simple fact is that considerable specialized training is required to administer and interpret psychological tests.

Mr. Insisto's demand for the data may reflect inadequate communication from Dr. Quandary and in that sense might have been prevented. If Quandary had met with the parents in advance to discuss the ground rules for providing feedback (for additional discussion, see chap. 4) or had met with the parents following the evaluation to review her findings and answer their questions in person, the demand for the data might have been forestalled. Even at this point, an offer to review the findings might address the parents' real needs. We also recommend providing parents with a copy of the actual test report. In many states, parents have full access to their child's formal records by law. Even where parental access is not guaranteed by law, one should assume that a parent with legal custody will at some point have access to the report. It is far better for them to have it handed to them by the author with the chance to ask questions than to see it later without benefit of interpretation.

On occasions when a parent continues to insist on copies of raw data or test protocols, despite appropriate efforts to address their questions and concerns, one should attempt to ascertain the reason for the request. If, for example, the goal is to provide information that would be helpful to a colleague, such as a psychologist treating the child who has been tested, the intent may be quite appropriate. We advise giving the following explanation in any case:

> Although my formal report is a part of your child's record and you are welcome to a copy of it, the notes I take and test forms I complete in the course of my evaluation are working notes. These are not finished products, and even the actual test responses could not be effectively interpreted without specialized training. Although I would be glad to share specific test response data with another qualified professional of your choosing, it would be unethical for me provide these materials to untrained individuals.

The preamble to *principle 8* on assessment techniques of the *Ethical Principles of Psychologists* (American Psychological Association, 1981) states that psychologists "guard against the misuse of assessment results," and section f of the same principle notes that psychologists "do not encourage or promote" the use of such materials by "inappropriately trained or otherwise unqualified persons." The best route to provide the data to another person Mr. Insisto might select would be first to secure a written release and then to telephone the intended recipient to determine the person's needs (i.e., which data are desired) and qualifications to interpret that data. If specific scores or responses are needed, this fact can be more easily determined.

It is not infrequent to hear accounts of clinicians who, angry about unpaid bills, refuse to release test data or reports. Consider the following case:

> CASE 3-16: Manual Profit, Psy.D., tested Billy Deadbeat 3 months ago and completed the testing report promptly. He filed a claim with Deadbeats' insurance company and has been advised by the claims department that payment has been made directly to the subscriber. Dr. Profit then receives a signed release of information from Billy's school seeking a copy of the report to use in educational planning. While the report is of valid interest to the school, Dr. Profit telephones the

Deadbeats, who assure him that "the check is in the mail." Profit tells them that he intends to withhold release of the report until the payment arrives.

In this case, Dr. Profit is clearly holding the reports hostage in an effort to collect his fee. No matter how reprehensible the Deadbeats may be in withholding the insurance money they have already collected, and no matter how recalcitrant they or any other client may be in paying a bill, Profit's behavior is unethical. It is never proper to withhold information to the detriment of a client on account of an unpaid bill. Dr. Profit would be within his rights to request payment at the time service is rendered (i.e., the day of the appointment) or to use appropriate legal means (e.g., small claims court) to collect a legitimate debt, but he should not use his report for retaliatory purposes or as a means to force payment.

GUIDELINES

1. When developing, administering, or interpreting psychological assessment tools, one must exercise caution to assure that the *Standards for Educational and Psychological Testing* are followed.

2. Be certain that reports or conclusions based on test results are reported accurately and in a manner that can be understood by the intended audience.

3. Take care to avoid making (or permitting others to make) decisions based on test data that are inconsistent with the normative base or usual intended uses of the instrument as described in the test manual.

4. Do not use test instruments that you have not been trained to administer and interpret, and do not permit individuals under your personal supervision to do so.

5. Do not undertake psychological assessment of a child without the consent of that child's parent or legal guardian.

6. Remove obsolete raw test data from private practice case files on a routine basis. If employed by a private institution or agency, encourage the appropriate authorities at that facility to cull obsolete data from their files on a similar basis.

7. On receipt of proper written consent, clinicians should release copies of raw test data to other mental health professionals as long as the intended recipient is trained to score and interpret such data.

8. Mental health professionals should never withhold assessment reports or data needed for clinical assessment, treatment planning, or educational program design because a bill has not been paid. Financial considerations should not impede the psychological needs of the client.

•

CHAPTER FOUR

Confidentiality and Clinical Competence in Serving Children and Families

This chapter addresses two important topics that may at first glance seem unrelated: competence and confidentiality in services to children. Both are linked, however, because they demand special understanding and sensitivity to developmental issues. In addition, these two areas include many pitfalls that are easily overlooked but that practitioners must avoid.

COMPETENCE

Professional standards cannot explicitly cover every situation, and one hopes that practitioners will be circumspect in their work with all clients. The *Ethical Principles of Psychologists* (American Psychological Association, 1981), for example, enjoins all psychologists to maintain high standards of competence and to recognize both the boundaries of their competence and the limitations of their techniques. For many of our colleagues in the mental health professions, however, enthusiasm (or arrogance) too often clouds or exceeds competence. In addition, there is no clear consensus within the field as to whether work with children and families is a specialty, a subspecialty, or simply a special proficiency. When it comes to child and family work, there are no written guidelines to follow with respect to establishing a basic threshold of competence.

It is possible to complete a doctoral degree program that is "fully approved" by the American Psychological Association from course work through internship in clinical or counseling psychology at many universities without ever assessing or treating a child and without any formal training in family therapy. Similar circumstances also prevail in the training of social workers, general psychiatrists, and other mental health clinicians. Consider the following case examples of professionals working beyond the scope of their training:

CASE 4-1: Karla Kinder, Psy.D., completed her graduate training several years ago. Her practica and internship experiences were all focused on adult populations, including stints at a Veterans Administration outpatient clinic, the geriatric unit of a state hospital, and a college counseling center. She has been in private practice for four years focusing on individual treatment of adults and occasional couples work. She has recently begun to take on family therapy cases, including some families with children.

CASE 4-2: Cicero Dolt, M.D., trained as an adult psychiatrist, has no training in child development or child treatment. He has been treating Maureen Parting in individual psychotherapy since she and her husband separated 2 years ago. The Partings' divorce has become contested, and the custody of their 6-year-old son is at issue. At the request of Ms. Parting, Dr. Dolt agrees to testify as to her parenting skills and emotional stability. While on the witness stand, Dr. Dolt is asked to offer his opinions about Mr. Parting's competence as a parent and the best interests of 6-year-old Billy, so far as custody is concerned. Although he has never met Mr. Parting and has seen the boy for only brief intervals in his waiting room, Dr. Dolt does not hesitate to express his views based on information gleaned only in sessions with his client.

Dr. Kinder is presumably a competent clinician with extensive training in adult work. She may also have acquired experiences in marital or couples therapy along the way. However, she appears to lack a background in normal human development and child psychopathology, yet she apparently sees no reason why this should preclude her from working with children in a family context. Will she have a realistic understanding of the family's problems from the child's perspective? Will she be able to separate issues of the child as an identified patient in the family context from actual psychopathological conditions in the individual child? Will she be able to address the parents' developmental expectations regarding their child's abilities and behavior? The answer to all these questions seems at best to be "unlikely." At the same time, it is doubtful that Dr. Kinder will be called to account for her poor judgment before a malpractice tribunal, licensing board, or ethics committee unless or until something goes seriously wrong with one of her cases.

Dr. Dolt is similar to Dr. Kinder with respect to his lack of child training, but he is far more foolish in that he seems willing to betray his ignorance in public and under oath before a stenographer. It would certainly be appropriate for him to testify regarding his client's emotional stability, acceptance of parenting responsibility, or other similar aspects of her abilities to be a good parent. However, his willingness to comment on the child's adjustment or to offer an opinion about the father he has never met based solely on his client's comments places him far beyond the bounds of competence and acceptable professional responsibility. Furthermore, his public display of such poor judgment is likely to be caught on cross-examination and could well result in complaints to a licensing board or ethics committee. Should Ms. Parting lose the case and attribute the loss to Dr. Dolt's poor professional judgment, he might also find himself a defendant in a malpractice action. (For additional discussion of ethical problems in child custody disputes, see chap. 7.)

Cases involving sexual abuse have been prominent in the press and in clinical literature for the past few years. Such cases have provided new and dangerous opportunities for psychologists to display examples of their incompetence.

CASE 4-3: Franklin Futz, Ph.D., was trained as a clinical psychologist and has practiced individual and marital treatment with adults for nearly 30 years. Recently, he published an anecdotal paper reviewing court records or media accounts of five adult males who had been accused of molestation in cases in which children provided victim-witness testimony. On the basis of his analysis of these cases, Dr. Futz concluded that three of the children (or 60% of his sample of five cases) had fabricated their stories of being abused. Because of this published paper, Dr. Futz has frequently been sought as an "expert witness" for the defense in molestation or sexual abuse cases involving children. He has often testified, "It is quite common for youngsters to fantasize about sexual activities and to believe that these fantasies are real. The only meaningful evidence of sexual molestation in young children is documented proof of physical injury or sexually transmitted disease in the child. Their oral testimony cannot be considered credible."

CASE 4-4: Kathy Klutz, M.S.W., was asked to undertake a "sexual abuse evaluation" in a case in which a 5-year-old had stated, "Mommy put a popsicle stick up my bum." When Klutz first interviewed the child, the little girl denied that she had been mistreated. Deciding that some abuse may have occurred but was being "repressed," Klutz "continued to work" with the child using anatomically detailed dolls. The child subsequently provided Klutz with "sufficient play content to conclude that she was sexually abused for a prolonged period of time." Klutz made no audio or videotaped record of her interviews but concluded that the child required long-term treatment to reexperience her abuse, "so as not to be destined to repeat it."

It was subsequently determined that the child was severely limited in language development and that her mother had taken her temperature rectally on several occasions during episodes of fever. The child was also later overheard calling a thermometer a "popsicle stick."

Dr. Futz is actually far more dangerous than his colleagues Kinder and Dolt. To begin with, he should not be seeking to address the ultimate legal issue of guilt or innocence on the basis of theoretical speculation

(Melton, Pertrila, Poythress, & Slobogin, 1987). In addition, he fails to recognize the limitations of his own "research" and seems ignorant of the significant body of literature on children as credible witnesses or children as witnesses in sexual abuse cases (e.g., Goodman, 1984a, 1984b). If he is believed by the judge, inadequately cross-examined, or not rebutted by other witnesses, his testimony could potentially result in a child's being left in the unsupervised custody of an abusive parent. As in the case of Dr. Dolt, he may well find formal charges filed against him, especially when a more knowledgeable expert called by the other side learns of Futz's testimony.

Like Dr. Futz, Ms. Klutz seems prone to leap to conclusions. She had her own agenda regarding sexual abuse issues and was blinded by these in her assessment and treatment in a forensic case. The consequences to the family involved could have been disastrous. The malpractice suit now in progress against Ms. Klutz will be disastrous for her professional reputation, even if she is not found liable for damages by the jury.

Many cases involving children in divorce situations, or as victims or witnesses, or in abuse or neglect actions, or before the juvenile courts, will place the psychologist under at least some degree of professional scrutiny. Several such cases are discussed in chapter 7. However, in most contexts in which psychologists serve children and families, their work is not monitored. In other circumstances, there may be power relationships that make psychologists reluctant to call each other to account for such behavior.

CASE 4-5: Sarah Senior, Ed.D., is a supervisor at a child guidance clinic with a psychology internship program. She was assigned to work with Irving Inept, a trainee whose competence with children was questionable. Although the trainee was able to relate effectively with adults, he was stiff and distant in his relationships with children and adolescents. He also showed poor clinical judgment in conceptualizing child cases, although he was not behaving in a manner that was clearly harmful to clients.

CASE 4-6: Alan Advocate, Ph.D., was a well-trained clinical child psychologist practicing in Smallville. The town's school department

73

had a reputation for underdiagnosing special educational needs in their public school system. This may have reflected an effort to keep educational costs down in the face of state and federal laws (e.g., P.L. 94-142) intended to mandate necessary educational services for such children. When Dr. Advocate encouraged parents to press the school system for better services and to seek legal remedies if necessary, school administrators began actively to discourage referrals to his practice.

These two cases illustrate some of the drawbacks of pressing for recognition of competence or adequacy of services in child-focused situations. Evaluating the competence of colleagues or supervisees is always a sensitive task. In Dr. Senior's situation, there is no urgent problem, but Mr. Inept is clearly going to have continuing difficulty adequately serving the population he is now training to work with. Dr. Senior is in a critical position both to provide him with guidance in a timely manner and to advise him regarding problems he will face should he decide to pursue practice in this area. Presenting this feedback will be interpersonally difficult and in some ways represents an added burden to the already difficult task of supervising this trainee. In many ways, it would be easy for Dr. Senior simply to let Inept muddle through the rotation and be rid of him. This would obviously have significant implications for the children whom Inept may treat in the future.

Both academic and practicum or internship training programs should have well-conceptualized guidelines of what constitutes acceptable practice and how routine feedback is provided both to trainees and to their academic departments. Such feedback systems should include the concept of "provisional pass" grades or recommendations for limited or supervised practice in the future. These guidelines should specifically address both general skills related to competent human service delivery and special skills related to serving children. By the same token, university-based programs should carefully monitor practicum and internship sites, especially those without formal accreditation. Case 3-7 in the previous chapter illustrated the difficult pressures sometimes placed on trainees to take on excessive responsibilities or perform procedures for which they are not well trained or properly supervised.

Dr. Advocate is in a similar role in the sense that he is confronted with ineptitude and must decide whether to press an "inept system" to provide legally mandated services of an appropriate quality. Unlike Dr. Senior, however, Advocate is not in a role of supervisory responsibility. He must decide whether his public responsibility or duty to his clients is sufficient to warrant additional intervention. He must also decide how vigorously to press the case or encourage his clients to press it. The potential adverse consequences to him in terms of time, aggravation, and the effect on his practice and reputation are clear. However, the best basis for making his decision is less evident. (See also the discussion of cases 3-10 and 3-11 [*Forrest v. Ansbach*] in chap. 3.)

The "Sick Doctor"

Like all other human beings, mental health professionals are not immune from problems of their own. Emotional problems and substance abuse do occur among professionals and in such circumstances may well impair their professional functioning. When the clients are children, this problem is more dangerous for two reasons. First, the child client is often more dependent and developmentally vulnerable to abuse or incompetence at the hands of a practitioner. Second, unlike many adult clients, children may lack the sophistication to realize early on that they are being ill served by an impaired psychotherapist. Consider these examples:

CASE 4-7: The mother of a 4-year-old girl complained to an ethics committee and to legal authorities that her child's therapist was sexually abusing the child during individual psychotherapy sessions. One evening following a session, the mother noticed as she bathed the child that the girls pubic area was swollen and reddened. After some questioning, the girl described a "game" that the therapist usually played with her. This consisted of having the girl remove her panties and sit on his face while he "tickled" her with his tongue.

CASE 4-8: Two parents complained to the supervisor of Ranta Rage, L.I.S.W., a social worker at a large community agency. Their adolescent children reported that Ms. Rage was "sometimes nice" but at other times yelled at them for no apparent reason, did not remember their names, and confused information that they had given her with facts apparently recalled from other cases to which she was assigned. One of the boys reported, "She started screaming that I should have gotten 10 years in prison for robbing a gas station. I've never been in any trouble like that. She's a real scary lady."

CASE 4-9: In an effort to "build rapport" with some of his older adolescent clients, Ralph Reefer, M.D., routinely offers to share tobacco or marijuana cigarettes with them during sessions.

Sexual abuse of a child client and providing harmful or illegal drugs to minors are probably among the most offensive of criminal acts. While the perpetrators of such acts may report some "rationale" for their behavior, personal psychopathology is more often the culprit.

Lest the reader be inclined to dismiss sexual abuse of children by mental health professionals as rare or isolated events, we suggest reviewing the results of a survey by Bajt and Pope (1989). Ninety of 100 senior clinical psychologists responded to their request to report anonymously on any instances of sexual intimacy between a psychotherapist and a minor client that they had personally discovered during the course of their professional work. A total of 81 instances was reported by 22 different respondents. An additional five psychologists reported hearsay accounts of cases for which they lacked firsthand knowledge. Age ranges were reported for 20 female patients (range = 3–17 years, mean = 13.75, and standard deviation = 4.12) and 18 male patients (range = 7–16 years, mean = 12.5, and standard deviation = 3.01). These findings suggest that mental health professionals treating children must be sensitive to the possibility of sexual abuse by prior therapists.

Ms. Rage is showing behaviors that may indicate an undiagnosed neurological impairment. Her episodes of apparent confusion, memory problems, and unprovoked temper outbursts are distressing to her clients and suggest that other areas of her professional work may also be out of control. Although she does have a right to privacy with respect to any medical problems, the agency is obligated to intervene should her condition place clients at risk.

In the case of Dr. Reefer, the offer of tobacco-based products would also be deemed unethical because of the well-documented adverse health consequences that could result from smoking or nicotine addiction. Offers of marijuana or other illegal substances add extra voliations. His quest for "rapport" is fraught with signs of poor judgment and shaky professional boundaries.

Bad Boundaries and Dual Role Relationships

Both of the cases mentioned above also reflect a degree of poor professional boundaries on the part of the psychologist involved. More subtle problems with personal boundaries are all too frequent in child work. Even the practitioner with usually good professional standards may get into ethical difficulty with dual relationship problems involving child clients and their families.

CASE 4-10: Felix Foster, Psy.D., was treating a 5-year-old child whom he believed to be emotionally deprived. The parents reported some behavior problems, but the child told the therapist that he was just trying to get some attention and that his parents "are always busy." The therapist reasoned that the child needed some affection and often patted the child's head, gave small hugs, or permitted the child to sit on his lap during both family and individual sessions. The parents became increasingly disturbed by the therapist's suggestions that their attitudes and behavior at home were the cause of the child's misbehavior and failed in their attempts to convince the therapist that the responsibility lay solely with the "rotten brat." The therapeutic alliance deteriorated, and the parents abruptly terminated the professional relationship, later writing to an ethics committee that the therapist sexually misused their child.

CASE 4-11: Oliver Obtuse, Ph.D., was called before a disciplinary panel on charges of having sexual relations with a female client. Dr. Obtuse protested that the woman, with whom he acknowledged having an extramarital affair, was not his client at all. He had met her while treating her 10-year-old daughter. The daughter required treatment because she was anxious and depressed by prospects that her parents might be about to divorce.

Drs. Foster and Obtuse both seem to have blind spots regarding their behavior. Dr. Foster has apparently developed countertransference feelings for his young client. These feelings may be contributing to an inability to assess and intervene effectively in the family dynamics. In the end, his warm positive feelings for the child are misinterpreted, and he finds himself in significant difficulty. Not only does Dr. Obtuse suffer from boundary problems, but he also seems oblivious to the dual relationship problem involved in having an intimate relationship with the parent of a child client. To make matters worse, his behavior may be contributing to the stress that precipitated the child's need for treatment in the first place.

Not all potential dual relationship problems are as dramatic or insidious, but even seemingly mundane ones may pose significant ethical issues, as illustrated in chapter 2 by cases 2-10 and 2-11. Neither of these situations described in chapter 2 has as yet become an example of unethical behavior, but both are problems waiting to happen. Dr. Pal (case 2-11) could certainly offer some informal helpful advice to her friend, but taking on the child in therapy could prove a disaster. Aside from the host of issues that could destroy a friendship, Dr. Pal could find herself in the midst of a child custody battle between two friends and find her professional objectivity and personal loyalty challenged. The rural colleague's dilemma (case 2-10) is complicated by the fact that she may be the only mental health professional (let alone qualified child therapist) in a wide geographic area. In her "small world," avoiding some degree of dual relationship, at least on the acquaintance level, may be impossible. For her it will be important to talk openly with her clients about the therapist-client roles, relationship, confidentiality, and boundaries. She will have to be extra cautious and set limits that are comfortable for both her and her clients. She will also have to exercise special caution in hiring and supervising her support staff (e.g., secretaries or file clerks) to be certain that they too show a high respect for the privacy of their neighbors in the area.

Although not specifically focused on children, more extensive discussion of dual role relationship problems may be found in Keith-Spiegel and Koocher (1985).

GUIDELINES

The following guidelines are suggested to assure minimal basic competence among individuals planning to provide mental health services to children and their families.

Competence to Serve Children and Families

1. Practitioners planning to undertake psychodiagnostic or psychotherapeutic work with children or families should have completed formal course work in developmental psychology or human development, including educational components on physical, social, and personality development as well as psychopathology of childhood and adolescence.

2. In addition, such practitioners should also have completed supervised practica or internships in educational or agency settings that include practice in all the skills and techniques that will be used in work with children or families.

3. Practitioners should make themselves aware on a continuing basis of statutes or regulations in their locale or agency that specifically apply to children (e.g., child abuse reporting laws).

4. Clinicians should strive to maintain an awareness of and sensitivity to the effect of their own emotional stability on their child clients.

5. While it may not be possible totally to avoid all possible dual role relationships, it is especially important to consider the potential effect of such relationships when working with children and families. The dual roles in these situations may grow out of relationships with people other than the identified patient and as such may go unnoticed until some crisis arises.

6. If a child client behaves in a manner that suggests that abuse may have occurred while in the care of a prior professional relationship, the current therapist should treat such indications as worthy of serious exploration.

CONFIDENTIALITY

Privilege versus Confidentiality versus Privacy

Mental health professionals who are not well versed in legal matters are often confused by the distinctions among the concepts of privilege, confidentiality, and privacy. *Privacy* refers to the basic rights guaranteed by the Fourth Amendment and other sections of the U.S. Constitution. It is chiefly the right of the individual to make decisions about how much of his or her thoughts, feelings, or personal information should be shared with others. *Privacy* is generally considered essential to ensure human dignity and freedom of self-determination. *Confidentiality* refers to a general standard of professional conduct requiring a practitioner not to discuss information about a client with anyone. The concept of confidentiality evolved from the notion of individuals' privacy rights, although privacy is a much broader topic. Confidentiality is based in statute, case law, or both, depending on the jurisdiction (Swoboda, Elwork, Sales, & Levine, 1978), but when cited as an ethical principle it implies an explicit obligation not to reveal anything about a client, except under certain specific circumstances agreed to by both the professional and the client. Distinguishing between privilege and confidentiality introduces some new elements. *Privilege* (or privileged communication) is a legal term that is used to describe the protection afforded certain specific types of relationships from being subject to forced disclosure in court or other legal proceedings. Privilege is granted either by statute or by common law and belongs to the client. Traditionally, privilege has been extended to attorney-client, husband-wife, physician-patient, and penitent-priest relationships. Some jurisdictions currently extend privilege to psychologist-client or psychotherapist-client relationships (for a more extensive commentary on these topics, see Keith-Spiegel & Koocher, 1985).

Differences between Child and Adult Clients

The distinctions among privacy, confidentiality, and privilege rights of adults and those of children may be considered from the perspective of either law or developmental psychology. In the legal arena, the rights assured to adult citizens under the U.S. Constitution do not necessarily apply to children. As discussed in chapter 1, it was not until the 1967 *Gault* decision that children were clearly recognized as "persons" in constitutional law. In most circumstances, the parents or legal guardians of children under 18 years old may make all privacy-related legal decisions for them. This includes signing for releases of information, securing and inspecting school and hospital records, and authorizing searches of the child's property. In the strictest legal sense, children are not generally entitled to have secrets from their parents unless the parents permit it. For this reason, it is important that mental health clinicians discuss the limits of confidentiality with both parents and children at the outset of their professional relationship.

From the developmental perspective, the issues are quite different. For example, can the child at the preoperational stage of cognitive development, who assumes that her parents are omnipotent and omniscient, conceive of another adult's withholding any information from her parents? In such a situation, the notion of confidentiality has little meaning. By the same token, autonomy and privacy are central concerns to the adolescent, and the clinician's fidelity to any promises made to the teenager will almost certainly be tested regularly. If the central purpose of confidentiality in a professional relationship is to facilitate a trusting therapeutic relationship, one should not be trapped by a rigid concept of secrecy. Treating children and adolescents with truthfulness, personal respect, serious consideration, and involvement in goal setting goes a lot further in establishing a trusting relationship than does any absolute promise of confidentiality (Koocher, 1976a). Creation of a therapeutic climate is the central goal of the clinician, and within that context it is reasonable to discuss with the child the nature and extent of material to be shared with others as well as the reasons for sharing it.

The mental health professional must also be prepared to make judgments that have subtle implications that may not be clear to the child or even the parents. For example, will release of a treatment report to a school lead to inappropriate stigmatization or labeling? Will a diagnosis released to an insurance company lead to the denial of coverage years later? How does one explain these long-term risks to a child for whom "next month" seems as far away as forever? Clearly, there is an important role for the exercise of professional judgment and consideration of individual case factors in making such a decision.

Although a mental health professional is not legally obligated always to seek permission of a child client before disclosing confidential information, it is ethically mandatory to attempt to get such permission. This implies a recognition of the child's cognitive, social, and emotional developmental levels with appropriate allowances. It also implies an understanding of children's special dependency and vulnerability with respect to adults and of the resulting levels of protection that confidentiality may afford.

The basic principles involved include discussing the "ground rules" for confidentiality in advance with the parents and child together. In such cases, prevention is far better than trying to undo a complicated web of expectations (see case 3-14). For example, we strongly recommend that mental health professionals disclose the limits of confidentiality at the start of psychotherapy, especially with adolescents. Behavior that is self-endangering or potentially harmful to others (i.e., suicide risk and *Tarasoff* situations) ought to be specifically addressed.

CASE 4-12: Donna Rhea, age 15, discloses to her psychotherapist that she is using drugs purchased from another student at her high school and is engaging in unprotected sexual intercourse with him in payment for the drugs.

CASE 4-13: Becky Splitsky, age 14, calls you, her psychotherapist, to report that she has run away from home. Her parents do not know whether their child is safe and are frantic with worry. You ask the girl whether she objects to your letting her parents know that she is all right, and she says that she does object.

Donna's behavior is risky on at least three counts: from the street drugs, from sexually transmitted diseases, and from possible pregnancy. By disclosing this to her therapist, she is in many ways asking for help. The therapist should discuss with Donna the need for appropriate treatment and parental involvement, encouraging her to be a part of the disclosure and helping her get the additional help and support she seems to need. In Becky's case, the risk is not necessarily so acute but is still genuine. It is certainly desirable for the psychotherapist to help Becky find a safe haven, although not in the same way as described in case 2-14. Asking Becky if she objects to her parents being notified at this point is the wrong question and sets up an unnecessary test. Parental notification can be dealt with after talking Becky into seeking safe shelter if she will not be talked into returning home.

Children and the Duty to Protect Third Parties

Although most mental health professionals are aware of the so-called *Tarasoff* (1976) doctrine, many are unaware of important "duty to protect" cases that involved child clients. Such cases do occur, and clinicians would be wise to be sensitive to the possibility and to formulate plans for dealing with them should they arise.

CASE 4-14: Lee Morgenstern, a teenaged client, told his therapist (a psychiatrist named Milano) of sexual adventures, acting-out behavior, and jealousy related to Kimberly McIntosh, the young woman next door. The therapist did not particularly believe him. Later, the teen shot the woman to death, and the psychiatrist was sued. He sought summary judgment, but it was not granted, and the case went on to a trial. The jury ultimately found no negligence on Dr. Milano's part (*McIntosh v Milano*, 1979).

CASE 4-15: A teenaged juvenile offender named James who was in county custody threatened to "off" someone when released from incarceration. Sent home on a leave in his mother's custody, he tortured a 5-year-old neighborhood boy to death. The parents sued the county and advanced the *Tarasoff* doctrine as part of their case. The court disallowed application of that doctrine because there was no specific identifiable victim of the teenager's nonspecific threats. In addition, the court ruled that the official decision to grant leave and similar correctional release decisions were immune from liability (*Thompson v. County of Alameda*, 1980).

CASE 4-16: The mother of a mentally retarded juvenile, who was also known to be a fire setter, sued state and county authorities for failure to warn, after they sent him home on a pass and he set a fire that killed one person and severely burned another. The case was dismissed in part because the plaintiff knew of the danger and there were no specific identified victims (*Cairl v. Minnesota*, 1982).

No liability was assessed against mental health professionals in any of these three cases, but that does not eliminate potential risk in future cases. In addition, no one wants to have a client responsible for a homicide or to face the significant stresses and costs of defending a lawsuit. Thoughtful assessment and sensitivity to risk and responsibility are the key issues to be evaluated, considering such factors as past behavior, impulse control, access to weapons, formulation of specific plans to harm someone, and delusional content related to threats of harm (Blau, 1987; Botkin & Nietzel, 1987).

Releasing Information on a "Need-to-Know" Basis

It seems obvious to note that, once data leave a clinician's office, the professional no longer has control over the material. Even when release of information is authorized, it is often wise to limit what is released on a need-to-know basis. That is to say, one would communicate more detailed information to a client's new psychotherapist than one would to a school guidance counselor.

CASE 4-17: Buster Loose was evaluated by a psychologist on referral because of "learning problems." The clinician uncovered that a history of heretofore undisclosed sexual abuse was contributing to Buster's problems. Although he has a release of information form authorizing a report to the school, the psychologist limited the sensitive aspects of the information on a need-to-know basis and did not discuss the details of Buster's emotional difficulties in the report that he sent to the school.

CASE 4-18: Harley Hegger, M.D., a psychiatrist working as a psychotherapist and consultant to child-care workers in a residential treatment setting, is often asked or expected to share information about his clients during treatment team meetings or in consultation sessions. He wonders how much of the clinical material should be appropriately shared.

Both of these cases illustrate difficult "judgment call" situations. It is clear that the school authorities do not need intimate details of Buster's emotional issues in order to develop an appropriate, individualized educational plan for him. Staff at a residential treatment program may be more akin to psychotherapists than to teachers, but still they need not have access to the same full data set as the individual therapist. When in doubt, it is good to have a consultant or senior colleague with whom to review the case and determine the essentials to be communicated.

Child Abuse Reporting

Every state has legislation that mandates the reporting of cases of suspected child abuse to authorities for investigation (Garbarino & Gilliam, 1980). Mental health professionals are usually cited specifically as obligated to report. Too often, however, one hears of colleagues who ought to file a report in a specific case but decide not to. Usually, those reluctant to report will rationalize, "I thought it was better to keep the family in treatment than to file a report and risk losing the case for good." Such reasoning implies a naive sense of omnipotence on the part of the therapist, suggesting that somehow keeping the family in treatment will prevent further abuse. Not only is such failure to report illegal, but it puts the vulnerable child at risk and as a result is unethical on both of those counts. Sometimes, however, the situation becomes even more complicated.

CASE 4-19: On answering her office telephone one morning, Nellie Rigor, Ph.D., was told by the anonymous caller, "My pediatrician, Dr. Harris, suggested I call you. I saw a television show the other night about the signs of sexual abuse in the family, and I am concerned that my husband might be abusing our 12-year-old daughter. I don't know what to do. Can I get some confidential advice from you?" The psychologist replied that she would be glad to assist the family. However, she also advised the mother that she might be obligated under state law to report the case to authorities if there seemed to be reason to believe that abuse was indeed occurring. The mother then hung up the phone.

What are Dr. Rigor's obligations? Although she does not know enough to identify the caller, she does know the referral source. She could call Dr. Harris, the pediatrician, and ask his help or advise him to file the mandated report if he has specific data. However, Dr. Harris may not want to report the case and may stop referring clients to Rigor if she insists on pressing the issue. How far to push the matter in such a case must be a personal decision, but a concerned call to the pediatrician should be the minimum step taken.

CASE 4-20: Sarah Childers, Ed.D., regularly gets referrals for assessments from a local preschool. While conducting such an assessment with parental consent, she finds reason to believe that the child is being neglected and malnourished. State law would require her to report this case, but Dr. Childers knows that the state agency responsible for acting on such reports is staffed by ill-trained and overworked people. The parents are wealthy and influential in the city. She wonders whether it would be best not to report the case but instead to try to accomplish more by engaging the child and parents in treatment.

As in the case of Dr. Rigor, Dr. Childers must confront the matter of child abuse reporting and whether such reporting risks destroying a professional relationship or whether not reporting endangers the child. In this case, it seems wise first to consult with the family in order to share her concerns. Perhaps there is a valid alternative explanation for what she has observed.

Even when a clinician is correct in assessing abuse or neglect and must report the case, it does not have to be a totally untherapeutic experience. Dr. Harris and Dr. Rigor, for example, could tell the worried mother, "If it turns out that we are obligated under law to file a report on this case, we will stick by you and help to see that you and your family get the support and treatment that is needed." Reporting such cases does not necessitate terminating the professional relationship in every case (Harper & Irvin, 1985).

Sometimes it is clear that reporting a case will result in the child being removed from parental care and will create considerable disruption in a situation that is not necessarily terrible from the child's current perspective.

CASE 4-21: In the course of his psychotherapeutic work with an 8-year-old who was depressed following the death of a grandparent, a psychotherapist became aware that the parents were selling cocaine and other illicit drugs from the family home. This information was casually revealed by the child, who had observed many drug sales.

CASE 4-22: An 11-year-old boy whose parents were divorced was placed in the custody of his mother, although his father had frequent visitation. During the course of psychotherapy, which focused on helping him adjust to the divorce, the boy told with great glee of riding on a piece of carpet that his father would tow along over the snow behind his car.

In both of these cases, the child's-eye view of the adventures described may be benign. Disclosure would result in severe adverse consequences for loved ones as the direct result of parental behaviors that the youngster had not necessarily seen as problematic. Neither of these last two cases involve clear abuse or neglect of a child, but both involve parents who are putting their child at some risk, both by their direct risk taking or illicit behavior and by the role modeling they provide. Caution is indicated in both situations, as the child might feel quite guilty should the parents be arrested in the former case or should the mother seek to terminate the father's unsupervised visiting in the latter case.

GUIDELINES
Confidentiality Issues

1. Establishing trust and therapeutic alliances with child clients is not dependent on confidentiality in precisely the same way as it does with adult clients, and these developmental differences must be carefully considered.

2. Mental health professionals must be aware of the legal requirements and limitations placed on their relationships with child clients, including

such matters as child abuse reporting, duty-to-protect issues, and access of family members to children's records.

3. With respect to mandated child abuse reporting laws, it is particularly important for professionals to understand the threshold for filing formal reports with state authorities. Use of "professional discretion" as a rationale for not reporting is ethically unacceptable.

4. Discussion regarding confidentiality with parents and children at the start of a professional relationship is an important step in clarifying relationships and avoiding misunderstandings later.

5. Careful consideration should be given to the potential consequences of releasing confidential material in reports to "third parties" (e.g., health insurance carriers, public schools, etc.). Information should be provided on a need-to-know basis. This is a particularly important matter for child clients because of the potential that some data might have with respect to educational tracking or self-fulfilling prophecies.

•

CHAPTER FIVE

Research with Children:
Planning and Recruiting
Participants

This century has witnessed rapid and dramatic changes in the ethical guidelines and government policies regulating scientific research using human participants. The horrifying spectacle of science gone insane in Nazi Germany was most certainly the catalyst for the development of formal research policy here and abroad. It was to take the United States another generation, however, formally to adopt regulations that dealt specifically with research conducted on children.

As a result of the National Research Act (P.L. 93-348) signed into law in 1974, the National Commission for the Protection of Human Subjects of Biomedical and Behavioral Research was created. Based largely on the commission's report, *Research Involving Children* (1977), a small section outlining special considerations with child research participants is included in the latest federal regulations for human subject research (Department of Health and Human Services, 1983). The final version of this brief "subpart" and how it came to be has generated considerable scholarly comment (e.g., Leikin, 1985; M. Lewis, 1981; McCartney & Beauchamp, 1981; Mishkin, 1982; Porter, 1985; Reatig, 1981; and Wilson, 1982), largely because so much interpretive and decision-making power has been accorded to those who are empowered to evaluate individual research proposals. The federal regulations themselves offer investigators only very general operating parameters and little specific guidance, leaving the gates wide open for debate. Unfortunately, professional association ethics codes addressing children as participants in research are either outdated or too scanty to take up the slack by providing guidance.

Federal regulations governing research apply *only* to those projects funded in whole or in part by Department of Health and Human Services (DHHS) grants, contracts, cooperative agreements, or fellowships. Although funding from most any source would not likely be available to institutions that had not demonstrated a dedication to the protection of human research participants, there is no clear legal mandate to comply with federal policy for nonfunded projects or for projects funded from other sources.

This chapter and chapter 6 offer an analysis of the DHHS regulations for research using child participants (Department of Health and Human Services, 1983) as well as additional discussions of ethical matters not addressed by federal policy. However, it is important to note again at the outset that federal regulations accord considerable decision-making authority to institutional review boards (IRBs), which are composed of a small group of individuals at the site where the research will be conducted. This situation complicates our task of offering guidance to our readers in that we cannot presume to second-guess what any given IRB will decide to demand, recommend, or allow on any specific project.

RESEARCH VERSUS PRACTICE

For our purposes, *research* is defined as a category of activity designed to develop or contribute to generalizable knowledge. Such activity is conducted in a systematic, controlled fashion on the basis of accepted scientific principles. In contrast, *practice* refers to a class of activities designed solely to enhance the well-being of an individual. Routine and accepted practice is characterized by an expectation of success. Despite the uncertainty of a successful outcome owing to variabilities in the human response, such activity does not qualify as research since this uncertainty is itself considered routine and acceptable (Levine, 1978).

Between these two classes of activity is an ambiguous category variously referred to as *innovative therapy*, *novel practice*, or *unvalidated practice*. Though experimental in nature, such activities do not qualify as research unless they are formally constructed as a research project. The National Commission argued that significant deviations from acceptable practice should be incorporated into a research project in order to establish safety and efficacy while, at the same time, retaining therapeutic objectives.

During the deliberations of the National Commission in the late 1970s, the distinction between *therapeutic* and *nontherapeutic* research that was earlier popularized by many commentators was carefully reevaluated. Basically, the notion was that research proposals designed to benefit those with some illness or other problem directly might be evaluated very differently in terms of what could ethically be "done to" children (including how consent was to be obtained and the acceptable level of potential risk) than was research conducted for the sole purpose of obtaining generalizable knowledge about children.

Opinion about conditions under which children could, or whether they should ever, be enrolled in nontherapeutic research has varied markedly, often in the form of lively debate (e.g., Ackerman, 1979; Campbell, 1974; Comiskey, 1978; Cooke, 1977; Gaylin & Macklin, 1982; Glantz, Annas, & Katz, 1977; Langer, 1985; Lowe, Alexander, & Mishkin, 1974; McCormick, 1974, 1976; and Ramsey, 1976). Here the usual assumption that parents know what is best for their children and thus may "consent" for them is inapplicable because there is no direct beneficial intent to begin with. Is it ethical to use children for the "social good" even if the parents give their permission? The issue does not resolve easily because research application is a process that tracks across time, with findings overlaid on each other as the knowledge stockpile grows. No one can say for certain what information will ultimately be beneficial regardless of the initial intent.

Use of the terms *therapeutic research* and *nontherapeutic research* was ultimately abandoned by the National Commission; they were replaced with a conceptualization of levels of acceptable risks depending on the potential benefits accruing to the participants themselves or to others. This hierarchy is detailed in chapter 6.

Many professionals working with children have often found themselves in a position of being involved in a research or evaluation project and at the same time being entrusted with children's care or treatment. Referring to pediatric oncology care centers specifically, van Eys (1982) contends that "this new generation was taught to deliver care by research and to perform research in the process of delivering care. They honestly can't tell the difference anymore" (p. 421). Those working in hospitals and agencies serving the mental health needs of children, or those involved in primary prevention or intervention programs, may experience the same confounding roles. The "professional helper" role requires one to make an individualized decision in the client's best interests, often at least partially based on hunches, faith, and the client's wishes. The "investigator" role requires a commitment to carry out the demands of the research protocol in a competent, precise, and objective manner to assure that data are valid, interpretable, and generalizable. With careful planning that includes safeguards and contingencies, many of the treatment/research goal, role, and ethical conflicts can be minimized. (For an excellent analysis and account of an effort to tackle the ethical problems inherent in a controlled clinical trials psychotherapy research project, see Imber et al., 1986.)

INVESTIGATOR COMPETENCE

Ideally, *all* investigators studying children should possess competencies in research methodology, statistics, developmental psychology, family studies, and child/adolescent mental health. Some do, but most may be weak in one or more of these areas because traditional institutions training developmental psychologists emphasize experimental and research methodology skills and deemphasize or neglect altogether clinical skill training, and the reverse usually holds for clinical psychologists and other mental health professionals.

CASE 5-1: Dr. Hy Bomb, a somewhat inexperienced developmental psychologist, designed a cross-sectional study to assess 10–14-year-old children's reactions to the threat of nuclear war. Children of different ages were shown a short but graphic dramatized film depicting the results of a nuclear attack on an American city. Afterward, each child was given a brief questionnaire. Many of the children were upset after the film, and a few were crying. One vomited. Those who were able to work on the questionnaire seemed distracted and uncomfortable. Many left questions unanswered, and some questionnaires seemed to have been filled in randomly.

Those with more experience around children could have foreseen the problem and offered alternative study methods that may not have had such a powerful effect but that could have better protected the children while still yielding meaningful data. Experts who conduct research with animals have issued strong mandates to "know your species thoroughly" before proceeding (e.g., Lea, 1979). We recommend the same grounding for those working with children. Investigators should be thoroughly familiar with what causes children distress, what is known about their competencies at various stages, and so on *before* conducting research on them. We must be careful to separate out what we believe they are like from what we know they are like. For example, an investigator who believes that children are "tough" and "resilient" may design a study much differently from one who believes that children are "impressionable" and "easily vulnerable to the enduring effect of negative experiences":

CASE 5-2: Ann Naive, a school counselor, wanted to "test out" her hypothesis that poor study habits were caused by aggressive tendencies. She asked junior high school students who were sent to the guidance office for fighting on the playground if they liked to study and how much time they spent studying. Twenty-three out of 31 students said that they did not like to study, and most of the children studied less than 3 hours a week. She therefore concluded that her hypothesis had proved to be fact.

93

This ludicrous example shows a number of design and interpretive pitfalls. We recommend that those who study children consult with appropriate colleagues to assure that all competency bases are covered. Those who spend the bulk of their professional time working with children and their families are an excellent resource for identifying significant research needs, evaluating any assessment or experimental techniques as to their appropriateness, and intervening if difficulties arise during or after data collection. Those with strong methodological skills can assure that the design is strong, that data are appropriately analyzed, and that the findings are properly interpreted and generalized.

INVESTIGATOR VALUES AND BIASES

No researcher is without values, biases, and strong opinions or attitudes about his or her area of expertise. Collegial consultation, especially from those known to have theoretical or value differences from one's own, is a useful way to assure that one's biases have not, even unintentionally, jeopardized the integrity of the design or the welfare of the participants or perpetuated innaccurate stereotypes. The next case offers an example of value/theoretical bias:

> CASE 5-3: Dr. Edith Blame was interested in studying the mothers of daughters who were abused by their fathers. She created an interview schedule designed to assess the knowledge the mother had of what was occurring, the mother's sexuality, and the steps the mothers failed to take to protect their daughters.

This researcher was attempting to collect empirical data to substantiate her theoretical notion that the mother is the pivotal cause of the family dysfunction that leads to abusive incidents. The interview was not constructed in a way that allowed for disconfirming information to emerge. de Chesnay (1984) warns those who conduct research involving or treat families of incest victims to be especially wary of sexist stereotypes that permeate assumptions about incest.

Finally, just as for those who deliver psychotherapeutic services, professional boundaries must remain clarified and salient in the research investigator's mind. Children evoke strong emotional reactions, ranging from intense caring and compassion to disdain. Investigators must be objective and evenhanded in their work while still remaining alert to the welfare of the research participants. We also agree with Rae and Fournier (1986), who insist that researchers should always be kind to the children they study.

ETHICAL ISSUES WITH RESEARCH DESIGNS

Whether the participants are adults or children, the quality of a research design is itself an ethical issue (Edsall, 1969; Rutstein, 1969). Poorly designed studies yield uninterpretable, easily misinterpreted, or useless findings. Participants at best have wasted their time and at worst were needlessly put at risk or harmed. Future participants may also be harmed if the findings are generalized and applied. Overall, the scientific knowledge stockpile has been contaminated.

A difficult dilemma arises when a fully competent researcher faces a conflict between ideal methodology and ethical considerations:

CASE 5-4: Investigators were interested in the effects of pain and nonpain stimuli on grade school children in aggressive and nonaggressive settings. The investigator demonstrated the use of a device, which was basically a box with a large padded button. The box was painted with expressionless eyes, and the button was placed where a nose would be. The box was wired to "respond" to being "hit in the nose" by producing cries of pain (e.g., "Ouch," "That hurts," and "Ow").

This design, which we have only partially described, is adapted from a study by Dubanoski and Tokioka (1981). It was rejected for publication by the editor of one journal because the reviewers did not believe that striking an inanimate object could be termed aggression, or that the indicators of pain were meaningful to the children, or that the results could be generalized to children's behavior in response to hitting a person. However, the researchers had purposely chosen their methods to *minimize* any psychological stress or mental discomfort by using an inanimate object rather than a real or more lifelike victim. Dubanoski, who felt caught in a "catch-22" situation, asks the chilling question, "Does one conduct possibly unethical research in hope of publication or ethical research in fear of nonpublication?" (1978, p. 8). This dilemma of "good science" versus "participant welfare" is most evident in research involving control groups and randomized assignment to conditions.

Controls and Randomization

History reveals numerous examples of disastrous applications of findings from uncontrolled experimentation (Edsall, 1969). Thus, from a strictly scientific point of view, the use of control groups provides an ethical advantage. Unfortunately, the use of control groups can also involve profound ethical dilemmas.

Generally, a pure "no-treatment" control group should be avoided for ethical and methodological reasons. The following case reveals both flaws:

CASE 5-5: The Tiny Folks Clothing Company commissioned a study to evaluate the effectiveness of their line of boys' padded knee pants. Two groups of boys, one with the new protective pants (experimental) and the other with shorts (control), were observed for 2 weeks on an afternoon playground. Instances of physical mishaps were documented. The experimental group suffered no wounds or lacerations on their knees or legs, but the control group suffered several instances of scratches and open wounds. The difference between the two groups was statistically significant at the .001 level. Therefore, the manufacturer concluded that the new line of boys' wear was scientifically proven to be safe and protective.

The meaningful use of a control would have been, of course, to have boys wear long pants minus only the knee padding. Despite the impressive significance level, we have no findings of value. Although this particular case is rather silly, inappropriate conclusions are likely unless a control group is used properly.

Fetterman (1982) presents a case illustrating more profoundly how a control group of youngsters, in this case high school dropouts, was used as a "negative-treatment" group, thus biasing the meaning of the results. Teenagers who expressed interest in an experimental "second-chance" program funded by the government went through an elaborate screening program. Through a lottery process, one-fourth were not admitted to the experimental conditions. Fetterman cogently argues that this group of youngsters, who now felt resentful and demoralized, did not constitute a nonbiased group with which to compare treatment groups.

When a control group is necessary, its members should normally be exposed to whatever treatment or resources are already available. However, no-treatment control groups can be ethically justified under some conditions. For example, if the research does not involve participants in need of benefit relative to the experimental topic area, and if the consignment of some not to be exposed to the experimental variable causes them no risk or loss, a baseline control group can be ethically justified. Another acceptable example occurs when participants in research intended to be beneficial agree to be placed into a no-treatment control group and are, as a result, put at no additional risk. This practice can be justified so long as consent was properly obtained and the participants understood and fully agreed to this assignment. Finally, investigators may be able to justify a no-treatment control when resources limit services to fewer than the available participants, no other options or resources are available to participants, participants realize and accept from the beginning that not everyone can be enrolled in the treatment, the treatment has not been proved effective, and assignments to the treatment are made equitably (adapted from Conner, 1982). Staggered treatment, dose response controls, and other innovative designs that may help reduce ethical conflicts should be considered (e.g., DiTomasso & McDermott, 1981; Garfield, 1987; Veatch, 1987).

The ethical issues embedded in the use of randomization in assigning participants to experimental and control groups, varying only the independent variables, are discussed most frequently relative to biomedical research, usually in the field of oncology. This fact is not surprising because the consequences to at least some participants could prove lifesaving or fatal. However, the same general issues apply to social and behavioral research despite the fact that the outcomes for participants in any assigned group do not often involve the potential for any physical disability or deterioration.

Under two conditions, randomized designs pose few if any ethical complications. In the first instance, a "nontherapeutic" no (or minimal) risk study usually causes no harm to participants since they are not chosen on the basis of need and the study itself carries virtually no risk to them:

CASE 5-6: Dr. Peter Player, a developmental psychologist, randomly assigned 9-year-old male children into four groups to assess play behavior. One group received an automated space robot to play with alone for 15 minutes. Another group received a "GI Joe" doll, another a teddy bear, a third blank paper and crayons, and a final group a puzzle book. All children were observed and rated on a "play behavior" schedule.

Here the time period was brief, no child was deprived of anything known to be beneficial, and the only "risk" was that some boys may not have as much fun as others.

The second instance in which randomized designs pose few ethical complications occurs when research intended to benefit children in need, even when risk may be present, involves an *honest* null hypothesis. That is to say, it is absolutely unclear and unknown whether one treatment or procedure is any better than any other (or possibly even any better than *no* treatment or procedure that would acceptably allow for a no-treatment or placebo group as well). However, we must quickly add that this seemingly ethical problem–free situation rarely occurs. Usually, an investigator has some pilot data, a data-based trend, or some other reason that leads him or her to suspect that one treatment may be superior to the alternatives.

Randomized designs present ethical dilemmas for researchers when the participants have some problem that requires amelioration, the methods of treating or dealing with it either do not exist or are not fully satisfactory or efficacious, and some degree of risk (often unknown) is inherent in placing participants in one or more of the experimental groups. By its very nature, randomized designs do not allow for "selective placement," that is, the investigator's careful considerations of which group assignment might be the best for each particular participant. To determine placement in a study by coin flip runs counter to one's role as a caring advocate for a particular participant (Schafer, 1982). To meet the full scientific requirements of a randomized design, the study must be allowed to run its full course until all relevant outcome data are collected. This practice presents moral conflicts when early trends indicate that one group is improving rapidly or one group is deteriorating as compared to the others (see chap. 6).

Can this conflict between scientific quality, which may impartially consign participants to risky and suboptimal care, and concern for the welfare of individual participants and their unique needs be reconciled? Many authors have considered this dilemma thoughtfully, but no consensus or easy answers have been (or probably ever can be) proposed (Angell, 1984; Dupont, 1985; Lacher, 1981; Schafer, 1982, 1984).

Most of those looking for an answer concentrate on the nature of the consent requirements. If the investigator informs the prospective participants (or their proxies) of every detail of the scientific requirements and risks and the need to have the study run its full course despite early trends (and possibly obtain consent to have early trend information withheld), then ethical obligations will have been met. However, this "complete consent" approach is not without its shortcomings. It has been argued that long explanations, particularly if they are in writing, may not be understood or even attended to. Thorough consent procedures have also been seen as an intrusion on the caretaker-client relationship. Many participants or their parents may decline to get involved, and those who do continue may compose a biased sample about which later generalization may be hazardous. Finally, putting the responsibility for the decision onto the participants may be viewed as an easy escape from a dilemma that is not appropriately transferred to anyone else, least of all the participants and their parents, who may be vulnerable and prone to deference.

Others have suggested the use of alternative techniques to mitigate the dilemmas inherent in randomized designs. The use of historical control groups (data previously collected using one or more of the treatments proposed) is a technique that reduces the requirement of putting new participants at possible risk again (Wikler, 1981). However, to the extent that definitions of the problem, diagnostic criteria, or treatments have changed over time, or to the extent that the historical data are in error or are incomplete, bias can distort the validity of the conclusions. Historical control groups, when available, may be able to serve as a useful comparison when gross differences are found, but when important yet subtle nuances are at issue the use of such groups may lead to inappropriate conclusions (Dupont, 1985).

Longitudinal and Other Designs

The longitudinal design, whereby the investigator collects repeated data sets on the same participants over time, provides a valuable tool for studying developmental changes. Thus, children are often the participants in longitudinal studies. Despite the logistical problems (e.g., expense, following whereabouts of participants, dropout bias), this valuable design is the only one to result in a "true" developmental curve.

Ethical issues that may accompany the use of the longitudinal technique are often related to the fact that the participant-experimenter relationship exists for an extended period of time, often many years. Identifying information must be maintained yet kept secure. Participants or their families who decide to discontinue their involvement in the project pose a major disappointment for investigators since it is not possible simply to insert replacements. Thus, an attempt to clarify any misunderstandings or to check back to assure that the desire to disengage was not due to a momentary mood state is understandable, but heavy-handed coercion must be avoided.

Finally, the longitudinal design sometimes involves the creation of dependencies, and the investigator must be sensitive to this situation when the data-gathering phase has been completed. For example, if participants and their families were given special counseling or educational experiences, as may occur in long-term intervention projects, the time frame for terminating the services and the participants' needs may not coincide. To abandon these families, who had come to rely on such interventions over a period of time, may cause them even more hardship than had they been left alone all along to their own coping strategies. In a sense, this situation is similar to the termination process in psychotherapy relationships, which requires that therapists feel reasonably assured that the clients are capable of managing their lives independently of therapy. Investigators should review the situation of each participant and either make appropriate referrals, give information about alternative resources, or continue the services for an additional period of time.

Other designs where participants serve as their own control, such as the baseline comparison technique, can raise profound ethical dilemmas when risk is associated with participants being in the baseline condition (Noonan & Bickel, 1981):

CASE 5-7: Investigators at a large state hospital facility designed an experimental technique to reduce the frequency of self-injurious behavior in autistic children. In order to assess the effectiveness of their experimental technique, it was necessary to gain information about each child's rate of self-injurious behavior. Each child was observed and videotaped individually for 1 hour without any intervention unless it was judged that the child was engaging in a behavior that would cause permanent injury. Instances and time sequences were recorded.

The development of a minimally restricting method of reducing self-injurious behavior in psychotic children is a worthy challenge, and assessing the technique's advantage over the child's baseline behavior is methodologically important. Alternatives to observing the child in a potentially dangerous state should always be considered and may include approximations of baseline behavior available in records or from hospital staff observations. It may also be possible to use the current method of controlling injurious behavior as the baseline (if it is other than restraint). If only a baseline recording period is feasible, it should be as short as possible. For a child who is actively self-injurious, an hour is obviously too long.

Carts before Horses: Trivial Research and Samples of Convenience

Minors are often readily available in bunches at schools, day-care centers, hospitals, agencies, and so on, which makes them attractive to anyone attempting to locate an easy-access sample. Indeed, college freshmen and sophomores have been referred to as "psychology's fruit flies" (Rubenstein, 1982) because of the ease with which they can be recruited for research purposes. Captive populations tend to minimize logistical complications, which may invite more risk taking by investigators (Rae & Fournier, 1986).

Ethical problems lurking with convenient samples also include the potential that participants may be used in a trivial manner and that the research problem may be identified *after* the sample becomes available. Uninspired research clogs the literature with unimportant material and is also, by definition, an inappropriate use of research participants.

CASE 5-8: Dr. Harry Hurried, a psychologist who taught at a university and was in need of publications for tenure review, had a friend who ran a small after-school program. The friend told the psychologist that she was amenable to having research done at the school and that the parents were all very cooperative types. Dr. Hurried had just read an article on adult reactions to jokes containing aggressive themes and quickly adapted the methodology to use with children.

Although the risks of conducting such a study may or may not be at issue, the motivation for doing it and the meaning of the work can more certainly be questioned. Unfortunately, as long as professional advancement and recognition are linked to publication output, trivial research and poor use of convenient samples are difficult to discourage. Yet, because of the myriad ethical dilemmas involved in conducting research on vulnerable populations, it seems essential to use children only in those instances in which, after thoughtful planning and justification, the primary component of the study is the interest in learning more about the behavior of immature human beings.

Practical Problems Affecting Data Validity with Children

Minors, particularly younger ones, pose some practical problems that must be taken into consideration when planning research. Their limited vocabularies and potential for misunderstanding verbal instructions, coupled with the experimenter's possible misinterpretation of the meaning intended by the minor's verbal responses, may create "noise" in the communications. Children's variable moods (e.g., silliness, anxiety, or shyness around strangers) and their often limited attention spans can affect data quality. Situational variables, such as experimenter's physical appearance, personality style, or the setting in which the data are collected, may influence children's performances even more than adults' and should be carefully considered and controlled for at the onset:

> CASE 5-9: Thickly bearded Dr. Thor Conan hired a young female graduate student to assist him in interviewing young children about their opinions of adult authority figures such as police, teachers, and parents. Dr. Conan interviewed the second graders, and the assistant interviewed the fourth graders. Results indicated that second graders had very few opinions to express and gave terse responses to the questions whereas the fourth graders had many elaborated opinions to share. Dr. Conan concluded that significant developmental and cognitive changes occurred between the ages of 7 and 9.

In fact, we cannot be at all sure that this finding is valid because of the way the research was conducted. It is probable that many of the second graders were somewhat intimidated or overwhelmed by the whiskered male investigator and that the fourth graders were more relaxed talking to a woman, the sex they are typically more familiar with in terms of daily interactions. Preferably, one interviewer would conduct all the interview sessions, or, at the very least, the interviewers would have divided their duties in a random or split-group fashion.

Sampling Bias and Dropouts

Fussiness, fatigue, and short attention span are conditions that frequently plague experimental trials involving young children. Even if a very sleepy or anxious participant persists to the end, the validity of the data is in doubt. In many cases, these conditions make it necessary to terminate the trial prior to its conclusion. Data analysis generally excludes these "dropouts."

In studies of infant perception, it has been estimated that between 25% and 70% of the participants cannot maintain an alert or nonfussy state long enough to complete the experimental sessions (Caron et al., 1971). Thus, as Richardson and McCluskey (1983) note, random assignment requirements may be met at the onset of the trials, but the results are based on a selected sample whose data may not be representative of the original population. Although most investigators do report reasons and rates of participant attrition, few analyze the available data of those who started but did not complete the procedure. Richardson and McCluskey (1983) present examples from infant research that reveal how those who did complete the experimental session differed from those who could not. In such cases, the participants are no longer a random sample; "rather, the procedure selects those subjects who remain in the study" (p. 238). Although such sampling biases and dropouts cannot always be prevented, it is important to consider these factors when interpreting findings.

CONSENT: PERMISSION AND ASSENT

Even fairly recent history reveals that children from orphanages and foundling homes were commonly conscripted as research participants or as candidates for experimentation with unproved therapies. Early research accounts rarely make mention of asking parental permission, even from those participants who had parents readily available (Mitchell, 1964).

The Nuremberg Code (1946), adopted as a judicial summary after the trials of 23 Nazi physicians for crimes against humanity, provides the first clear statement of the necessity to obtain a research participant's voluntary and informed consent. Although never used as a legal precedent, this statement of human participants' rights to understand and then freely choose whether to be used for research purposes is the backdrop from which subsequent codes and policies were developed. No provisions for child participants appeared in the Nuremberg Code, although Alexander (1970), one of the authors of the first draft, noted that the proxy consent provisions for incompetents was dropped from the final version, probably because it did not apply to the specific cases being tried.

Early federal policies in the United States adopted a proxy consent model whereby parents or legal guardians were empowered to make all decisions regarding their children's participation in research. The proxy consent provisions were replaced in the 1983 DHHS guidelines with two more appropriately conceived procedures. *Consent*, a legal concept implying full competence to make a binding decision that affects oneself and in most circumstances reserved for those who have reached the age of majority, cannot be appropriately delegated to others. Thus, currently it is *permission* that is sought from parents or guardians. The affirmative agreement, termed *assent*, is to be obtained (with exceptions) from the children themselves.

Parental or Guardian Permission

The permission of the parents or guardians must typically be documented in a way that assures that the provisions for consent have been met as if the permission granters themselves were actual participants. The major thrust of the consent provisions in the federal regulations is to ensure that participants know exactly what they are getting themselves into before deciding whether to proceed. As will be discussed, however, the difficulties that competent adults often have with comprehending the information offered by investigators (Taub, 1986) and the allowance for exceptions to obtaining full consent-type agreements muddle the reality of what actually happens in research.

According to current federal policy (Department of Health and Human Services, 1983) for research generally, information given to the prospective participants must be in a language that they or their representatives can understand. The circumstances when seeking consent must be free from coercion and undue influences. No exculpatory language that creates a situation in which the participants or their representatives waive or appear to waive their legal rights or release the investigator from liability for negligence can be allowed.

Basic elements of a general the consent agreement include a clear statement that research is involved; the purpose of the research; the expected duration of participation; a description of procedures to be used (including the identification of any that are experimental); a description of any foreseeable risks or discomforts or any reasonably expected benefits to the participants or others; disclosure of any appropriate procedures or treatment alternatives that the participants may wish to consider; a statement regarding the extent to which the participants' identity will be kept confidential; an explanation of the steps that will be taken should any risks manifest themselves; the identity of a contact person should the participants have any questions about the research or their rights; and assurance that participation is voluntary and that refusal or a desire to later discontinue will not involve any penalty or loss of benefits to which the participant is entitled. Additional elements may also be appropriate in some cases, such as a statement explaining that there may be risks that cannot currently be foreseen and outlining any consequences of the participants' desire to withdraw or the conditions under which the investigator may unilaterally terminate the participant's involvement.

Children who are wards of the state or some other agency or institution are discussed separately in federal regulations. Research may be conducted on such children only if the project is related to their status as wards or is conducted in settings in which the majority of the children involved are not wards. If an IRB approves a project conducted on wards of the state, an advocate independent of the IRB or research team is appointed for each child to assure that his or her welfare is protected.

Under some circumstances, the federal regulations allow for an IRB to determine that permission need not be sought from the parent or guardian at all. If such permission is not a reasonable requirement to protect the participants (with neglected and abused children cited as examples), consent requirements may be waived so long as another mechanism for protecting the children is substituted and no applicable state or other laws are violated by the waiver.

CASE 5-10: It is well known "on the streets" that Jack Needle, 15-year-old Marcia's father, deals drugs in the neighborhood and gets into many fights. Marcia's mother's whereabouts have been unknown for years. Marcia regularly attends a well-supervised, community funded after-school drop-in recreation and "rap" center. The center has received a small grant to assess attitudes and personality characteristics of their clientele and to hire consultants to use the results to better understand and serve the children who frequent the center. The group leader informs the children generally about the study, which the children react to favorably, and distributes information and permission materials for the children to take home to their parents. Marcia approaches the group leader to beg him not to contact her father, who she fears would only express anger toward her and the center, but to let her be in the study anyway. She is interested in the study, and she would feel embarrassed if she were excluded from participation.

Marcia's age and maturity and the minimal risk involved, coupled with the purpose of enhancing the children's well-being, are important factors in this case. The risk of inflaming a marginal and potentially dangerous parent as well as the discomfort Marcia would feel at being excluded from the activities would possibly allow for Marcia's assent to be sufficient to allow her to be involved in the research without parental permission.

CASE 5-11: Ann Active, age 15, contacted a community birth control center for services. She and her boyfriend are frequently sexually intimate, but she fears that if she were to become pregnant her very strict parents would follow through on their threat to kick her out of the house. She lives in a state where she can receive these services without parental awareness. The agency is conducting an evaluation research project that involves the usual and a new approach to counseling sexually active teenagers. Ann is given information about the study and is assured that continued services are not contingent on research participation. She agrees to participate and to be assigned randomly into one of the groups and to be interviewed periodically about her perceptions of the experience.

Here is another example where an assent only *may* be acceptable since the federal regulations define children as those who have *not* attained the legal age for consent to treatments or procedures involved in the research yet the state in which Ann resides requires only her consent. The research has beneficial intent, although one group may receive more benefit than the other. Yet, since the "control" group is receiving the standard services and the untested approach has no known risks, an IRB may approve Ann's participation in the absence of parental permission. However, once again investigators must assure themselves that state laws do not preempt federal policy. Just because a minor is legally authorized by state law to consent to certain treatments, it does not necessarily follow that the authorization extends to the research component of the treatment received. For example, granting authority to minors to consent to treatment is often intended to protect either the state or the minor who would not otherwise be able to obtain treatment, not to promote the autonomy of minors. Thus, extending the independent consent provision to a research component of a treatment may be inconsistent with legislative intent. For a thorough discussion and interpretation of conditions under which a minor's assent to behavioral research can be sought without parental permission, see Grisso (1989).

Next, we present a case in which some children may unwittingly be a part of the data gathered for a research project, but neither parental permission nor the assent of the children is sought for some of the children about whom data will be collected:

> CASE 5-12: Complete permissions and assents have been obtained to observe on the school playground the behavior of several *specific* children who are having trouble socializing. However, in the course of recording the behavior of the target children, notes are taken on the behavior of nonstudy children, but only when they interact with the target children. The other children (and their parents) are not aware of the fact that any study is being conducted on the playground. Nonstudy children are not identified by name.

Here is an example of probable "acceptable" lack of permission and assent from those children and their parents who circumstantially connect with the study pool children. If the other nonstudy children were informed that they were being observed on occasion for research purposes, they might become self-conscious. The target children might also be embarrassed if all the other children knew that they were being studied. Observations of specific children may be of extreme benefit to understanding those children's social interaction skills and patterns, and such observations are best made in completely naturalistic surroundings. The other children were not specifically identified and were placed at no risk, and the setting was completely nonobtrusive. The 1983 DHHS regulations permit IRBs to waive permission and assent when the research presents no more than minimal risk and involves no procedures for which written consent is normally required. Further, observation of children who are not specifically identified in a public setting is exempt from DHHS regulations.

The next case involves a situation, based on a part of the *Merriken v. Cressman* (1973) case, illustrating a form of inappropriate permission seeking:

> CASE 5-13: A research firm was contracted by a school system to identify and then assist children who were at risk for drug abuse. Students were to fill out lengthy questionnaires that delved into sensitive and private issues relating to the children's feelings and home life. The school sent each parent a letter informing them in very general terms of the program, extolling its purpose, requesting their cooperation and support, and noting that if they did *not* wish to participate in the program they should contact the school. The letter ended with, "We will assume your cooperation unless otherwise notified by you."

Children were not consulted as to their feelings, and parents were given virtually no information about what the project would entail or how their privacy would be invaded. The "Book-of-the-Month Club" solicitation technique, placing the responsibility on the dissenting parent to disengage from the project, is unacceptable. (For a detailed description and analysis of the full case, see Bersoff, 1983.)

The Child's Assent

The process of assent allows the verbal child input into the decision-making process. The 1983 DHHS regulations define *assent* as the affirmative agreement to participate in a research project. That a child fails to object or explicitly to dissent should not be construed as sufficient to claim that assent has been obtained. The next case illustrates an insufficient response:

> CASE 5-14: After describing the tasks that would be involved in his research, Mr. Rush asked 11-year-old Harold, "Do you mind doing these things?" Harold replied, "I guess not."

The investigator asked the wrong question. He should have queried Harold in a way that allowed for the boy to respond comfortably either positively or negatively, for example, "Would you be willing to try these puzzles? You don't have to if you don't want to."

The DHHS regulations do not specify what kinds of information should be presented to the children in the course of obtaining assent, leaving such matters up to the IRBs. We recommend conforming as closely as is appropriate to the DHHS consent requirements, although investigators should make necessary alterations, depending on the age and vulnerability of the children. We believe that children should be offered as much information as they can comfortably absorb so that they may give informed assent or dissent. Explanations for young children can focus on what the child will experience in simple, straightforward language, as illustrated in the next case:

> CASE 5-15: Dr. Pia Jay developed a cross-sectional design study to assess children's ability to conserve quantity. Obviously, the 4-year-olds would not be enlightened by a theoretical explanation. Instead, she approached her young participants by saying, "We're going to be guessing about things. Like, I'll show you two glasses of water, and you tell me which glass has more water in it. Would you like to do some things like that with me?"

Obviously, infants and young children cannot engage in the assent procedure because of language and comprehension barriers or other limitations on the child's developmental capacities (Lewis, 1983). Institutional review boards are empowered to determine when and if the children are capable of providing assent, taking the age, maturity, and psychological state of the children involved into consideration.

More recently, research on the capacity of children to weigh benefits and risks to requests to participate in research or treatment decisions has revealed much of what common sense would suggest—namely, that older teenagers still legally defined as minors are no less capable than are adults (Grisso & Vierling, 1978; Weithorn, 1983a, 1984; Weithorn & Campbell, 1982). Even younger children (between 6 and 9 or above) are often capable of expressing a reasonable choice with regard to research participation (Lewis, Lewis, & Ifekwunigue, 1978; Weithorn & Campbell, 1982) and often offer decisions and reasons for their choices that cannot be distinguished in major ways from those of adults (Keith-Spiegel & Maas, 1981).

What is becoming increasingly clear is that consent in not an all-or-nothing entity in terms of an individual's ability to weigh all factors carefully and make an autonomous decision in his or her own best interests. Various standards of competency have been proposed, ranging from the level required for children's assent (the capability of evincing a choice to do something about which they have a rudimentary understanding) to an ability not only to understand all the facts and issues and assimilate these into the decision-making process but also to appreciate one's own immediate situation and how the decision is affected by it (Appelbaum & Roth, 1982; Roth, Meisel, & Lidz, 1977). Concepts of *variable competency* also take into account such factors as the person's experience, age, intelligence, and rationality (Gaylin, 1982) as well as a host of other factors such as cultural and personality factors (Keith-Spiegel, 1983) and the nature of the types of decisions to be made and their potential consequences (Drane, 1984; Guyer, Harrison, & Rieveschl, 1982; Taylor, Adelman, & Kaser-Boyd, 1984).

Despite the complexity of the issues surrounding the assessment of the capacity to make consent decisions, despite the increasing recognition that in many circumstances minors may be as capable as adults, and despite the concerns that even "competent" adults may not meet the stricter tests of consent capacity, no movement is underway to remove protective scrutiny from parents or guardians (except in very unusual circumstances) or from IRBs. However, IRBs are empowered to approve a project that does not seek the child's assent at all, even for populations that are quite capable of providing it. This situation would be most likely to occur when the research offers the hope of direct benefit to a child who needs it, the treatment is available only in a research context, and other treatments have been tried and have failed.

When Parents and Children Disagree

In actuality, we would not often see situations in which the child assents to research participation but the parents refuse permission. One example of an exception would be instances in which permission forms are sent home from the school and the child wants to be a part of the project but the parent refuses to allow it. Far more typically, the parents are the first to be approached, and if they refuse permission, that is the end of it.

We may lament the parents' decision to refuse permission, especially when a child or children in general may have greatly benefited from participation or the investigator believed the parents' reasons to be unfairly biased. For example, contemporary parents may be reluctant to enroll their autistic children in research that purports a psychogenic component because of resentment over past characterizations of "refrigerator" or cruel and unloving parenting as the cause for the disorder (Lapin & Donnellan-Walsh, 1977). On the other hand, such parents may uncritically enroll their autistic children in research seeking evidence for biochemical etiology.

Another dilemma that may actually be fairly common occurs when those empowered to give permission are divided in their opinions (Plotkin, 1981; Thomasma & Mauer, 1982):

CASE 5-16: Mr. and Mrs. Split express sharp disagreement in the assessment of their hospitalized teenage son's enrollment in a research project using aversive conditioning to eliminate his cocaine addiction. Mrs. Split vigorously rejects the idea of "causing my boy any more pain than he has already endured." Mr. Split thinks that the project is a "great idea" and may even "make a man out of him" as well.

Both the Splits appear to be looking at the research opportunity from their own perspectives rather than from that of the merits of the project or the true treatment needs of the boy.

For research on children judged to involve *minimal risk* or research with *greater than minimal risk* (terms that are defined and discussed in chap. 6) but presenting a prospect of direct benefit to the participants, an IRB may find that the permission of one parent is sufficient, and assent from the child may or may not be required. For research involving greater than minimal risk but unlikely to benefit the participants, both parents must give permission unless one is deceased, unknown, incompetent, unavailable, or no longer has legal custody. It appears possible that an IRB may allow the Splits' boy to participate in the research anyway, although in this case the members may well be cautious since neither parent is properly focused on the project. Such conflicts are unfortunate, especially when a child who could benefit from the research is caught in the middle. Families with strong and healthy relationships may pose fewer consent-related disputes than families with limited trust among themselves (Northern Health Region in Current Medical/Ethical Problems, 1986). Thus, children from more dysfunctional families are far more vulnerable from the onset since we cannot be sure that the parents will act in the best interests of their child (Kinard, 1985).

When the parents approve of their child's participation and the child does not offer a clear assent or openly dissents, the researcher faces ethical dilemmas (Pence, 1980). Even when an IRB rules that assent is not required, an unhappy, defiant, or hostile child is difficult to justify enrolling (not to mention the potential for contamination of the quality of the data, which, in social and behavioral research, are often influenced by participants' emotional states or by a "bad attitude").

Investigators who have successfully negotiated parental permission are understandably disappointed when their minor subjects put up a block by refusing to assent. However, *unless* the research holds out the prospect for benefiting the child participant in some way that is available only in the research context, the investigator appears to be obligated to excuse the child. The investigator must refrain from heavy-handed cajoling (see the following section), which may be difficult, especially if the child's reason for not giving assent appears to be trivial or stupid.

CASE 5-17: Mickey Katz declined to stay after school to take an interest inventory that was part of a research project on career development stages, despite the fact that Mickey's parents had enthusiastically signed the permission forms. Mickey told the experimenter that he could not stay because he did not want to miss the afternoon cartoon shows on television.

The investigator may be inclined to ask, "Couldn't you miss *just one day*? This is an important study, and I would very much appreciate your help." But a strict adherence to the philosophy of assent, that is, granting to the minor some measure of autonomy and self-determination, renders the reason for refusing to give assent irrelevant and beyond scrutiny.

A related problem occurs when the parents who gave permission use their power as parents on their reluctant offspring. Indeed, parents may be embarrassed when their child refuses to comply and may react to the child's differing wants in much the same way as they would to any other act of defiance or noncooperation. Here, the investigator witnessing such a dispute or sensing that censure may be forthcoming later may be obligated to intervene on behalf of the child. This can usually be accomplished by reassuring the parent that the child's reaction is acceptable and that no one or the project is in any way jeopardized by this child's nonparticipation.

COERCION TO PARTICIPATE

Contemporary ethical standards require that participation in research be voluntary as well as informed. Neither parents nor their minor children should be heavily pressured, cajoled, inappropriately enticed, or "blackmailed" to participate. Some have argued for the support of a concept called *acceptable persuasion*, which varies somewhat depending on the study purpose. For example, if an investigator has objective information to indicate that an experimental treatment has some potential for alleviating a specific child's problem and that the procedure itself is available only in the context of experimentation, then stating this belief and rationale is acceptable (and will likely be persuasive). "Forcing" participation of dissenting children, whose parents have given permission, may also be deemed acceptable under certain circumstances, as described earlier.

Subtle pressures on prospective research participants are largely unavoidable. Parents, especially those whose children are especially vulnerable because of physical or mental disorder, may be easily persuaded even when the investigator does not intend to do so. The investigator's prestige and authority, enthusiasm, empathy or sensitivity, and charm may be decisive factors, especially if parents are guilty, desperate, or insecure. To children, any grown-up who seems to know what he or she wants may elicit compliance. Thus, with children it is important to seek assent that is not merely an acquiescent or deferent response to authority (Grisso & Vierling, 1978). Fortunately, according to a sample of active researchers in developmental psychology, children are often enthusiastic about the opportunity to participate in research (Keith-Spiegel, 1983).

Various types of coercion of the people granting permission (usually parents) are illustrated in the following cases. These range from subtle and possibly unintentional maneuvers to brash, controlling tactics.

CASE 5-18: Investigators approached parents for permission to utilize their disabled children in a longitudinal assessment of school performance. Parents were told that a unique and beneficial aspect of participation was the assessments that their children would receive, free of charge, which the parents might find helpful.

Failure to disclose that the assessments, all based on widely used and easily available screening tools, could be obtained for little or no cost elsewhere may have misled parents to assume that this package was available only in this particular research context. In general, failure to offer alternatives to participation increases compliance (Rosen, 1977).

CASE 5-20: Babies who had febrile convulsions were conscripted into a research project by the staff of a health maintenance organization

(HMO). Parents were told that the babies would be given an EEG "to assure that brain damage had not occurred." When a parent declined permission for her baby to be in the research but requested that the EEG be performed, she was told that this would not be possible unless her baby was enrolled in the study.

Here parents were made anxious (i.e., the possibility of brain damage was revealed), and then the assessment of the infant was held hostage by the HMO because the test would not be performed unless the parents went along with the total package. This tactic is blatantly unethical. The only reason why an indicated procedure could be ethically withheld is if it were available only in the research context.

CASE 5-21: Nate Sneaky, M.A., gained the cooperation of mothers and their children to be observed in a playroom for a brief period. At the conclusion of the session, an assistant asked if the parents would now fill out a lengthy and sensitive family history questionnaire and agree to come back with their spouses for an interview.

This tactic is known as "foot-in-the-door" coercion (Freedman & Fraser, 1966). It is based on the assumption that a small-scale commitment can be expanded to a larger commitment, which is likely to yield a higher participation rate than had the investigator initially revealed the full scope of the project. Although additions to the original plan can sometimes be justified, the use of "bait and switch" from the onset is inappropriate professional conduct.

CASE 5-22: Parents of children seen in a clinic for speech impediments were told by Dr. Samuel Chat that participation in his study would "almost certainly result in improvement of the children's speech."

Almost by definition, the outcome of an experimental treatment is unknown or else it would not be "experimental." Although Dr. Chat chose his words carefully enough to worm out of any less than dramatic results, the "almost promise" of benefit constitutes heavy-handed coercion.

CASE 5-23: Recently relocated parents from Korea and Vietnam were contacted and told that their school-aged children would likely fail to adjust to their new environment and would make few American friends unless they were enrolled in a special program. The researcher's project consisted solely of interviewing and testing the children at several intervals over a period of 2 years as part of a cross-cultural longitudinal comparison between these children and their American-born counterparts. No other interventions were planned.

As in the previous case, playing on parental anxieties by suggesting that consequences of nonparticipation are high (save, perhaps, for those instances in which the child's condition is grave and all other known treatments have failed) is inappropriate and coercive. This case is particularly reprehensible because the parents are misled to believe that some beneficial intervention will occur when, in fact, the likely effect on these children is trivial.

CASE 5-24: Normal, healthy infants were solicited from lower socioeconomic neighborhoods to serve as a control group in a longitudinal study of babies with a serious allergy. Although the control babies were not given any experimental medical procedures, they were hospitalized on several occasions to undergo a series of tests, some of which were uncomfortable, invasive, and painful. Parents were paid several hundred dollars for their cooperation.

This project (adapted from *Neilsen v. Regents of the University of California et al.*, 1973) was primarily concerned with the rights of parents or researchers to subject babies to repeated discomfort when no potential for direct benefit to the infant participant is possible. However, the element of monetary coercion is also at issue because parents may have been more cautious in their decision making had there been less financial incentive.

The current ethical climate with regard to monetary compensation for parental involvement indicates that reimbursement is not unethical per se. However, the amount should be in a range that compensates modestly for inconvenience and time and never so large as to sway persons to participate when they might otherwise have chosen to decline.

Obtaining assent from children to participate in research is apparently not that difficult to accomplish (Keith-Spiegel, 1983). It seems unlikely, however, that very young children value the opportunity to "contribute to science" as might adolescents or adults. However, the novelty, special attention, and unusual or interesting features of the task appear to be attractive enough to elicit assents from younger children, although one also needs to remember that children may not believe that "no" is ever the "right" answer regardless of how they feel. Children may certainly be purposely pressured into assenting to participation in research. The following cases illustrate potential problems:

> CASE 5-25: Children were told that, if they agreed to be in a study and tried hard to do their "very best," they would get a special surprise as soon as they were finished. If a child asked what it was, the grinning investigator chirped, "You'll see!"

The study involved problem-solving tasks. However, motivation was not part of the research design. Had it been, slight changes could have turned this example into an appropriate procedure. Assent to do the problems would have been obtained first, prior to the announcement of the surprise. All children, including those who were not promised anything, should ultimately receive the same surprise. As presented in case 5-25, however, the surprise is solely a vehicle for influencing assent. An announcement that something special but mysterious will occur is probably overwhelming to most children (and perhaps to many adults). We submit that offering rewards during the assent phase that will not materialize unless the investigator's demands are met is not ethically appropriate:

> CASE 5-26: Peppy Bounce, the investigator's assistant and an affable and bubbly person, spent several minutes praising and playing in an attractive playroom with each potential child participant prior to attempting to elicit assent. Even though she did tell children that the

study trial would be a little physically uncomfortable, no child refused to assent.

We cannot be sure that the assistant's toys and charm altered the children's response patterns. Some would certainly argue that children, especially younger ones, are susceptible and gullible. A "to-the-point and pleasant-but-business-like" approach is above ethical reproach:

CASE 5-27: Children were told that their participation in a project requiring a rather tiring and long session was very important because the results would help other children not as fortunate as they. It was further suggested that people who did not care enough to help others were selfish and self-centered.

Altruistic appeals during an assent phase are not uncommon, especially when the research purpose is to solve a problem or alleviate some condition. According to a survey, such appeals have been described by developmental psychologists as "persuasive" (Keith-Spiegel, 1983), especially when the investigator personalizes the pitch (e.g., "I really need your help badly"). Ferguson (1978) contends that mild altruistic appeals are acceptable and may even contribute in constructive ways to the child's social development. However, to pressure participants into feeling bad about themselves (e.g., selfish, weak, uncaring, etc.) should they exercise their right to dissent is not ethically appropriate.

Are children more susceptible to coercion involving altruistic appeals or opportunity for monetary gain than adults? Keith-Spiegel and Maas (1981) found that strong altruistic appeals, even when risk was present, resulted in similar patterns of agreement or refusal to participate among 9–16-year-old children and adults over age 21. For example, 42% of the children and 53% of the adults would consider participating in a somewhat bizarre study purporting to benefit "starving people" by developing untapped food sources. Participants were told that they would be asked to take a bite of some unusual edibles, such as "baked mouse." Despite the altruistic tug, however, 58% of the children and 47% of the adults registered a definite "no" regarding any interest in this culinary experience. Thus, on the basis of these preliminary data, altruistic appeal is persuasive to some children and adults and unpersuasive to other children and adults in roughly similar proportions.

As for monetary enticements, Keith-Spiegel and Maas (1981) found that the comparisons between adults and children revealed more diversity. Whereas both groups were eager to participate in low-risk projects with high monetary reward, more children than adults would agree to participate in low- or moderate-risk research with minimal financial gain. For example, 39% of children and 44% of adults asked agreed to sit in a room alone all day for $2.00, but none of the adults listed the money as the reason for agreement, whereas a third of the children who agreed to be in the study stated that the money was the primary factor in their decision. However, 23% of the children dissenting from participation did so because the monetary value was too low!

When investigators face low enrollment rates in their research samples, sampling bias may occur. How can researchers make the "best connection" with potential participants and their parents and still refrain from using unacceptable forms of coercion? Available information indicates that a personal touch, that is, direct communication with parents as opposed to a form carried home from school or a mailed letter, greatly enhances the rate of permission granted by parents (Thompson, 1984).

FREEDOM TO WITHDRAW

Generally, research participants are offered a kind of exit hatch even after they have agreed to engage in a research project. Participants can change their minds at any time and withdraw from the project without penalty or loss of benefits to which they may have otherwise been entitled (Department of Health and Human Services, 1983).

It is not clear that federal regulations would always allow child participants to discontinue because the assent requirement may be altered or overridden by the IRB. The National Commission (1977) recommendations specify that an objection to continuing should normally be respected. If the project involves a potential benefit, the intervention is available only in the research context, and the child is not viewed as mature enough to act in his best interests, then the child's wishes to disengage can be overridden.

There is yet another limitation to children's freedom to withdraw, and it is inherent in the children themselves. Most children have been socialized to do what they are told, and, once having affirmed their intention to do it, they follow through. Unless a child has an extreme negative reaction to an experimental situation that leaves no question in the investigator's mind that the child does not want to continue, child participants may not voice their right to leave. Data from a survey of highly experienced developmental psychology researchers have lent support to this point. Only a few of the researchers sampled had ever experienced a specific request from a child to be excused from participation, and this happened to these few investigators only rarely (Keith-Spiegel, 1983). The next cases illustrate what is more likely to happen when a child participant wants to disengage from a research project in midcourse.

CASE 5–28: Dr. Cog presented second graders with a large stack of cards to sort into piles according to shape and color. Gary Bored began increasingly to look around the room, pick his nose, and pay less and less attention to the task. Natasha Tense began sorting so fast and vigorously that her rate of error was extremely high.

CASE 5–29: During an interview session, 6-year-old Clyde Balk responded with, "I don't know," when asked his age and asked, "When will this be over?" after the second question on a 20-question schedule.

Although none of the children asked explicitly to be excused from participation, their behavior and verbal indicators betray their desire to be somewhere else. As opposed to clear requests to withdraw, which children apparently make only rarely, implicit signs of "wanting out" are quite common (Keith-Spiegel, 1983). The common clues that indicate a child's desire to discontinue include off-task or random behavior and verbal responses; hand and foot dancing; excessive yawning; inattentiveness; muteness or inappropriate answers to age-appropriate questions; fussiness, crying, or puckering; going to sleep; and lack of eye contact with the investigator.

Thus, it is the investigators who must often assess cues and assist with the exercise of their children's right to withdraw. This wish can usually be confirmed by the answer to the investigator's question, "Would you like to stop now?" Although one may feel a little tug to try to get the child to continue, this feeling must also be countered with a concern for her rights to some autonomy even though she does not clearly state her apparent wishes. It may also help to remember that unhappy, bored, or inattentive children produce poor-quality data.

In this chapter, we have focused largely on the important facets to consider in the preparation of research projects up to the point of data collection. The next chapter reviews the various risks that may accompany social and behavioral science research as it is being conducted or that may result directly or indirectly from research participation.

GUIDELINES

1. Investigators should be thoroughly knowledgeable about federal research regulations in general and more specifically about how these relate to child participants. In addition, investigators must be aware of any more restrictive state or local laws within their jurisdiction that may preempt federal regulations.

2. Investigators are often placed in dual role or conflict-of-interest situations when they are simultaneously part of the care or treatment team. In such instances, they must explore any contradictions in these roles and minimize them to the greatest extent possible while striving to protect the welfare of the study participants.

3. Ideally, investigators working with children possess expertise in both research methods and child development as well as considerable direct experience working with the population under study. Any deficiencies in these realms require the addition of appropriate collaborators or consultants to the project.

4. Researchers must explore their own values and biases to assure that they have not distorted the potential for objective or disconfirming results.

5. The choice of research design poses a number of ethical dilemmas. Investigators should utilize the most appropriate design while, at the same time, assuring that the welfare of the participants remains protected.

6. Except for a few extraordinary circumstances, permission from parents or legal guardians and assent from the children (whenever appropriate) are necessary conditions for conducting research with children.

7. Permission and assent should be negotiated in a manner that provides all relevant information in a way that can be understood by the recipients.

8. Coercion of children or their permission granters is to be avoided during the consent to participate phase.

9. Generally, children should have the same rights to withdraw from research trials as do adults. However, investigators must be sensitive to the special difficulties that children may have in exercising that right.

•

CHAPTER SIX

Research with Children:
Risk Potential
and Management

Social and behavioral science research does not typically present the more serious consequences to participants, such as pain or a worsening of a physical condition, that can arise in biomedical research. In fact, the risks in social and behavioral research often appear trivial. Yet we must quickly note that psychological risks are also difficult to define, detect, and assess for long-term effects.

Among the less significant risks for children in the experimental setting itself are tedium or boredom, confusion, inconvenience, temporary anxiety due to the presence of strangers or the novelty of the situation, and disruption of normal routine. Such risks are much like other "downside" aspects of a child's average day.

Risks that may present more disturbing experiences for children include induced anxiety or stress, fear of failure, a lowering of self-esteem, reactions to intrusions of privacy, conflict or guilt caused by opportunities or temptations to behave counter to values or expected rules of conduct, embarrassment, physical discomfort, and adverse reactions to the investigator or to the true purpose of a deception experience on being "debriefed."

Other risks of participation in social and behavioral research can manifest themselves over the longer term. Many of these may harm children significantly. Withholding or delaying needed interventions, breaches of confidentiality, "social injury," "labeling" that unfairly stereotypes or stigmatizes the participants, and loss of trust in adults as a result of investigators' thoughtlessness or on learning that one was lied to or manipulated are among the more troublesome risks in this category. The effects may linger long after the study has been completed, allowing no opportunity for the investigator to ameliorate the problem or even to become aware that a harm had materialized.

Although the risks noted above are potentially operative in social and behavioral science research with any population, including competent adult humans, the vulnerabilities inherent in minor status place additional responsibilities on investigators. We have much to learn about children. Yet current knowledge allows for the assumption that traumatic or emotionally upsetting experiences are problematic for one whose tender age and accompanying immaturities preclude a full understanding of causes and dynamics related to events. Assessment and coping strategies are less fully developed in children than in adults. What experiences trigger negative reactions or what factors determine their intensity may vary as a function of age alone.

It must also be kept in mind that most minors who are sought out as research participants possess vulnerabilities beyond those imposed by age. Disadvantaged background, emotional disturbance, developmental disability, mental or physical illness, stressed, judged "at risk" for school failure or other problems, school dropout, and criminal or acting-out behavior are among the relatively common criteria for minors conscripted into research activities. Unfortunately, more vulnerable target research populations also tend to be subjected to more risks (Wells & Sametz, 1985). As Fisher and Tryon (1988) have noted, "nonnormal" participants are more likely to be exposed to more deficit-oriented stimuli that may be more uncomfortable (thus, more risky) than stimuli used with "normal" participants. For example, research on aversive conditioning techniques is difficult to justify using normal children, but their use with psychotic children is often viewed differently. This may be because research on vulnerable people often has a beneficial intent, thus increasing, as is discussed below, the margin of "allowable" risks.

Recognizing the vulnerability of minor research participants whenever an attendant degree of risk exists, a general ethic holds that investigators initially work with alternative populations. Animals, competent adult humans, adolescents, and older children, in that order, are to be considered prior to performing risky research on younger children or infants. Because we are certain that children are neither complicated animals nor simplified adults, this seemingly tidy and rational progression is often useless. So many phenomena of interest to social and behavioral researchers manifest themselves only in the human being and only during a certain developmental period. Even to contemplate the use of alternative study groups is often impossible or ridiculous (e.g., trying to toilet train a rat or observe primary language acquisition in human adults) because the data could not yield any meaningful knowledge or lend themselves to any valid application. Biomedical researchers face the same problem when investigating conditions that are uniquely human and pediatric (e.g., developing feeding protocols for infants who have not previously taken solid food or studying bone development during the preadolescent growth spurt).

ALLOWABLE RISKS WITH CHILD
RESEARCH PARTICIPANTS

The Department of Health and Human Services (1983) guidelines place considerable responsibility for risk-level assessment and approval in the hands of the IRBs. So long as a proposed research project involving minors poses "no greater than minimal risk," DHHS-sponsored research can be deemed acceptable even if no benefit to the child participants or to children in general is anticipated.

As for the definition of "minimal risk," the DHHS guidelines offer us only the following: "Minimal Risk means that the risks of harm anticipated in the proposed research are not greater, considering probability and magnitude, than those ordinarily encountered in daily life or during the performance of routine physical or psychological examinations or tests." Although the National Commission for the Protection of Human Subjects of Biomedical and Behavioral Research (1977) offers examples of minimal risk techniques (which include questionnaires, psychological tests, and puzzles), the definition remains ambiguous. It even lends itself to the possible interpretation that a research protocol may include risks as great as the sort that a child might encounter in an average day (Furlow, 1980), which could include being run down by a car or sexually molested on the way home from school. The loose definition also leaves room for the disturbing interpretation that the standards of risk can be adjusted up or down depending on the life situation of the population under investigation. That is to say, one might attempt to justify the use of more risky procedures under a "minimal risk" standard if the child participants live in dangerous families or neighborhoods. The DHHS definition could benefit from clarification, although we assume that the standard level to be used implicitly envisions a relatively safe and caring home and environmental context. Thus, in our estimation, an example of a "minimal risk" study with those risks actually manifesting themselves would look something like this:

CASE 6-1: One hundred children in several age groups were compared in a reaction-time experiment. They were asked to push a button as fast as they could every time a blue light appeared on a panel. All went well, except for 9-year-old Johnny, who complained of a sore finger after he slammed the button vigorously, and 6-year-old Tammy, who started to cry on becoming confused about when she was supposed to push the button.

Johnny's temporarily sore finger and Tammy's stress would seem to fall into the realm of children's "everyday" risks, similar to tripping over a toy or feeling upset after a failed attempt to get juice into a cup. As such, this study would very likely be judged in the minimal risk category.

Research involving "greater than minimal risk" but presenting the prospect of direct benefit to the child participants is also appropriate according to the DHHS guidelines, as long as the IRB determines that the risk is justified by the anticipated direct benefits and that the anticipated risk/benefit ratio is at least as favorable as that of other available procedures or approaches. Research that involves greater than minimal risk but that holds out no prospect of direct benefit to the child participants may also be appropriate if the risk is judged to be a "minor increase over minimal risk," the intervention or procedures experienced by the children are reasonably commensurate with those "inherent in their actual or expected medical, dental, psychological, social, or educational situations," and the intervention or procedure is "likely to yield generalizable knowledge about the subject's disorder or condition which is of vital importance for the understanding or amelioration of the subject's disorder or condition." Ambiguous terms persist, however, not only in the definition of what is a "minor increase over minimal risk," but also with respect to what constitutes "direct benefit," important "generalizable knowledge," or even a "disorder" or "condition" that requires the alleviation that the "direct benefit" may provide. In social or behavioral research, such concepts are not easily operationalized, and opinions among professionals may clash. If the child learned something or felt good about being a research participant, is that sufficient to claim that a "direct benefit" has resulted? Some would support that argument (e.g., Bower & de Gasparis, 1978). If the child becomes nervous when taking school exams, is this a "condition" or a normal (albeit troublesome) human characteristic? Where lines are drawn becomes critical in the assessment of research protocols because allowable risk varies accordingly.

A fourth category in the DHHS guidelines allows the possibility of "research not otherwise approvable" to be conducted if it provides a reasonable opportunity to understand, prevent, or alleviate a serious problem affecting the health or welfare of children, such as a rapidly spreading and dangerous virus. However, far more rigorous external review, including the opportunity for public review, is mandated in such instances. It is unlikely that a social or behavioral science study would ever fit appropriately into this category.

INDIVIDUAL DIFFERENCES AMONG
RISK ASSESSORS

A given design can often be evaluated for risk in different ways, depending on the values and perspectives of those empowered to make such assessments. For example, in a survey of pediatricians, Janofsky and Starfield (1981) found remarkable variability in risk assessment levels assigned to very common and routine pediatric procedures. The next three cases illustrate how such differences may arise among social and behavioral scientists.

> CASE 6-2: Investigators studied the relation between children's first names and their popularity with peers. Children were asked, in private, which three classmates they liked the best and which three they disliked the most. Each child's sociometric choice was compared to his or her name category, such as "common," "old-fashioned," "odd," or "trendy."

It is not readily apparent how this study could benefit the children involved, and the project also seems a bit trivial. Some risk is attendant, at least for the less preferred children, who were made more salient in the other children's minds and may have been teased or gossiped about (e.g., "Who did you say you didn't like?"). However, some have contended that less popular children are not placed at any additional disadvantage by participating in a sociometric procedure (e.g., Hayvren & Hymel, 1984). It can also be argued that the results of such a study may benefit children in the future, if certain types of given names are consistently linked to more or less peer acceptance, by sharing the findings with prospective parents.

> CASE 6-3: A group of children identified as mildly shy and "quiet" by teachers was enrolled in an experimental program designed to build assertiveness, enhance self-esteem, and teach the children how to stand up for themselves and defend their points of view.

Benefits for the children appear potentially substantial, and no risks are readily apparent. However, it could be argued that children who reach the program goals could be put at risk at school or at home since some teachers and parents may consider the children's newly emerged behavior "stubborn," "arrogant," "rebellious," or "disrespectful." Thus, such children could conceivably face censure and punishment as a direct result of successful participation in a program with beneficial intent.

CASE 6-4: A group of parents whose unborn child was identified through amniocentesis as showing the XYY genotype was selected for an intensive child-management class. This experimental program was designed to better prepare the parents to cope with any behavioral disorders that might materialize.

Such a program may well assist parents in approaching their genetically different child from an informed and sensible perspective. At the same time, however, some untoward effects are possible as well. Critics of this program contended that these "educated" parents may become unnecessarily alarmed, especially if they also familiarize themselves with the flashier "criminal gene" literature. Parents may even create a self-fulfilling prophecy by interpreting normal child outbursts as ominous and menacing, reacting inappropriately, and thus creating an abnormal upbringing that could foster the development of a behavior disorder in the child (adapted from Dickens, 1984).

We can hope that, when clashing views on the presence and intensity of risk emerge during IRB review, the same diversity that led to the differences of opinion also assures the ultimate protection of the participants. The more conservative or protective points of view deserve to be heard and should be carefully considered before rejecting them as unnecessarily stifling.

DEVELOPMENTAL AND INDIVIDUAL DIFFERENCES IN CHILDREN'S RESPONSIVITY

Risks must be viewed from a developmental perspective because minors, ranging from those with tiny, incompetent bodies and nearly content-free minds to large, highly skilled, and competent beings, can be affected in many areas and in many ways by manifested risks. The infant and young child, for example, may be distressed by unfamiliar surroundings and strangers and the absence of a primary caretaker, whereas adolescents often seek novel experiences and prefer that their caretakers are nowhere to be found. However, younger children are generally less aware of and affected by breaches of confidentiality and thus less susceptible to any embarrassment that may ensue than are adolescents, who are more sensitive to what others know and may be talking about. Developmentally based analyses of risks will not completely predict the effect on minors of different ages since individual differences among children of the same age can be marked. For an excellent and useful discussion of the developmental nature of research risks, see Thompson (1989).

CASE 6-5: In a study of startle response patterns, 8-year-old children were asked to open several Jack-in-the-box type containers. Objects inside of the boxes included a curly wig, a plastic spider, a rabbit's foot, and a live lizard.

Some children remained nonplussed or even amused with these stimuli, whereas others flinched. A few were frightened or repulsed.

CASE 6-6: To learn more about children's reactions to "strange" dogs, responses of 6-year-olds to the introduction of a small, unleashed, friendly, and harmless terrier into a playroom situation were observed.

Again, although actual risk may be nil, an occasional child may experience extreme terror and thereby be at risk as a direct result of the experimental manipulation. When it is possible that sensitivity or past events may elicit discomfort or fear, prescreening is recommended. Fortunately, the permission-seeking phase should accomplish this goal much of the time since, for example, a parent would know that her child is terrified of lizards or any kind of dog.

When the minor participants are vulnerable in other ways, research procedures that would be comfortable for the "average" child may be distressing to those with special characteristics (Fisher & Tryon, 1988). For example, a questionnaire concerning family lineage may be uncomfortable for the adopted child. Thus, special characteristics should be ascertained whenever possible before proceeding and the research procedures evaluated and amended accordingly.

THE USE OF DECEPTION WITH MINORS

The intentional use of deception constitutes one of the most hotly debated practices in social-behavioral research and, according to Adair, Dushenko, and Lindsay (1985), has become a normative research practice in the field of social psychology. Deception techniques come in many varieties and include misleading participants about the study purpose, failing to give participants complete information about the study during the consent phase, inducing false expectations, and giving false feedback on performance. The use of deception has been justified as necessary to assure valid findings that might otherwise be contaminated had the participants possessed complete forewarning. Supporters argue that data could not be gathered for some important types of research unless deception is used. Critics argue that deception compromises the consent agreement, condones lying to participants, and undermines the public's opinion of researchers. (For excellent discussions of the issues related to deception in research, see Sieber, 1982a, 1982b, 1982c.)

Surveys indicate that about 20%–25% of behavioral-science research involves some form of deception. A 1976 survey conducted by the SRCD reports about the same rate of deception technique use with children. In a survey of highly productive developmental psychologists, Keith-Spiegel (1983) found that about one-third of the sample generally condoned the use of deception. Another third found deception techniques acceptable under some circumstances, although they were not in favor of techniques that would make the child participants feel foolish, guilty, betrayed, or a failure. The remainder of the respondents were opposed to any use of deception with child research participants.

Despite the harsh criticism of deception, ethics codes (such as those of the American Psychological Association, 1981, and the Society for Research in Child Development, 1973) allow its use, with qualifications. The APA insists that the study should be sufficiently significant to justify the use of deception, that alternatives should be considered and abandoned only if they prove unfeasible, and that participant "debriefing" (an explanation of how the deception occurred and why it was necessary) should occur in a timely manner. Any upset participants may elect, at this point, to have data they provided withdrawn (American Psychological Association, 1982). Thus, in a sense, "voluntary and informed consent" is to be obtained after the fact.

The 1983 DHHS regulations make no direct reference to deception research. However, deception techniques are apparently provided for since IRBs are allowed to alter or waive requirements to obtain informed consent in certain cases when the "research could not practicably be carried out without a waiver or alteration." A related provision states that participants will, "whenever appropriate," be "provided with additional pertinent information after participation." Thus, debriefing is suggested but not strongly mandated. The child-specific section of the DHHS regulations notes the possibility of no necessity to obtain parental permission for "critically important research" if informing the parent might place an already endangered child's welfare at greater risk, thus allowing for deceiving parents under certain conditions.

The use of deception with children raises concerns and complications that have not been clearly addressed in ethics codes or federal policies, nor have its ramifications been empirically explored. Since a two-track consent process is usually involved when participants are minors (i.e., gaining permission from parents or guardians and gaining assent from the child), the use of deception can occur in three different ways: (a) children only are deceived, but complete information is given to parents, who then also give permission to have their child deceived; (b) both parents and children are deceived; and (c) parents only are deceived, but the children are given complete information.

The first pattern noted above is of interest because it provides a possible additional safeguard for children who are not at risk from their parents. Parents may be more attuned to how their child would react in specific situations or to learning the truth during debriefing and thereby make appropriate protective decisions. The other two patterns are particularly problematic because the parents are deprived of knowing exactly what they are agreeing to allow their children to do. Because of the lack of child-specific guidelines, it is also not clear whether only the children (i.e., the actual study participants) or only the parents or both are to be fully "debriefed."

The next case illustrates the potential problems that could ensue when parents are deceived about the nature of a study in which their children participated:

CASE 6-7: Investigators obtained consent from parents, who agreed to complete a battery of personality tests and gave permission for their children to be interviewed as part of what was described to them as "a study of contemporary families." Parents were told that the children would be asked questions about "attitudes towards school, interests and hobbies, and other aspects of their routine daily experiences." In actuality, the interview focused largely on the child's observations of their parents' behavior, such as displays of anger and affection, discipline techniques, alcohol and drug use, and so on. Many questions were quite intrusive, such as, "Has either of your parents ever hit you hard?" and, "What do your parents argue about?" After receiving feedback from their children, several parents complained. The investigators defended their interview schedule content by referring the parents back to the obtained permission to ask the children about their "daily experiences."

Here the parents were misled by the use of concealment; as a result, their privacy was certainly invaded. It is also likely that the children were placed in an uncomfortable position and experienced guilt or anxiety when asked to "tattle" on their parents.

We strongly recommend that the permission-granting authorities, who are usually the child participants' parents, not be deceived in all but the most extraordinary of circumstances. Considerable consultation and peer review should be undertaken to determine the acceptability of misleading parents under any circumstance, with special attention paid to the potential risks of deception to the parents and their children.

Hazards of Deception

The inherent potential for harms and wrongs in the use of deception techniques is found in two aspects of its use, and these are often interrelated. First, the deception manipulation itself may be stressful or humiliating, as when participants are told that they did poorly on an intelligence test (when in fact they did very well, or the test itself was not an intelligence test, or the test was not even scored). Second, even though the deception itself may not have elicited any reaction (or it may have been experienced as positive as in cases in which bogus feedback about performance was highly flattering), a negative reaction may occur on the "debriefing" when the participant learns of the deception. Sometimes debriefing may bring forth feelings of relief, but the "inflicted insight" (as Baumrind, 1976, calls it) can also be painful or unwelcome. Negative consequences for adults of either facet of deception have been described in the literature and include feelings of degradation, loss of self-esteem, embarrassment, anger, disillusionment, anxiety, and mistrust (Baumrind, 1976, 1977, 1985; Cupples & Gochnauer, 1985; Kelman, 1967; Seeman, 1969; Striker, 1967; Weinrach & Ivey, 1975).

Because we do not possess solid data on child-specific risks of deception, our comments must be considered speculative. Many children are extremely sensitive and suggestible. Because of their less mature capabilities of processing information and their still-emerging self-concepts, children may be more vulnerable than are adults to manipulations involving deflation of self-esteem, negative false feedback, induced anxiety or stress, or the berating of cherished attitudes, values, beliefs, people, or institutions. The following case illustrates how children, in particular, may feel unsettled as a result of being deceived:

CASE 6-8: In a study of the reactions of 8-year-olds to "failure to live up to a responsibility," children were asked to stay alone to watch over a box of four live kittens for a 5-minute period. They were admonished to make sure that the kittens stayed safe and in the box. During the second minute, a buzzer was set off directly behind the child, causing a reflexive orienting response. While the child's eyes were diverted, an investigator's confederate slipped his hand through a slot in the wall and removed one of the kittens. For the next 5 minutes, the child's reactions to the missing kitten were observed through a one-way window. When the investigator returned, he listened to the child's story about what happened and told the child that "the kitten would show up and couldn't have got very far." He then thanked and excused the child.

It may be useful for us to know more about how failure to live up to adult standards feels to children and what effect it has on them. A structured and controlled laboratory approach to the matter is potentially more useful than are anecdotal or clinical reports. Nevertheless, this study method raises several ethical questions. The children were put in a position that may have caused near panic in the more sensitive ones, and the problem was dismissed but not resolved at the end of each child's participation. Many children may have worried about the kitten's safety for a very long time, and the guilt could be potentially harmful. The acceptability of this design could be markedly enhanced by altering the "failure" experience to something more emotionally neutral, collapsing the "failure observation" time to a minimum, and either fully debriefing the children (running the risk here of reinforcing the notion that adults pull mean tricks on little kids) or, at the very least, assuring them that the problem is completely resolved (i.e., finding the kitten, perhaps with the child's assistance).

On debriefing (or "dehoaxing," as Holmes, 1976a, 1976b, calls it), the mere reassurance that things were not as they seemed may not fully (if at all) "disabuse" or "desensitize" the participants or restore them to their "former sense of self." This is especially true if the participants were "set up" to behave in ways that would make them feel ashamed, embarrassed, or guilty on learning that they were manipulated or observed. Because of the more vulnerable status of children, it seems reasonable to suspect that the failure of debriefing to resolve any emotional residue is more likely and profound than for adults:

> CASE 6-9: A child confederate of the investigator tells several other children a contrived "secret." The child confederate also elicits promises that the secret will remain unshared. Later, a teacher's aid (also a

confederate) asks each child individually if they know anything about a specific "secret-related" matter. Secret content was varied to see if children would break their promises more readily when a secret involved a misdeed (i.e., she stole another child's toy) than when it involved a personal matter in the sharer's life (i.e., her parents were getting a divorce).

Even if proper permission was obtained from parents, some useful information about children's promise-keeping behavior emerged, and the children were all told later about the true purpose of the study, ethical concerns persist. On debriefing, children may have felt guilty about telling on their friend, and this may be difficult to desensitize easily. Impressions that adults (including one of their own teachers) mislead them may cause resentment, not to mention poor role modeling.

An example of a children's "honesty assessment" (many of which, ironically, use deception) also illustrates debriefing risks:

CASE 6-10: A child is asked to look at a diagram of an extremely complicated maze for 1 minute. Then, with pencil placed in the start box, the child is asked to close her eyes "real tight" and to negotiate through the maze "without any peeking allowed." The maze itself is purposely so complex that an adequate performance would be possible only if one disobeys the rule and peeks.

Debriefing children who peeked may well cause some emotional reaction such as guilt or embarrassment and shame on learning that they were found out. A decision not to debrief in this instance (even if it were ethically justifiable) creates unfortunate effects as well. That a good performance can be achieved by cheating is reinforced in the "peekers," and honesty is punished by a poor performance.

The "shift in realities" that emerges during debriefing may be especially confusing to younger children. They agree to do one thing under one set of expectations and then are told, in effect, that "that isn't what happened." Rather than emerging enlightened, they may emerge feeling confused, tricked, stupid, or unsure of themselves.

The 1981 APA ethics code does specify that debriefing should be done "as soon as possible." Although the allowable time lag may be interpreted variously, the general ethic is that research participants should not hold misconceptions for an extended period. This is especially important, of course, if the misconception affected the participant negatively. Children's sense of time is subjectively different than that of adults. A lack of timely feedback to children could exacerbate or intensify any negative aftereffects:

> CASE 6-11: A study of the effects of negative feedback about ability on classroom behavior and attitudes toward school involved selecting one group of students who normally performed very well academically. They were told that they scored poorly on an "important abilities test." A month later, teachers were given rating scales focusing on the assessment of changes in the students' behavior since "failing" the test. The children were given the same rating scale that was administered 2 months earlier about their attitudes toward school. Afterward, children were told that a mistake had been made in calculating their test scores and were given honest performance feedback.

Certainly, there are better ways of studying the effect of school evaluations than resorting to ethically objectionable tactics. Children who take pride in their school abilities would likely be devastated on being evaluated as "dumb." The inordinate amount of time that the children were forced to carry around false beliefs about themselves, however, is particularly abhorrent. A month's experience in the life of a child, and the unfortunate shifts in self-concept that could have germinated, may not so easily be undone by the less-than-honest declaration that a mere scoring error was later discovered.

Ironically, the APA commentary on its 1982 ethics code section dealing with research practices specifically allows the option *not* to debrief children and even supports the use of additional deception if it helps ensure that a child emerges with positive feelings toward the experience:

> With children, the primary objective of the post-investigation clarification procedure [debriefing] is to ensure that the child leaves the research situation with no undesirable aftereffects of participation.

Attaining this objective may mean, for example, that certain misconceptions should not be removed or even that some new misconceptions should be included. If children erroneously believe that they have done well on a research task, there may be more harm in trying to correct this misconception than in permitting it to remain. Conversely, ameliorative efforts are needed when children feel that they have done poorly. In some circumstances, such effects may include using special experimental procedures to guarantee the child a final experience of success. [pp. 65–66]

The 1982 APA code also generally condones the acceptability of withholding damaging information from participants if it does not affect the participants beyond the experiment itself. This "what kids don't know won't hurt them" approach to managing deception and other risks can be justified from a humane, paternalistic perspective. Unfortunately, this view also officially sanctions lying to and deceiving children. It can be argued that those who have dedicated their professional lives to working with children, and who also benefit professionally from the children they study, are obligated to treat children with openness, honesty, and respect.

The following case is illustrative of the APA commentary recommendation in operation:

CASE 6-12: Children were asked to respond to a number of figure-matching items. Regardless of the child's actual accuracy score, each one was told, "You did very, very well on this task."

Here the study methodology itself involved no deception, but the experience was "fictionalized" after the fact, at least for those children who did not actually earn a high score. The children probably did feel good about themselves on leaving the room (save for those who may have realized that they were not very good at the task and may have been very confused by or suspicious of the feedback). The argument that no harm was done may be valid, although conceivably the bogus feedback could give the children a false sense of security about their abilities that could backfire later. The risk of "true" feedback is that children who scored very low might leave the room feeling deflated and stupid.

We suggest that there may often be a reasonable compromise with child participants between stark honesty and benevolent lying. In case 6-12, for example, a different approach during the closing phase may have still allowed the poorly performing children to feel "okay" about themselves without resorting to false feedback. The focus could be not on their performance but rather on expressing appreciation for their assistance with the research project. Because we all *should* be grateful to our participants for their help with our projects, and because the receipt of appreciation is warming to humans generally, this communication does the job honestly and positively.

Alternatives to Deception

Alternatives to the use of deception should always be carefully explored before proceeding. Critics have argued that deception techniques have often provided a quick, noncreative, and undesirable shortcut to more ethical and scientifically sound experimentation. Role playing and other simulation alternatives have been developed (e.g., Diener & Crandall, 1978; Geller, 1982) that may be appropriate for use with older children. Alternatives may well present new methodological problems, but they do diffuse the ethical ones to a great extent.

Forewarning deception techniques (see Sieber, 1982a) or partial disclosure methods during assent may also alleviate many of the potential risks of total deception. Here participants are informed at the onset that full disclosure about the study will be offered after the experiment is completed. Thus, permission or assent to be deceived is obtained at the onset. Or, if several different manipulations are involved, participants may be given complete information about all conditions but not know which condition they are in until later.

An effective use of partial disclosure is adapted from Baumrind (1976) in the following case:

CASE 6-13: Lionel Byte, a graduate student, planned a study using a modified "prisoner's dilemma" game, played by two children at computer terminals. Baseline cooperative data were to be gathered by using a standard sequence of computerized plays followed by a series of actual interactive plays with the human partner. The investigator wanted the children to assume that the "partner" was always a real person rather than a computer. To diminish deceiving the children while at the same time maintaining the integrity of the study purpose, the children were told that part of the time they would be playing a computer and part of the time they would be playing their human partner but that they would not know when they were playing which partner.

Here the children knew at the onset that something would remain unknown. The dilemma of the use of misinformation regarding their peer's cooperative and competitive strategies was completely avoided. Later, the children were told that the first 125 plays were with a computer and the last 75 with their human partner, but this information did not conflict with the information given at the time of obtaining assent.

Fortunately, most deception techniques used with children in social or behavioral research are quite benign, and long-term harm seems unlikely. Nevertheless, we highly recommend avoiding the use of deception, proceeding with it only if the study has extraordinary merit, cannot be approached in an alternative way, and the plan for removing any negative effects is carefully and compassionately considered in advance. We submit that the risks of deception (and debriefing) may be very subtle or undetectable in children but nevertheless interfere with their emerging and developing self and sense of trust in themselves and others. We also note that many see the critical issue as the wrong involved in deception, a wrong that cannot be defended simply by proving that no harm was done.

PARTICIPANT PRIVACY AND DATA CONFIDENTIALITY

A tendency to retreat from the position that parents or others have an *absolute* right to know anything and everything about minor children (especially teenagers) and an increasing recognition of a minor's rights to privacy are steadily emerging. The concept of obtaining a minor's assent acknowledges the child's right to know that she is a subject of a research study and her right to accept or reject this opportunity to be "intruded on."

Generally, ethics codes and federal policy admonish investigators to protect the privacy of their participants and to maintain the confidentiality of data. With child participants, however, complications can include (a) the parents' desire for feedback or their belief in their rights to know the details of their child's study behavior or performance; (b) pressures by school personnel, other agencies, or other second-order permission granters to have access to data; (c) the researchers' beliefs that they have discovered findings about specific and identifiable children that should be shared with others; and (d) questions about minors' capabilities to give "voluntary and informed consent" to allow the data that they contribute to be shared with others.

Sharing Research Data with Parents

When parents give permission for their children to participate in research, it is not uncommon for the parents to request or expect detailed feedback, especially if the study topic involves an area of specific interest or concern to the parents. Under what conditions, if any, is it ethically acceptable to share a specific child's "data" with that child's parents?

Principle 5 of the 1981 APA ethics code allows for the sharing of any information originally gained in confidence as long as the "person or the person's legal representative" gives consent. This principle offers a guideline about sharing data with someone other than the parent (i.e., consent from the parent must be obtained), but it does not address the question of keeping any data from the parents. In principle 9, which deals specifically with research participants, investigators are admonished to keep data confidential "unless agreed upon in advance." In the 1982 elaboration of that principle, it is noted that instances may arise when sharing data with parents, teachers, or therapists could greatly benefit the participant; however, this should not be done without the participants' "free and informed permission."

Even assuming that an investigator can meet the "informed" test by explaining the situation to a child in a way that can be fully understood, the child is likely to be placed in an intensely difficult situation when it comes to "voluntariness." If the parents are demanding feedback, and the child refused or expressed a desire for her parents not to be informed, how does the investigator share the child's reluctance with the parents in a way that protects the child from pressure or even possible censure? Abused children may be particularly at risk in this regard (Kinard, 1985). We maintain that children's potential for exercising their right to dissent from having data shared with their parents is greatly limited by parents' power as parents. This situation cannot be easily resolved. The investigator may attempt to wriggle out of the conflict by agreeing to lie to the parents, although such a tactic raises other ethical issues. Another more appropriate resolution that may be useful in some situations is for the investigator to excuse the child who exhibits considerable conflict, explaining to the parents that their child did not meet study criteria. Investigators are generally encouraged to excuse any participant who appears stressed or upset and would presumably wish to withdraw. Any irritation that the parents may feel is diverted onto the investigator.

We suggest that the ground rules for sharing data be clearly established at the outset, with both the parents and the child participants (if they are competent to give assent). This way, either the parents agree to not being informed, or the minors realize before they contribute data that their parents will receive information about their performance. This allows the minors a chance to protect their privacy, either by withholding assent or by choosing or attempting to alter their performance or to restrict their answers to questions.

> CASE 6-14: After their 10-year-old daughter completed a series of achievement and personality tests as part of a cross-sectional study, Mr. and Mrs. Curious showed up at the researcher's office requesting detailed feedback on their daughter's performance. They reminded the investigator that during the permission phase she offered to answer *any questions* about the study.

The investigator was initially vague about the boundaries of her offer, and this came back to haunt her later. If the researcher wished to keep the data confidential, she could have said something initially like, "Whereas we do not share the findings on any particular child with others, including the parents, we will supply you with a summary of the overall findings and will answer any questions you may have about our results."

Investigators must also be prepared to face another type of parental ploy:

CASE 6-15: Mr. and Mrs. Manipulata inform the investigator that they will permit their 7-year-old daughter to participate in a research project if and only if they are given detailed feedback and interpretation of information obtained during her study trial.

These parents are essentially holding their permission hostage. Researchers should not feel comfortable with this ploy, and many would not enroll the child in the study at all. Others may promise parents a copy of the final report, based on aggregate data, in the hopes that this would be acceptable as an alternative.

Certainly, in those instances when a child may be at risk for some problem and the research purpose involves—at least in part—assessing that risk, it would typically be inappropriate to withhold any findings from those who could be of assistance in alleviating the problem or to inform others that there is no need for concern. This situation can usually be handled very effectively by making it clear to all parties during the consent phase that such information will be shared as soon as it is available.

PROTECTING CONFIDENTIALITY FROM
ACCESS BY SOMEONE OTHER THAN THE
CHILDREN'S LEGAL GUARDIANS

Ethics codes and policies involving data access by someone other than parents are straightforward. Whereas the child participant, if appropriate, should still be informed at the onset about who will have access to any individualized data (e.g., the school or a therapist), consent must also be obtained from the parents.

When multiple data sets are collected on minors over a period of time, as is frequently done with longitudinal research, information about the identity of a specific individual must be maintained in connection with his or her data for an extended period of time. Here identities should be coded in the data file and the master file made available only to the principal investigators. Parents and the minors, if appropriate, should be informed at the outset of the procedures for maintaining confidentiality and any foreseeable limitations of such procedures (e.g., the possibility of a subpoena).

One of the drawbacks of our rapidly developing technology is that information that may be potentially damaging, and that could be used to participants' disadvantage, could possibly be stored in data banks that do not include proper safeguards. The 1982 APA guidelines suggest that investigators may not wish to contribute data in such instances because of the possibility that they may be accessed by people who cannot or will not interpret them accurately. This situation may be especially disturbing when it concerns information contributed by minors because such data more rapidly reach obsolescence yet could be used to the participants' disadvantage at some later date.

On occasion, an investigator's data may be of great interest to other agencies that wish to know the identity of the participants or what information the participants supplied to the investigators. With child participants, examples of sought-after data may include drug dealing or use, gang activity, ongoing sexual or physical abuse by adults, or children involved in litigation. Investigators working in sensitive or controversial areas should strongly consider applying for confidentiality certificates from the Public Health Service (see Gray & Melton, 1985; Melton, 1988a, 1988b; Melton & Gray, 1988; and Reatig, 1979). These certificates are intended to provide immunity from subpoena and offer the best protection of data confidentiality currently available. It is important to note that the certificates do not provide an absolute guarantee that data cannot be accessed by others. Names and other identifying information are protected, *not* the data. Therefore, if somebody already knows the identities of participants, say in a study of abused children, it is not clear whether a subpoena of the data provided by particular participants could be enforced. It is also unclear whether reporting laws are abrogated by the certificates. Melton (personal communication, 1988) recommends that, when litigants may know who is in a study, a certificate of confidentiality and a protective order or memorandum from the presiding judge be obtained in advance of any issue of subpoena (or threat thereof).

Investigators should also be aware that statutory privileges are preempted in cases of conflict with a constitutional right. Say, for example, that a criminal defendant alleges that the data are relevant to the case at hand and that to deny access to them would deprive her of due process. In such an instance, Melton (personal communication, 1989) recommends that the investigator attempt to have discovery limited by *in camera* review of the data for relevancy and necessity. Other helpful sources of data protection techniques include American Psychological Association (1982), Boruch and Cecil (1982, 1983), Carroll (1973), and Knerr (1982).

Published case studies of children tend to be about very unusual or exceptional ones or involve specific details of the process of psychotherapy or treatment. Here it is always possible that a child (and the parents) can be identified by at least some readers. Again, any such risks should be shared with the relevant parties in advance. Also, as far as is possible, individuals should be disguised and sensitive material deleted, without, however, jeopardizing the integrity of the work (American Psychological Association, 1982).

Third-Party Contacts

Some types of research require contact with others for the purpose of gaining information about children. Parents, teachers, school counselors, therapists, classmates, neighbors, or other family members may be involved. Here, two risks present themselves. First, these parties may reveal information about the child that the child would not want told to an outsider (i.e., the investigators). Second, in the course of interviewing, sensitive and previously unknown facts about the child participant (e.g., that the study is on sexually abused boys or friendless teenagers) may be revealed to interviewees (APA 1982). Although one should obtain the

147

participants' assent to solicit third-party information, children may not fully understand the ramifications of such privacy invasion. The 1982 APA guidelines suggest that, for this type of research, the investigator should proceed only after a careful analysis of the ethical problems and with outside consultation to assure that the project merits the potentially serious ethical hazards.

Disclosure of Research Data without Permission

In chapter 4, we discussed how information gained in confidence can be disclosed without the permission or even over the objections of the child in cases in which children are in imminent danger to or from others or themselves. Researchers may also be included by most states under the statutory categories that mandate reporting of specific circumstances or conditions. These categories are not necessarily limited to mental health issues. In this age of concern regarding acquired immune deficiency syndrome (AIDS), investigators should also thoroughly familiarize themselves with public health reporting laws. The ethical responsibilities of researchers are similar to those of applied mental health professionals. The 1982 APA guidelines note that researchers are not excluded from the requirement to disclose information to avoid harm to a research participant or to protect others from a participant. Further, the participant should be informed that information may have to be disclosed, given the rationale for the disclosure, and be counseled about the limits of confidentiality.

When the study purpose and techniques are benign and the study population has not been selected because its members are "at risk," elaborate procedures to ensure confidentiality are not necessary. In such instances, the likelihood of the need to disclose is infinitesimally low, and one runs the risk of needlessly scaring away potential participants. However, if it is known in advance that certain sensitive information may emerge, verbal children can be informed about confidentiality limitations at the onset. For example, in a study of depressed or highly aggressive acting-out children, the investigator should reasonably suspect that revelations of contemplated danger to self or others may be discovered. In their survey of researchers who studied childhood depression using self-report inventories in community (nonclinical) samples, Burbach, Farha, and Thorpe (1986) found that about 25% of the investigators had not even considered the possibility of actually locating seriously depressed or suicidal children. Over two-thirds of the sample either made no plans in advance should such children be identified or planned not to intervene at all. More than one-third of the investigators ultimately did experience a need to intervene directly on a child's behalf, although their efforts were often not thoroughly thought through.

CASE 6-16: Teenagers were administered a widely used and standardized self-report depression scale as part of a larger battery of assessments. Ned Blue's test indicated such an elevated score that the researcher was seriously concerned about the young man's welfare.

Because the young man was identifiable, the researcher should seriously consider taking action, after consultation with an assessments expert if needed and without revealing the participant's identity at this point. With teenagers, a direct conference may be appropriate to assess the matter, including learning if the minor is already receiving therapy, if the parents are aware of and dealing with the depression, if the school's professional staff has knowledge and is involved, and so on. Given the dynamics in a particular instance, the investigator may assist by providing resources or making contact on the participant's behalf. If the conference leaves the investigator unsatisfied, additional consultation with experts and other avenues of action should be immediately explored.

Suppose the assessments as described in case 6-16 were taken anonymously and, at the bottom of the answer sheet, the participant also wrote, "These items are like I feel all the time and I'm going to do away with myself. I mean it!!!" As Burbach et al. (1986) put it, here is a time when ignorance is *not* bliss! Would the researchers have any duty to attempt to locate the individual from the total pool of anonymous participants? Such a note may be an attempt at adolescent black humor or sarcasm, but it may also be a cry for help to someone the youngster perceives as a professional and as such should be taken seriously. If the data are collected in such a way as to prevent the identification of individuals, the investigators should consider extending a general invitation for "the person who wrote us a note to get in touch with us for more information."

When research participants threaten harm to another, researchers are not excluded from the potential obligation to take protective action, if there is an identifiable victim. If there is no specific victim (e.g., an adolescent research participant says, "I hate girls and I intend to tear up as many of 'em as I can"), then one must attempt to assess the significance of the threat and possible risks. (Readers interested in the general issue of threats of violence against unnamed others by juveniles are referred to the discussion of *Thompson v. County of Alameda* in chap. 4.)

Intervening on behalf of children or others poses some risks to the investigator, however, such as the possibility of assessing the situation incorrectly and divulging information to parties who will use it in a way that increases the child's risk. As with any study, the higher the quality and validity of the study techniques and the more competent the investigators, the less likely the possibility for errors in judgment. Similarly, the more carefully thought out the plan for dealing with any contingencies, the more likely the success of the intervention. We must also note that research investigators do not have reporting obligations involving children or adults that *exceed* those of others working with similar people who are not research participants. Thus, "inflicting" information on others, even others in trouble, is not necessarily a legal or an ethical responsibility. The investigator must be especially sensitive in making any decisions to disclose information not related to ethical or legal reporting mandates.

Naturalistic Observation

Observing children's behavior in their everyday environment has advantages. The behavior is natural, unstilted, and therefore potentially more generalizable than is the frequently inhibited or withdrawn behavior that can occur in the unfamiliar setting of a laboratory. However, issues of invasion of privacy can arise, particularly if the children are unaware of the investigators' presence and "mission."

The 1983 DHHS guidelines allow for observations in public settings without permission or assent so long as there is no interference or manipulation of the situation. Yet, the meaning of *public* is not clear cut. Sieber (1982a) defines public behavior as activity that others may freely observe. However, *private* behavior (that intended not to be observed) often occurs in public settings:

CASE 6-17: Bart Acne, M.A., sat in a booth in a restaurant known to be a teen hangout. He surreptitiously took notes on the customers' conversations and antics as part of a study of contemporary adolescent social behavior. Topics dealt with problems with parents, experimentation with drugs and sex, various plottings to gain the attention of admired peers, and considerable unflattering gossip about classmates.

Even though the teens were personally unknown to Mr. Acne and therefore unidentified except for their sex and general physical description, the young people were most certainly under the assumption that they were not being monitored. Since minors are probably less aware of and concerned about their immediate surroundings, except for their immediate focus of attention, than are adults, their privacy is easier to invade. We are uneasy about exploiting this type of opportunity.

UNEXPECTED AND EARLY FINDINGS

Once a project is designed, investigators typically assume that data collection will go smoothly to its planned conclusion and that only information relevant to the study topic will emerge. However, unanticipated surprises are always possible and may plunge investigators into dilemmas with which they are unprepared to deal:

CASE 6-18: Research assistant Sonja Shock interviewed school-age children about their career aspirations as part of a longitudinal study of career choice patterns. When she asked a girl what job she wanted to hold at age 25, the girl replied, "Police woman." When the research assistant inquired about the basis of the decision, she replied, "So I can help girls who are being beaten up by their mother's boyfriends like I am." The flustered Ms. Shock asked if this was still going on and if anyone else knew about it. The girl began to weep and said, "My mom knows, but she doesn't do anything to stop him."

Here, the incident was entirely unexpected, as opposed to the known potential for problems discussed in the previous section. Depending on the principal investigator's profession and state law, reporting to officials may be mandatory. Even if such reporting is not legally required, however, ignoring the girl's plight would likely not be morally acceptable to any investigator. Immediate consultation with experts is advised, and some action to protect the girl should be instituted.

Other situations can arise when the reasonable course of action is unclear. This can happen when the investigator does not possess the specific competencies necessary to evaluate the situation thoroughly or when the expected finding is equivocal. The case presented below encompasses both these features:

CASE 6-19: While collecting crayon drawings for a benign cross-sectional study of school-age children's artistic creations, Dr. Pat Surprise noted that an 8-year-old boy drew pictures that were startlingly at variance with the array of houses with chimney smoke, flowers, trees, animals, happy people, and suns produced by the others. One showed a blood-soaked, dismembered, male adult figure. Another was of a man hanging by a rope from a tree with a large dagger in his chest.

Dr. Surprise was a bit shaken with the boy's drawings and very uncertain about what, if anything, she should do. Some past course work on children's drawings alerted her to the possible pathology, but she had no significant expertise in this type of assessment. She did not know the boy at all, and for all she knew he was reflecting some morbid recollections from a movie or news broadcast.

Investigators working from a strictly experimental model have permission (and assent, if appropriate) only to collect data and do not typically obtain in advance any consents to intrude into the participants' private lives further. Dr. Surprise could opt to ignore the discrepant drawings, although this may cause her lingering concern. A first course of action would be to share the materials (without identifying the artist) with a colleague who is expert in the area of clinical assessment of children's drawings. At this point, she may get a better understanding of what they could mean and what other options are available to her. If the consultant also expresses concern, the investigator may opt to share the information with the school psychologist or some other appropriate person who may be in a position to advocate or protect the boy. We do not recommend, in this instance, going initially to the parents since the drawings could indicate a negative or abusive home situation that could place the child in further danger. However, in other types of instances the parents could be informed of a potential problem, such as when a participant performed in such a way as to indicate a possible perceptual dysfunction, and further evaluation suggested. The general rule of thumb here is to make a decision based on the child's overall best interests as carefully weighed against any agreements about data confidentiality. It is also strongly recommended, if the child is old enough to understand, that an explanation for the investigator's actions be offered (Kinard, 1985).

Another type of unexpected dilemma is experienced when early data analysis suggests clear indications of positive or negative results even though the study itself is not yet completed. This potential exists when information is collected on individuals over a period of time (longitudinal designs). For example, in recent studies of a new clot-dissolving drug TPA (i.e., tissue plasminogen activator) for heart attack victims, results were so overwhelmingly favorable that it was deemed unethical to continue withholding the drug from patients in the control group (TIMI Study Group, 1985).

In less dramatic instances—that is, situations not involving life-or-death consequences—investigators engaged in longer-term research could still be faced with this dilemma. If an experimental group flourishes in, say, a study comparing innovative versus standard methods of teaching children to read, should the technique be offered to the control group and/or should the early results be presented in the literature despite the fact that the initial plan was to keep the project going for another year? The codified ethical obligations are not clear. The 1982 APA guidelines suggest that findings deemed beneficial should be offered to the control group members if at all feasible, but they do not address the problem of "early" findings in a long-term project. When the participants are children who are developing at a rapid rate, to delay offering a beneficial treatment may not have much meaning by the time the study has run its planned course.

What about the opposite situation, one in which the experimental group is not benefiting or is even deteriorating? Again, the available guidelines are not explicit. The APA ethics code does note that psychologists should terminate a clinical or consulting relationship when it seems reasonably clear that the consumer is not benefiting and that alternative sources of assistance should be offered. Research participants are not explicitly included in this mandate, although the thrust of the entire code is to protect the welfare of consumers as a primary concern.

In research, it is not uncommon for manipulation effects to show up in fits and starts or for it to take some time before the full effect is known. Indeed, the research model itself is predicated on the belief that a systematic and complete investigation is required before a valid finding can be issued. A number of historical precedents illustrate how the adoption and practice of a treatment that is not fully tested can have results that are as bad or worse than the original problem the treatment was intended to alleviate.

The early finding issue does not resolve easily. However, we offer a general suggestion. If the risks are relatively minor, were validly assessed in advance, were understood and accepted by all parties concerned with evaluating and participating in the study, and were not exceeded during the course of the investigation, then the investigator cannot be faulted for proceeding. However, if manifested risks to any participants are more serious than or exceed those that were originally projected, then a reconsideration of the situation is mandated.

PREVENTION/INTERVENTION RESEARCH
PROGRAM RISKS

Many research programs designed to avert risk of harm or to remediate preexisting damage involve children as the primary target group. Educational, psychotherapeutic, and coping or other skill-building techniques are frequently used intervention strategies. The research component usually involves assessing the efficacy of different approaches and/or evaluating the outcome of the intervention and comparing it to the "status quo" situation. Direct benefit to the participants in the experimental group is virtually always intended. Therefore, prevention/intervention research has generally been regarded as humanitarian, socially relevant, and an unlikely candidate for ethical pitfalls or criticism. As Gray (1971) put it, "It was taken for granted that a program with clear implications for human welfare was rooted in positive motives and intent" (p. 80). Indeed, today the need for prevention and early intervention programs seems more critical than ever before. Drug abuse, family and gang violence, high teenage pregnancy rates, environmental damage, and AIDS are among the many woes within our borders that threaten the very fabric of our society.

More recently, however, research concerns and risks that may attend prevention and early intervention research have gained attention. Some of the case examples that we have already presented are relevant to these issues (e.g., cases 5-10, 5-11, 5-13, 6-3, and 6-4), and much of the material already discussed generally applies to this type of work as well. However, sufficiently different conditions and concepts pertain to warrant a separate enumeration of some of the major ethical dilemmas.

The focus of our brief discussion will be on the more common type of prevention/intervention project, which involves participants judged to be at risk for the manifestation or worsening of some malady, disadvantage, or other negative consequence should the individual remain on an unaltered life course. Sometimes the children are judged to be at risk primarily because they reside in risky families or environments (e.g., with substance-abusing parents, a stressed single parent, divorcing parents, or a mentally ill parent or in poverty). At other times, children may be judged to be at risk because of indicators that can already be observed in their behavior, performance, or physical state and that suggest likely adverse consequences should intervention not occur. Examples here include poor school performance, hanging out around gangs, membership in some social group that is often victimized by discrimination, being overweight, or frequent fighting with other children.

The usual child target study populations for prevention/intervention research are often vulnerable in more ways than simply tender age. The children are often from ethnic minority groups and/or underprivileged families. Parents are often a factor in the children's deficit condition, if, for example, they are unable to nurture or provide for their offspring properly. Whereas such children are most certainly in need of supportive resources, they and their proxies are often at a distinct disadvantage when it comes to negotiating the traditional requirements for voluntary and informed consent, avoiding even subtle coercion from a seemingly helping hand or authority figure, and assessing research risks in the context of perhaps an even riskier everyday life.

The fact that the children and families under study are often unlike those of the research team creates the potential that the team will be insensitive to, ignore, or even disparage or destroy the cultural traditions or values of the study population. Sometimes, whatever it is that is to be prevented reflects the political orientation or the values of the programmers, and these may run counter to the welfare of the participants or deprive them of their civil rights. The ethical investigator in this line of work becomes thoroughly familiar with and respectful toward the study community, its values, and its traditions and includes consultants from the community during all phases of the project.

Although all research may have some direct or indirect political implications, this fact is most obvious in prevention and intervention work. As Kessler and Albee (1975) have noted, political, social, and ethical implications accrue whenever things are done to large groups of people. Because change is the goal, and because this type of work usually takes place in the community and is often focused on more vulnerable and powerless groups, it comes under the scrutiny of many eyes. Who has the right or the power to decide what should be prevented or interfered with? Is one person's notion of prevention another's notion of the loss of self-determination or choice? How does one balance the benefits of intrusion into people's lives against their civil rights? Do the target populations have clear rights and/or the capability to withhold consent from being intervened on? Can any prevention or early intervention program be truly effective without first abolishing injustice and poverty?

Intervention work with children, as Melton (1987) has discussed, poses special confusions. There has been, on the one hand, an increasing recognition of children's rights ("child advocacy") and, on the other, an increasing justification for coercive intervention in the lives of children and their families as social problems become redefined as public health problems ("child saving"). Those who become involved in intervention work with children can expect to confront a number of clashing policies and values.

Powerful people are often interested in the results of prevention/intervention work and often favor a particular outcome. Sometimes the reason is as simple as wanting to maintain a job or position, but sometimes it is more insidious, such as a desire to support a preconceived belief (e.g., unfounded beliefs that black children are inherently more aggressive than white children or that lesbians make bad mothers). Investigators must be sensitive to their own biases and vigilant to any attempt by others to pressure or coerce them. In reality, such sensitivity and vigilance can prove very difficult to accomplish. Investigators who are able to specify data ownership and procedures for the dissemination of results clearly and in advance are less likely to face political pressures to suppress their findings.

Prevention/intervention research is often expensive, which means that it must be funded by some private foundation or government agency. Another political agenda can arise here in that the granting agency is often in a position to determine what could or should be "prevented" or "remediated." Considerable agreement often exists about these decisions (e.g., the acceptability of programs designed to prevent drug use among teenagers or intervention programs for children who have been the victims of sexual abuse). Yet across-the-board agreement is not always the case. Sometimes the offensive condition reflects value judgments about which rational people can disagree greatly (e.g., "masculinizing" boys with traditionally feminine interests, providing easy-access abortions to unwed teenagers, or the early tracking of young schoolchildren into academic or trade school pathways).

Prevention/intervention research is more often conducted in the community where the target population resides than in a laboratory. Scientific control is usually compromised in some way, which, as we have already discussed, bruises the validity of the data, often to an unknown extent. People other than the investigators themselves are often involved, and assuring their competence and adherence to the program is difficult. The variables being measured and the program being administered are often complicated and difficult to operationalize (e.g., building self-esteem), resulting in, as Cowen (1982) described it, a rhetoric and a conceptual field that are far ahead of the data base.

Prevention/intervention programs run a considerable risk of stigmatizing the participants through labeling because the focus is often on some presumed or potential deficit rather than on what strengths the individual also possesses. Since people other than the investigators may know or learn of the project and its purpose, participants may become generally known as "those underachievers," "delinquents," "dummies," and so on. It may not matter that, as in primary prevention work, the labels are not accurate because the problem has not even manifested itself. That the child is at possible risk, say for a mental disorder, may be sufficient to lead others to label her as already afflicted. Negative labels can affect the children's self-esteem and even possibly lead to a "self-fulfilling prophecy." In some cases, the procedure for conscripting participants into the program may itself cause them to label themselves, as when the previously unaware child is told that she is at risk for a future unwanted pregnancy. Attempts to camouflage the study purpose by referring to such programs by acronyms (e.g., "KIP," for Kindergarten Intervention Project) or using upbeat names (e.g., the Sunshine Club) may be only partially successful in combatting the tendency of others to label the children. Since this problem may be difficult to avoid and most certainly involves an ethical problem, investigators should consider whether the potential for averting the risk outweighs the consequences of labeling.

Besides the problem of protecting the participants' confidentiality by overt revelation or unintended leaks about the study, other privacy issues present themselves. What criteria should be used to determine whether an intrusion into the life of a child and her family is justifiable, particularly if the study poses risks to the children and the potential benefits accrue to society rather than to the participants? Much of this kind of work is highly sensitive and requires the disclosure of extremely personal matters that might embarrass or upset participants. Primary prevention research presents an additional unusual twist in that the participants are judged to be at risk for a problem that has not yet manifested itself. Can any degree of coercion or invasion of privacy, however slight, be ethically justified under this circumstance? Certainly, one obvious condition must be a thoroughly adequate consent phase, and yet, as we have mentioned, the target populations involved are often the very ones who will have the greatest difficulties protecting their own welfare.

Sometimes prevention/intervention work creates dependencies in the participants that must be handled carefully and compassionately on completion of the formal research project. Contemporary ethical standards would not allow for abandonment of participants simply because all data of interest to the investigative team have been collected. The assumption that the children and their families are at least as well off as they were when they were conscripted into the study may not be a valid one, especially for long-term support projects that may leave participants more resourceless than they would have been had they been left to cope on their own all along.

For a more intensive discussion of the risks of community intervention programs with minors, see Sieber (1989).

MINIMIZING RISKS

Prior to undertaking any research activity, investigators would be wise to analyze each feature of their proposal carefully to determine its risk potential. Most researchers will not have to go to the impressive extremes detailed in Hyers and Scoggin's (1979) remarkable account of the safeguards instituted prior to running a high risk-to-benefit ratio study involving minors. Yet simply to assume that "all will go fine" or that "the chances of a problem are too small to worry about" betrays professional responsibility. As Pearn (1981) declared, "The unexpected is more likely to happen with children than with adult subjects" (p. 115).

Generally, the investigator would be wise to evaluate the potential for risk from several vantage points. What does common sense reveal about the potential for harm at various developmental stages? What does the investigator's experience with similar interventions or procedures contribute to an understanding of the proposed risks in this particular study? What is the situation of the proposed participants? That is, what might be vulnerable about this specific group (Levine, 1978)?

Other basic considerations involve an honest assessment of questions about the importance of the research. If no knowledge that would benefit humankind and/or generalize and integrate into the knowledge stockpile is likely to emerge, the research project (regardless of risk level) cannot be justified.

The literature should also be searched to learn what has already been contributed and what has been learned about risky procedures and their sequelae. It has never been easier to accomplish such searches, thanks to computerized abstract banks.

If risks are not expected but are conceivably possible, or if the potential for risk is simply unknown, one should consider running a small pilot test on the least vulnerable but still appropriate sample to check out risk elements before proceeding. For planned risks, that is, when procedures to be used are known or expected to put the children at some degree of risk, every effort should be made to assure that these are as noninvasive and mild as possible without compromising ethics or data validity.

All experimental equipment should be assessed for safety from the "child's-eye" view. The physical environment in which the study is to take place should be appropriate to the age and size of the children for reasons of comfort as well as safety. For example, electrical outlets may require safety covers; child-sized furniture is desirable; and sharp, easily broken objects or those that might be swallowed should be removed. In a well-publicized incident at a large university, electrical equipment used with children was alleged to have faulty and exposed wiring, thus posing a potentially fatal hazard.

It is, unfortunately, not uncommon to find incidental risks materializing owing to the failure of the investigators to be sensitive to the possibilities or their putting convenience ahead of participant welfare. For example, in one study schoolchildren were pulled out of their classes on several occasions for assessments by an unfamiliar investigator wearing a white lab coat. Rumors quickly circulated among the other children that the "dumb, bad kids were getting shock treatments."

Other efforts to remove incidental risks include a consideration of unintended and/or unnecessary psychological harm. For example, if the data collection involves any discomfort, departure from routine, or extended duration or involves very young children, the presence of a parent (or another person known or trusted by the child) should be considered an ethical necessity in most cases. Investigators must be mindful that the younger child's sphere of social comfort is usually far more narrow than that of adults and that even routine events can cause wariness and uneasiness in unfamiliar surroundings.

GUIDELINES

1. Research investigators should be thoroughly knowledgeable about federal policies and ethical guidelines related to risk assessment and permissibility. In addition, they should know their state laws to assure that no federal policy or ethical mandates are preempted. They should also be thoroughly knowledgeable of state laws relevant to their obligations to report information uncovered in the course of their work, such as child abuse reporting mandates.

2. Prior to undertaking any research activity, investigators should make every attempt to minimize planned, potential, or incidental risks. If the potential for risk remains high, investigators must assess whether proceding with the study can be ethically justified.

3. Investigators should carefully plan, in advance, procedures to follow should any risks manifest themselves once the study is under way.

4. Minors who have vulnerabilities in addition to age alone require

an especially sensitive consideration of additional types of risks that may accrue.

5. Deception techniques should be avoided if at all possible.

6. Investigators must strive to protect the privacy of their research participants and maintain the confidentiality of the data they provide. Prospects of sharing data with others, including disclosures within the family, should be carefully considered before participants are conscripted into the study. In some cases, more extraordinary measures, such as application for confidentiality certificates, should be taken.

•

CHAPTER SEVEN

Children and
the Courts

While there is mention of legal issues throughout this book, the ethical problems covered in this chapter focus specifically on the involvement of children with the judicial system. These issues include criminal or delinquency actions, children as victims of and witnesses to crime, child custody decision making, and other civil litigation (e.g., full voluntary commitment as opposed to parental commitment of minors to psychiatric hospitals). Children's rights issues are one interface of behavioral science and the law where the evolution of psychological concepts and changing legal decisions has been very rapid. The result is a growing body of psychological research and increased invitations for mental health professionals to become involved in the legal system as experts in matters dealing with children and families. Unfortunately, the actual state of knowledge in the behavioral sciences does not always lend itself to answering the precise questions the legal system would like to have addressed (e.g., Who abused this child sexually? Which parent will do the better job of raising this child? Was that 12-year-old competent to waive his *Miranda* rights when he was arrested?).

Ethical difficulties often arise when mental health professionals are not fully cognizant of the legal procedures and issues involved in a case, when they are not sufficiently knowledgeable regarding current psychological research on the matter at hand, or when they inappropriately try to "wing it" or speculate without solid foundation when called on to give an expert opinion. Such problems are particularly distressing since they may result in decisions with enduring consequences for the children and families involved.

THE CHILD AS A RESPONDENT UNDER JUVENILE LAW

A considerable body of work has evolved focusing on juveniles' exercise of their *Miranda* rights. In *Miranda v. Arizona* (1966), the Supreme Court established the constitutional requirement that persons accused of a crime have the right to counsel and the right not to incriminate themselves. The Court subsequently extended the rights of accused adults to minors when it rendered the *In re Gault* (1967) decision (see also *Fare v. Michael C.*, 1979, discussed below).

In a series of empirical studies, Grisso (1981, 1983) concluded that the vast majority of juveniles age 14 and under do not grasp the meaning of the *Miranda* warnings they are given on arrest. Likewise, 15- and 16-year-olds with IQ scores of 80 and below are unable to comprehend the presentation of these rights at adult levels of understanding. Studying juveniles of 15 and 16 with low-average or better intelligence, Grisso discovered that their comprehension of the *Miranda* warnings did not differ significantly from that of adults. This does not necessarily mean that adults fully understand their rights. He also found that 25% of adults lacked an adequate understanding of the warnings and their implications. Interestingly, the same set of studies reveals that "prior experience" with the courts and police, race, and socioeconomic status were unrelated to comprehension of these rights by juveniles.

Using specific examples, Grisso (1983) summarizes the problem of integrating knowledge of human development with the facts in such legal cases very well. The message is simple. No matter what the technical minimum requirements of a law, there are always some jurisdictions that will be sensitive to these children's rights issues and some that will not have the time or the inclination to attend to them. In these latter cases, it is not at all clear that knowledge of relevant psychosocial data would necessarily change the situation.

Within the juvenile court system, mental health professionals may be asked to serve as evaluators, to address criminal forensic questions or amenability to treatment issues, or to serve as consultants or psychotherapists. An analysis and critique of the juvenile courts and the roles that mental health professionals can or should play in them are far beyond the scope of this volume, although some authors have questioned whether the mental health and juvenile justice systems belong together (Melton et al., 1987). We shall limit our discussion of such issues to the most prominent national concern regarding this population. How should the violent juvenile offender be managed in the current system?

In the criminal arena, there is an increasing tendency to treat juveniles charged with major crimes (especially homicides) as adults rather than in the juvenile or family court system. The legal procedure for accomplishing this shift is often referred to as a "transfer" or "waiver" hearing to move the case from juvenile to adult jurisdiction. This is not an issue of competency to stand trial, which involves the ability to comprehend the roles of court officers, cooperate in one's own defense, and appreciate the potential consequences of the proceedings. Rather, the trend reflects a growing public sentiment that dangerous children (i.e., violent juvenile offenders, especially in highly publicized cases) should not to be "let off the hook" simply by virtue of their age. Some states have lowered the age of jurisdiction for criminal court, either for all juvenile offenders or for selected types of offenses. Other states have expanded the basis for transfer of cases from juvenile court to adult criminal jurisdictions by either expanding the criteria for transfer or by shifting the burden of proof from the state to the defendant. Still other states have established concurrent jurisdictions for selected offenses or offenders, giving prosecutors great latitude in selecting the judicial forum in which to adjudicate adolescent crimes (Fagan & Deschenes, 1988). Traditionally, transfer decisions have been based on criteria such as the adjustment of the juvenile in the community (i.e., at home and at school), the juvenile's supposed amenability to treatment, and the nature of the offense.

CASE 7-1: In *Morris v. Florida* (1984), a state appeals court upheld a ruling that a 13-year-old murder defendant must undergo an evaluation to determine her competence to stand trial before her presumed incapacity could be overcome. Previously, juveniles under 14 were presumed incapable of criminal acts under Florida law, but following this decision youthful offenders are to be examined to assess their ability to be tried as adults.

Mental health professionals will undoubtedly increasingly be called on to perform such evaluations on children in the future. This will present interesting professional problems in terms of both training and practice since the professionals who are called on to conduct such evaluations may be court consultants trained predominantly to work with adult clients, not with children. Such clinicians would obviously need to acquire a substantial background in child development, including cognitive, social, and emotional development, as well as a solid grasp of childhood psychopathology before undertaking such assignments. Regrettably, not all our colleagues are appropriately sensitive to this issue. By the same token, child clinicians are often not trained to think of their clients in terms of criminal responsibility or forensic competency and would need to acquire this knowledge before they could assist in such determinations. The following case reflects some of the complexities involved in assessing children who are charged with crimes.

CASE 7-2: The burglary conviction of a mentally handicapped 17-year-old with an IQ of about 80 was overturned when his confession was deemed involuntary (*Illinois v. Berry*, 1984). The judicial panel cited the defendant's age, education, mental capacity, emotional characteristics, and relative inexperience in criminal matters in determining the voluntariness of the confession. The panel noted that the youth was below average in intelligence, had little education, was dependent on his parents, lacked a history of criminal experience, and respected the police. At police headquarters, he was isolated from his mother, did not have an attorney, and was subjected to some deceptive questioning. In addition, his *Miranda* warnings were never given because Berry was told that he was not in custody.

Although psychological testimony was a necessary and constructive part of the *Berry* case, we wonder how psychologists would feel about being asked to perform an evaluation in a case such as *Morris v. Florida*, where the death penalty may be at issue. During its 1988 term, the Supreme Court ruled narrowly in *Thompson v. Oklahoma* that it would be cruel and unusual punishment to execute a young man who murdered his brother-in-law at the age of 15 in the belief that he was protecting his sister. During its 1989 term, the court is expected to rule more broadly on cases involving 16- and 17-year-old murderers who are facing the death penalty. The defendants in the other pending cases are not so sympathetic as was Thompson. The ultimate outcome for children who commit murder in states with the death penalty is by no means clear. Florida is one of a number of states with a large death row population and an increasing rate of actual executions. Do child mental health professionals want to participate in a legal system that might ultimately execute children? Is the state of psychological data on competence determination of sufficient rigor to warrant predicating the death penalty on such evidence? Such questions may well confront mental health professionals with increasing frequency before the current decade is over.

The Child as Witness

What about the child as a witness in court? Here competence is also a central issue. While children have been offering testimony in courts of law for centuries, questions are often raised regarding the value of their statements (Goodman, 1984b). A review of the historical background and current research dealing with the child witness is presented in a special issue of the *Journal of Social Issues* (Goodman, 1984a). Topics include the reliability of children's memories, children as eyewitnesses, their ability to differentiate fact from fantasy, testimony by the child victim of sexual assault, and jurors' reactions to child witnesses.

The data suggest that children can indeed be competent and credible witnesses, but they also suggest that special factors must be considered in questioning them. A number of complex and interrelated factors related to suggestibility, semantics, social demand characteristics, developmental phenomena, and other situational factors may influence the accuracy of childrens' testimony (Goodman, 1984a). This has become an area of intense interest among both clinical and developmental investigators. The resulting progress is likely to be beneficial both to the children who are involved in the legal process (i.e., by making it possible to reduce stress) and to those who are seeking justice (i.e., by establishing optimal circumstances and methods for eliciting the most accurate testimony).

Several states have passed laws providing means for children to testify in nontraditional ways. For example, some states provide for defendants to be out of the courtroom when a child victim of sexual assault is called to testify to provide a more comfortable climate for the witness. While appellate courts in at least seven states have upheld such laws, the Supreme Court of Massachusetts voided that state's statute on constitutional grounds (*Commonwealth v. Bergstrom*, 1988).

CASE 7-3: Robert Bergstrom was convicted of two counts of rape and two counts of indecent assault and battery on his two daughters, who were 6 and 8 years old at the time of trial. The judge had permitted the girls to testify by closed-circuit television from a jury room while their father, the jurors, and the spectators viewed the testimony through monitors. The law at issue was barely a year old at the time and permitted a child under 15 to testify by such means when the judge finds through a "preponderance of the evidence" that the child is otherwise "likely to suffer psychological or emotional trauma." In striking down the conviction and sending the case back for retrial, the Supreme Judicial Court of Massachusetts ruled that the law violated the defendant's right "to meet the witnesses against him face to face" and provided for an unconstitutionally broad category of victims.

In a 30-page opinion on this case, the court interpreted the words of the state constitution *to meet* and *face to face* as guaranteeing a direct confrontation with the witness. The underlying theory is that a witness will be more truthful in the presence of the accused. This theory, of course, is based on the notion of a confrontation of equals and unfortunately takes no account of developmental issues such as the child's dependency on parents and the extreme demand characteristics of the unequal power distribution between the child victim witness and the adult defendant. The decision also noted that, under the state constitution, no distinction could be drawn between a child witness and any other class whom the legislature might designate as requiring special treatment in the future, again missing the point of a child's unique vulnerabilities. The court was also troubled because the judge at the Bergstrom trial had told the children neither that they were testifying against their father nor that he was observing them from a nearby room. The court also ruled that the level of proof required to permit testimony in a protected circumstance under the existing law (e.g., preponderance of evidence) was insufficient. Instead, the prosecution would be required to prove beyond a reasonable doubt that the children would suffer psychological or emotional trauma before permitting the use of the video testimony.

A few weeks after the Massachusetts ruling in the Bergstrom case, the U.S. Supreme Court reversed the conviction of an Iowa man at whose trial two female victims of sexual assault testified as he sat out of view, watching them from behind a one-way screen in the courtroom (*Coy v. Iowa*, 1988). The screen was in place to avoid "frightening the girls" by having to look at their alleged assailant during the testimony. Once again, the right to meet one's accuser face to face was cited as the prime basis for the ruling. This decision is likely to void most state laws enacted in recent years to shield young victim-witnesses from direct confrontations in courtroom testimony.

Consider the role of psychologists in the following cases in the light of the clear message from the courts that direct testimony of child victim-witnesses will be necessary to obtain convictions.

CASE 7-4: Helena Heal, M.S.W., has been treating a 6-year-old who was the victim of a sexual assault a year earlier. The alleged perpetrator of the molestation is now coming to trial, and both Ms. Heal and her patient will be called as witnesses. The child will be asked to testify regarding the events, and Ms. Heal will be asked to testify regarding the child's competence and veracity as well as the trauma the child has suffered (all with appropriate consent granted by the child's family). Ms. Heal has worked with many sexually abused children in the past and knows that reliving the molestation under direct and cross-examination will be especially stressful for the child since the defendant will be sitting in court while the child testifies. Although she does not believe that testifying is in child's best interests, she also knows that the defendant cannot be convicted without her client's testimony.

CASE 7-5: Hy R. Gunn, Ph.D., is a professor of psychology who has published widely on the potential inaccuracy of eyewitness testimony. He has been approached by the attorney representing the alleged perpetrator of Ms. Heal's client. The lawyer would like Dr. Gunn to assist him in framing questions to discredit the reliability of the 6-year-old's testimony in the minds of the members of the jury and to give expert testimony raising doubt as to the validity of the eyewitness accounts of children in general.

Ms. Heal is a conscientious social worker who is concerned about the welfare of both her client and society at large. She wants to see the person who so traumatized her young client put away, but she also does not want to see the child hurt further. Ms. Heal must consider her client's best interests and make her views known to the child's parents and the appropriate authorities. The ultimate choice, however, is not hers to make, and she must be prepared to support the decisions of her client (and the parents) in this matter.

One wonders what Ms. Heal would say if she knew that Dr. Gunn were being consulted? For his part, Gunn is a rigorous scientist who earns a good living interpreting scholarly research to lawyers and juries. Gunn knows that each accused person is entitled to a vigorous defense, and he has considerable doubt about the innocence of the defendant in this case. Yet does he have the right to base his willingness to testify on his own opinion regarding the guilt or innocence of a particular defendant? Is he entitled to judge the defendant? Does he have the right to provide his expertise selectively? Will the result be a lopsided chess game between a 6-year-old and a Ph.D. or an objective presentation of hard data that the trier of fact may use to find the truth? Loftus (1987) has eloquently addressed very similar issues and has concluded that Gunn must follow his own conscience and common sense. He must also be prepared fully to respect the professional skills and knowledge of Ms. Heal. He should resist the temptation to use educational chauvinism (i.e., I have a doctorate, and she doesn't). So long as he competently and accurately represents theory and valid scientific research without *ad hominem* criticism of his colleague, his decision either way cannot be deemed unethical.

Aside from procedural changes that might grow out of psychological research or cases such as those discussed above, it does not necessarily follow that empirical data are well used by judges in making their decisions. In addition, there may be times when constitutional issues demand that a child's best interests be ignored while she is serving as a witness. A series of rulings on a case involving the *Boston Globe* between 1980 and 1982 (Melton, 1984b) may be used to illustrate the point.

CASE 7-6: A case known as *Globe Newspaper Company v. Superior Court* involved a test of the constitutionality of a Massachusetts law barring persons "not having a direct interest in the case" from courtrooms during the testimony of minors who were the victims of sex offenses (*Massachusetts General Laws Annotated*, chap. 278). The *Boston Globe* objected to having its reporters excluded from the trial of an adult defendant who was charged with the forcible rape and "unnatural" rape of three girls who were 16–17 years old at the time of the trial.

The early decisions at the state level upheld the exclusion, noting that the statute was intended to encourage young victims to come forward and to protect them from undue psychological harm at trial. The U.S. Supreme Court ultimately overruled the early decisions, thereby voiding the law, although this decision was not rendered until long after the criminal trial had ended. Part of the Supreme Court's reasoning was that the statute was overly broad in providing for mandatory closure in such cases. More interesting, however, was the Court's statement that there was "no empirical support" for the notion that such a statute facilitates the reporting of such crimes. In a dissenting opinion, Chief Justice Burger argued that the reality of severe psychological damage to child witnesses in this context was "not disputed" and that states ought to be encouraged to experiment in order to generate empirical data of this sort. It was not clear to the Court that thorough searches for meaningful data had been undertaken. Melton (1984a) notes that study of this case "does little to promote faith that the Supreme Court will make good use of social science data [in its opinions]" (p. 118).

CONSISTENCY IN COURTS' TREATMENT OF CHILDREN'S COMPETENCE

Courts' views of children's competence have been determined more often by context than by psychological data. This is best illustrated by the juxtaposition of two Supreme Court decisions handed down on the same day in 1979.

CASE 7-7: *Parham v. J.R.* was a class action case that revolved around the issue of the "reluctant volunteer." Although adults cannot be involuntarily hospitalized in a psychiatric facility without a court finding that such confinement is warranted, children can be "voluntarily" hospitalized by their parents without such a hearing even if the child objects. This class action lawsuit from Georgia brought the issue to the Supreme Court in the context of a "least restrictive alternative" argument. The suit was brought on behalf of several children who had been hospitalized at state psychiatric facilities on the basis of their parents' or guardians' consent and sought their release or placement in less restrictive settings.

CASE 7-8: *Fare v. Michael C.* involved an adolescent suspect in a murder case who was the same age as some of the patients in the *Parham* case. Michael C. was apprehended by the police and read his rights using the standard *Miranda* warnings. Tape recordings of the interview and his subsequent confession make it clear that Michael was in great emotional distress. In response to the standard offer of a lawyer's services prior to questioning, Michael asked for his probation officer. He was told that the man was unavailable and was again offered a lawyer. Michael expressed the fear that the police might try to trick him by having another officer pretend to be a lawyer. Finally, he confessed to the crime. At the time of trial, Michael's attorney sought to suppress the confession on the grounds that Michael had not been fully competent to waive his rights and confess without legal advice.

In the *Parham* case, the key legal question was whether a hearing is necessary prior to involuntarily committing a minor to an inpatient psychiatric facility (as would be required with an adult). Presenting a rather romanticized view of the American family, the Burger Court asserted essentially that parents know best and that they (in concert with the facility's admitting officer) were adequate proxies for the child. The adolescent patients were deemed incompetent to request a hearing or otherwise assert any legal right to make a decision regarding hospitalization.

Although the taped interview with Michael C. strongly suggests that he did not understand his civil rights fully, the Supreme Court's majority opinion nonetheless expressed the belief that Michael, as a young man "experienced with the criminal justice system," was competent to waive his rights and confess to murder without consulting an attorney. The court was apparently not persuaded by Michael's apparent belief that the police would be allowed to trick him into confessing.

Comparing the decisions, we find that the Court ruled that teenagers are not competent to object to involuntary psychiatric hospitalization but are competent to confess to murder without first consulting a lawyer. Both these opinions were rendered without benefit of psychological data. Furthermore, it is not at all clear that the Court would have attended to psychological data (e.g., the research on children's understanding of such rights by Grisso, 1981) had it been available. The common knowledge available to the justices seems their most relied on source in such situations. On the one hand, this might seem a situation in which mental health professionals would want their research to be considered.

On the other hand, we must be concerned about the quality of the work and the accurate interpretation of the findings in court if it is to be used in judicial decision making.

What of the role of the child mental health specialist in such cases? Do we have real answers available to us? Expertise and knowledge of the literature is of central importance, and not all our colleagues would be competent to serve in this capacity, whether they know it or not (for an example of misplaced self-confidence in this regard, see case 4-3).

CHILD CUSTODY DECISION MAKING

Melton et al. (1987) report that mental health professionals are typically involved in only a small fraction of child custody decisions. They note that 90% of such decisions are made by divorcing spouses either through bargaining or through mediation in the process of divorce. They report on a national sample of judges who hear such cases and note that 55% reported that opinions from mental health experts are presented in less than 10% of the cases they hear. Only 25% indicated that such testimony is presented in the majority of contested custody cases in their courts. Melton and his colleagues do not find this surprising because, unlike cases of delinquency or child maltreatment, custody cases are often not heard in family courts with strong traditions of mental health or social service involvement. Rather, they are often heard in probate courts, established to safeguard property.

Melton and his colleagues also observe that most mental health professionals have little expertise that is directly relevant to custody disputes. They note that many of the issues to be resolved in such cases (e.g., "parental responsibility") are more appropriately within the purview of the judicial fact finder than of the clinician. They also note that there is no scientific basis for addressing most of the questions that courts must decide in such cases (e.g., there are no rigorous studies of the effects of various custody and visitation arrangements on children and families). The problems of clinicians overreaching their expertise in such cases is a highly visible one. In summaries of cases adjudicated by the APA's ethics committee, substantial space is devoted to a discussion of such circumstances (Ethics Committee of the American Psychological Association, 1988; Mills, 1984).

The special context of divorce raises other interesting questions. Decisions to be made in the best interests of children are highly subjective in such situations and require complex reasoning skills to conceptualize, let alone resolve. In her doctoral dissertation, Greenberg (1983) studied the degree to which children of different ages are able to employ a rational decision-making process to arrive at a custodial preference between divorcing parents. The study involved the judgments of 144 children between the ages of 9 and 14. A group of 18-year-olds was included to provide the perspective of a legal adult, and 44 domestic relations judges evaluated the decisions reached by the children. The major finding of the study was that age, IQ, sex, and socioeconomic factors were not very useful in predicting competent decision making. Rather, process-oriented problem-solving skills and knowledge about divorce were better predictors regarding the competence of children to participate in the decision-making process regarding custody.

Greenberg found that children who were able to isolate relevant aspects of the problem and generate alternative solutions and those who were familiar with what a divorce involves (i.e., those with the capacity to reason and experience) exercised the most sound judgment. The data suggest that judges who seriously wish to attend to statutory guidelines for taking a child's wishes into account ought to consider these factors. A more critical issue that is not taught well in most training programs is how one communicates this information to judges in a way that is both comprehensible and useful.

What are proper roles for psychologists in such cases? The most articulate authors on this topic (e.g., Melton et al., 1987; Weithorn, 1987) cite two principal roles: that of evaluator or investigator and that of mediator. The mental health professional as a skilled investigator or evaluator is especially valuable to the courts when abuse or neglect has been charged. Mental health professionals can also assist the court by pointing out what is known or not known about psychological factors in the effects of various custody arrangements. The second principal role for mental health professionals is that of a mediator. Clinicians with specialized training in dispute resolution can assist families in the negotiation process while helping them to understand the needs and best interests of the child (to the degree that such interests can be reasonably determined). Both these roles involve potential ethical pitfalls that the practitioner must avoid. These ethical dangers often revolve around issues of competence and blurred roles or dual relationships. Although many of these issues were raised in chapter 4 as general themes (e.g., case 4-2), we shall highlight them here with a focus on children in a divorce situation.

Before beginning either evaluation or mediation of a child custody matter, it is critical that all parties involved understand the ground rules with respect to privacy and confidentiality (for a discussion of the distinctions, see chap. 4). Although one would expect that pledges to hold communications in confidence would encourage trust in a mediator and honesty by the parties, it is unclear whether courts will allow communications in mediation to be privileged ("Protecting Confidentiality," 1984). At the same time, the competent mental health professional will recognize the potential ethical problem of the parent who arrives for evaluation and during the sessions says, "Don't tell my spouse, but . . . ," then proceeds to disclose some significant material point on which a decision might turn. In anticipation of such problems, some clinicians ask all parties to sign reciprocating waivers prior to the start of the evaluation. The waivers specify from the outset that both parents and their attorneys will have access to any information disclosed to the evaluator. Similarly, if good-faith mediation is to take place in a context free of subsequent court disclosure, both attorneys and their clients could also execute a contract not to call the mediator as a witness in any future court proceeding.

Role of the Clinician as an Evaluator

A matter of great importance and great controversy for clinicians who function as evaluators in child custody disputes is whether they should address or testify to "the ultimate legal issue" in their work. That is to say, should the evaluator make an actual custody recommendation to the court or simply provide a listing of facts and opinions for the judge to consider? Many clinicians believe that specific recommendations are moral or legal matters beyond the expertise of the mental health professional (Melton et al., 1987; Weithorn, 1987). Child custody cases rarely involve questions of actual "parental fitness" in the sense that one or the other is grossly unfit to care for the child. Rather, the more usual issue is that of which parenting arrangement will serve the best interests of the developing child. In such instances, the term *best interests* is a moral or legal concept, as defined by state law, not a psychological concept. There is general agreement that mental health professionals in this role should conduct thorough and wide-ranging evaluations, point out strengths and weaknesses to the court, and help the court understand what is known or not known in the existing research or clinical literature.

Evaluation in such cases can become quite complex. Cases may involve a request for consultative input by parents in an amicable divorce, state intervention in cases of abuse or neglect, termination of parents' rights, contested adoptions (Schwartz, 1983), or charges and countercharges regarding alleged sexual abuse. It is critical that the clinician who agrees to take on the evaluation of such a case be knowledgeable regarding both legal and clinical aspects of these types of cases. In addition, it is important to be mindful of the appropriate role boundaries. In particular, one should take care not to slip from the role of evaluator to that of intervenor (i.e., therapist).

What factors ought to be considered in making child custody decisions? Are race, religion, or parents' sexual conduct valid factors to consider in making a custody decision? The fact is that such decisions vary widely both regionally and according to local preference. In some cases, psychological factors have been cited as bases for such decisions, and mental health professionals are likely to be called as expert witnesses in future cases on similar issues. In general, however, religion and parents' sexual preferences have not been deemed proper bases for making such decisions. Some case examples from family law illustrate the point:

CASE 7-9: When Linda Sidoti Palmore and Anthony J. Sidoti, both Caucasians, were divorced in Florida during the spring of 1980, custody of their 3-year-old daughter was awarded to the mother. A year and a half later, Mr. Sidoti sought custody because his ex-wife was cohabiting with a black man, Clarence Palmore, Jr., to whom she was married 2 months later. Among the various claims at trial were psychological arguments that little Melanie Sidoti would be vulnerable to adverse peer pressures and social stigmatization as the result of living in a biracial home. The Florida courts then awarded custody to the father, much to the public distress of little Melanie, as seen in the national news broadcasts.

Psychological testimony had been introduced at the local level in support of the father's position and was apparently heeded to some degree, even though it was not supported by any meaningful body of clinical or empirical data. Fortunately, the Supreme Court saw the issue as one that was of broader significance. Chief Justice Burger, writing for a unanimous Supreme Court, noted, "Whatever problems racially-mixed households may pose for children in 1984 cannot support a denial of constitutional rights" (*Palmore v. Sidoti*, 1984). The case was sent back to be reheard at the state level. As this book goes to press, Mrs. Palmore is still seeking to regain custody of Melanie, who has been moved from Florida to Texas by her father. The state courts in Florida ruled that they lacked further jurisdiction in the case because of the change in residence, and the matter is left to the Texas courts to decide. With a range of appeals possible, Melanie may attain the age of majority before a final decision is rendered in this case.

CASE 7-10: Mr. Feldman and Mrs. Feldman were 18 and 19 years old, respectively, when they married in 1962. In July 1970, Mrs. Feldman obtained a divorce from her spouse based on his "cruel and inhuman treatment" and a history of extramarital affairs. She was granted custody of their two minor children. In August 1973, when the children were 6 and 9 years old, Mr. Feldman was visiting his wife's home when he observed a copy of *Screw* magazine on her nightstand. (In his decision, the appellate judge refers to this as a publication possessing "dubious redeeming social value.") He also found letters and explicit photographs sent in response to a blind box ad his wife had run in the magazine seeking responses from "other . . . couples or groups . . . for fun & games." He immediately sought custody of his two children, asserting parental unfitness related to his ex-wife's apparent recreational interests.

There was no evidence that the former Mrs. Feldman was anything less than a fully adequate parent or that her children had any knowledge of or involvement in her sexual activities. The judge noted, "In my opinion the right of a divorced woman to engage in private sexual activities, which in no way involve or affect her minor children, is within the penumbra of that yet ill-defined area of privacy mandated by the specific guarantees of the Bill of Rights" (*Feldman v. Feldman*, 1974).

CASE 7-11: Linnea and Edward Quiner were married in Los Angeles in 1961, had a child in 1962, and separated in 1963. Edward was awarded custody of their son at least in part on the basis of Linnea's religious practices. She belonged to the Plymouth Brethren, also known as the Exclusive Brethren. There were approximately 220 members of this group in the greater Los Angeles area at the time, and their beliefs dictated that they keep "separate" from all those outside their church. This separation included prohibitions against eating in public, secluding oneself from schoolmates, not affiliating with any social organizations, disavowing all forms of entertainment, proscription of all reading material except the Bible, and opposition to medical insurance.

Although this would seem to be a case involving a custody decision based on religion, it is more properly regarded as one based on an assessment of the more global adverse effect that such a life-style could exert on a child's development. This is the sort of case in which specialists on child development might be called on to offer expert opinions regarding the long-term effect of specific child-rearing practices on the psychological well-being of the child. Although the local court granted custody to the father, the California Court of Appeals reversed the decision (*Quiner v. Quiner*, 1967). That decision was in turn nullified by the

California Supreme Court, at which time the parties made an out-of-court settlement with the child going to reside with the mother (Areen, 1985). So much for relying on the courts to protect the best interests of the child.

Who may legitimately request an evaluation? If a mental health professional is asked to evaluate or treat a child of divorced or separated parents, it is critical to obtain consent for the procedure from the custodial parent or from both parents in cases of joint custody. Other appropriate circumstances would include evaluation in response to a court order or following an appointment as a guardian *ad litem*. Proper access to and cooperation by both parents is generally needed for effective evaluation. While this is not a universal requirement, clinicians must exercise extreme caution before proceeding without such approvals.

CASE 7-12: Peter Parker, Ph.D., was approached by Mrs. Fish, who was in the process of a divorce. She reported that her two children (Freddy, age 14, and Franny, age 6) were showing distress about the current visiting arrangements. Mr. and Mrs. Fish have joint legal custody, although the children resided primarily with their mother. After the last visit to their father, he refused to bring the children back to her, and it was necessary for her to get a court order to have them returned home. Parker met with Mrs. Fish and the children for one session. It seemed clear to him that family counseling was needed, and he recommended this. He soon received an angry call from Mr. Fish, complaining that he had seen the children without authorization. Parker met with Mr. Fish and explained his recommendations. They parted on amicable terms, with Mr. Fish requesting that Parker not see the children again until he and his estranged spouse could both agree on the family therapist of choice and have the court approve. Dr. Parker agreed.

About a month later, Parker came out of his office following an appointment and was surprised to find Freddy Fish in his waiting room. His receptionist explained that Mrs. Fish had called while Parker was in the midst of his last appointment. She told the receptionist that it was urgent that Freddy see Dr. Parker, so the receptionist booked him into the available slot. Mrs. Fish had dropped Freddy off and gone on an errand for an hour. Freddy was clearly in great distress, and except for the single hour ahead Parker's schedule was full for the day.

Dr. Parker saw Freddy for a single appointment on that day and was subsequently brought up on ethics charges before a state licensing board for "continuing to treat the child over the father's objections." Parker argued that he had not agreed to see the youngster again without the father's permission, but he also noted that it would have been inappropriate for him not to see the child. At the very least, Parker felt an obligation to meet with and assess the emotional status of the distraught youngster. For example, if he had simply refused to see the child and the youth had been suicidal, Parker could have been deemed seriously negligent. The licensing board agreed that Parker's actions were appropriate under the circumstances and dropped the charges. By that time, however, Parker had already suffered considerable distress himself and incurred significant legal expenses.

CASE 7-13: Zelda Splitter, a recently divorced young mother, brought her 5-year-old child to see a psychologist because she was concerned about the joint custody and shared visitation plan then in place with her estranged spouse. She reported that the child alternated between the parents' homes on a weekly basis and that she feared that this was causing (or would cause) emotional harm to the child. She asked the psychologist to evaluate the child and offer an opinion without discussing the matter with the child's father.

CASE 7-14: Franklin Fret is a noncustodial parent whose child was visiting him for the summer. He asked a clinician to see the youngster in short-term therapy to assist him in coping with stresses related to the divorce. When contacted by the clinician, the former Mrs. Fret, who is the custodial parent, refused to agree in writing to this plan.

In both these cases, the clinician should have no further contact with the children described. Ms. Splitter may be shopping for an expert opinion to assist her in some maneuver against her ex-spouse, or her motives may be more innocent. However, so long as the child's father has joint legal custody, the clinician should not agree to perform any professional services in secret. While the former Mrs. Fret may not object to the short-term help her husband is seeking, she has legal custody of the child. Treating the child without her formal consent might subject the clinician to a technical charge of battery at some future time, should Mrs. Fret see an outcome of which she does not approve. If Mr. Fret is sincerely concerned about helping his child cope with the stress of divorce, there is nothing to stop the clinician from meeting with him alone to give consultation on how to handle various problems the child may be having.

Role of the Clinician as a Mediator

The two most significant areas of ethical concern to psychologists who work in the area of divorce mediation involve matters of competence and dual relationships. The former issues demand that the clinician doing such work be well trained in mediation techniques as well as having appropriate clinical knowledge to enable a reasonable focus on the developmental needs of the children involved. The latter issues require great care to assure that the clinician does not attempt a transition across roles (e.g., from mediator to therapist, or vice versa).

Mediation is rapidly growing in popularity as an alternative to adversarial contests in divorce and child custody disputes. Although there are many appealing aspects to mediation in these contexts, there are also many unanswered legal and ethical questions. Emery and Wyer (1987) describe a number of the issues in detail. First among these are the qualifications of the would-be mediator. Second is the question of whether mediation should be mandatory in some cases as a matter of public policy. Third is the issue of basic assumptions regarding custody alternatives (e.g., should mediators work toward joint custody?). Finally, what role (if any) should mediators play in subsequent court hearings?

Mediation is most often taught in schools of law or business rather than in programs training mental health professionals. Some clinicians have the misguided notion that, because they have some understanding of interpersonal dynamics, they can sit down and function as mediators.

This is the same error in judgment made by those trained only with adults who undertake child work. Specialized training should be required before work as a mediator is undertaken; however, no professional standards exist in the mental health fields to define qualifications clearly. As is often the case with practitioners who are attempting to function beyond their areas of competence, little is noticed by one's colleagues in the field until something goes very wrong and formal complaints are filed.

Although mental health professionals who act as mediators are not engaged in the unauthorized practice of law simply because they conduct divorce mediation in areas of child custody and visitation (Cavanaugh & Rhode, 1976; New York City Bar Association Committee on Professional and Judicial Ethics, 1981), they must certainly be careful to avoid offering advice in areas beyond their expertise (e.g., legal risks or tax consequences of various settlements). The linkage between child custody and financial issues cannot be ignored because such matters as child support payments or disposition of a family home may revolve around who has physical custody of the children. In such instances, it is critical that final decisions, even when mediated, be executed by competent attorneys. Fortunately, most mental health professionals do not become entrapped by this particular type of dual role problem.

On the other hand, consider these cases:

CASE 7-15: Melinda Moderate, Psy.D., agrees to act as a mediator in a child custody dispute between a divorcing couple. The parents are too angry at each other to make good use of her services, and mediation breaks down. She is then contacted by the attorney for one of the parents, who asks her to undertake an assessment of the family in order to make a recommendation regarding custody to the court.

CASE 7-16: Mark Muddle, Ed.D., undertook mediation between Irving and Isabelle Ire, who were in the process of a contested divorce. He subsequently began treating Irving, Isabelle, and their children (Isadore, age 8, and Ilene, age 6) in individual psychotherapy. During this time, Isabelle would frequently ask Dr. Muddle to call Irving on her behalf to request payment of child support and other expenses.

These two cases illustrate some common types of dual relationship problems that have grown out of child custody mediation work. Dr. Moderate is being invited to switch roles from mediator to evaluator. It is to be hoped that she will be sensitive to the fact that this particular transition would probably not be in the clients' best interest. She and they have failed at a mediation effort. Although it may not be her fault, there are bound to be both transference and countertransference issues as a result of that prior contact. It would be wisest for her to decline the invitation to change roles.

Dr. Muddle is already in over his head. Perhaps he was well trained as a mediator and is even competent as both an adult and a child psychotherapist. Although many mental health professionals who engage in divorce mediation can competently conduct individual psychotherapy, they must carefully avoid the dual role of mediator and individual therapist (Koch & Lowery, 1984). One simply cannot be an effective individual psychotherapist for sets of people with incongruent or competing interests. To flip and flop between being a mediator and being a psychotherapist will assure that neither job will be performed well. A good review of the issues and research on mediation in the context of divorce can be found in Kelly (1988b).

In recent years, a number of important public policy questions have been raised regarding mediation. Should mediation be made available to all who request it, or should referrals for such services be mandatory as a matter of public policy? When mediation is mandatory, as it currently is in contested cases in some jurisdictions, the role of the mediator is changed significantly. In that context, the basic presumptions of the mediator become very important, and these are sometimes dictated by law. For example, in some jurisdictions there is a clear preference that mediators work toward effecting an agreement on joint legal custody. The chief rationale given by those who prefer joint custody is the belief that it benefits the children, and some studies do support that view (Clingempeel & Reppucci, 1982; Ilfeld, Ilfeld, & Alexander, 1982), although other studies do not (for a review of the research on custody arrangements and post divorce adjustment of the children, see Kelly,

1988a). It is not always clear, however, where the threshold lies for focusing on a sole custody settlement.

Another important policy question is whether mediation is appropriate in matters of alleged child abuse or neglect or in the case of severe psychopathology or low intelligence (Folberg & Taylor, 1984).

CASE 7-17: Henry Crusher has a documented history of violence toward family members, has been diagnosed as having an "explosive personality," and has served time in a state penitentiary for armed robbery and dealing illegal drugs. He has subjected his wife, Helen, and his children to physical abuse resulting in the need for brief medical hospitalizations of Helen and one child on two occasions. Helen is seeking a divorce from Henry and sole legal and physical custody of the children. The Crushers live in a state with a requirement of mandatory mediation in the case of divorces that involve children. The mediators operate under a presumption of joint legal custody as the ideal solution. Henry states that he is looking forward to mediation and that if he does not get an agreement for joint custody he will "break heads!"

In this particular case, it seems unreasonable to force Helen and the Crusher children into mediation with the potentially dangerous and abusive Henry. The mental health professional who agrees to function as a mediator in this situation is placing herself in a position of great ethical vulnerability. She must either ignore the statutory mandates or work toward a mediated settlement that is clearly not in the best interests of Helen and the children, even if it is accepted public policy.

When should the child's own preferences be considered in child custody decisions, and how much weight should these be given? Consider the following scenario:

CASE 7-18: Sandra Solomon, M.D., is conducting a court-ordered child custody evaluation of the Perrier Family. She finds herself unable to discriminate between the parenting credentials of the two young urban professionals who are divorcing. They live too far apart to alternate living arrangements for their 9-year-old child. Both want primary physical custody of their child, although each is willing to share visitation with the other. The potential home environments, parenting skills, emotional stability, and other strengths offered by each parent are equivalent. No significant weaknesses detract from either one. When the child is interviewed, she tells the psychologist, "I love both of my parents, but I want to live with my father because he is going to buy me a puppy and take me to Disneyland."

Although there are legal precedents in some jurisdictions for giving significant weight to a child's preferences (*Goldstein v. Goldstein*, 1975; *Shapiro v. Shapiro*, 1983), many would argue that the Perrier child's preferences are superficial and unreasonable bases for tipping the scales. Such reasoning ignores the fact that many adults choose living partners chiefly on the basis of physical attractiveness or income. Should children not be permitted to make selections on the basis of purely hedonistic factors? We leave such determinations in the hands of the judge. Although a mental health professional can often assist the court by eliciting a child's preferences, the weight assigned to these preferences is a moral or legal matter.

Even when one is competent and thoroughly professional in doing child custody work, there are other ethical difficulties that may appear if one does not anticipate a potential risk and take steps to avoid it. Securing payment for one's professional services is a good example.

CASE 7-19: Attorneys for Arthur and Anita Arrears both asked Dexter Dupe, M.S.W., to undertake a child custody evaluation in the matter of their pending divorce. After spending more than 25 hours interviewing the parents and children and drafting a thoughtful and detailed report, he realizes that he is not certain about who is to be billed for his time. Both parties give him conflicting information regarding their degree of financial responsibility, and one party, who does not like the findings, refuses to pay anything at all.

It is not at all unusual for one or both parties involved in a contested custody case to be angry at the clinician involved, even if that person functioned competently and effectively. It is also not unusual for dissatisfied parties to react by withholding payment for services, even when the charges are reasonable and appropriate. Clinicians should anticipate this issue and clarify financial responsibility in advance with all parties, including legal counsel for the individuals in dispute. At the start of the work with the family, both adults should be asked to sign a note of understanding regarding financial responsibility. This often may be combined with a waiver of confidentiality form as discussed in chapter 4. Such a document would define in writing from the outset which parties will be responsible for which fees. If done in this manner, the clinician will most likely have the support of the parties' attorneys should collection later become a problem. Attorneys will not want to alienate a clinician whose services they may wish to call on in the future.

Another means of securing payment in such cases is to request a retainer or advance payment to be placed in escrow and drawn against as the clinician's time is consumed. Use of such mechanisms requires careful accounting practices and prompt refund of unencumbered funds.

One final financial issue of importance in child custody or other forensic work involves the use of health insurance as payment for clinical services. Clinicians must be mindful of the fact that a child custody evaluation or other forensic services are not necessarily "health services." As such, they may not be reimbursable under the provisions of health insurance policies. However, when the diagnosis or treatment of psychopathology is the focus of the clinician's work, health insurance coverage may well apply. This distinction is important for two reasons. First, if the client expects insurance to pay for clinical services, the clinician's bill will come as a rude and unfair surprise. Second, the clinician who bills a health insurance company for services that are purely court related, as though they were health services, may be subject to prosecution for insurance fraud.

OTHER CIVIL RIGHTS ISSUES

From time to time, mental health professionals find themselves involved in cases or public policy issues related to other civil rights of children. Many of these issues may seem to involve no psychological or mental health aspects at first glance; however, the future may find an increasing role for experts in child development to come before the courts as expert witnesses in such matters. We present a discussion of a few such cases in brief form simply to illustrate the range of circumstances and provoke thoughtful consideration by our readers.

Children and the First Amendment

What rights, if any, are children entitled to with respect to freedom of speech? Perhaps the classic case example involves the perpetual struggles between school newspaper staff members and their faculty advisers or administrators. Yet the best known case is focused on an issue more galvanizing and political than adolescent editorials.

> CASE 7-20: In December 1965, at the height of the Vietnam War, a group of families in Des Moines, Iowa, met to plan a peaceful public protest against the war and for a truce by wearing black armbands during the holiday season and holding two fasts. The principals of the Des Moines schools heard about these plans. They met on December 14, 1965, and adopted a policy that such armbands would not be permitted in school. Children who wore but refused to remove the armbands would be suspended until they returned to school without them. John F. Tinker, age 15, Christopher Eckhardt, age 16, and John's sister Mary Beth Tinker, age 13, were students in high school and junior high school, respectively. They wore the armbands to school on December 16 and were suspended, remaining out of school until the planned period for wearing the armbands had expired after New Year's Day 1966.

In *Tinker v. Des Moines Independent Community School District* (1969), the Supreme Court ruled that the wearing of the armbands was "protected speech" under the meaning of the Constitution, at least in part because the behavior was not aggressive or destructive and did not substantially interfere with the requirements of discipline and school operations. Justice Fortas, writing for the majority of the Court, noted, "Students in school as well as out of school are 'persons' under our Constitution [and they are] entitled to freedom of expression of their views." While this would appear to be a strong case of advocating children's rights to free speech in schools, Waddlington, Whitebread, and Davis (1983) note that the case may actually have less to do with children's rights than with inculcated family values since the children's parents were activists in the peace movement at the time. Interestingly, two other defiant pupils, Paul Tinker, age 8, and Hope Tinker, age 11, were not enrolled as plaintiffs in the case. We wonder whether one of the parties feared that inclusion of children that young might have lead to a loss based on developmental assumptions.

Unreasonable Search and Seizures?

If children are indeed persons under the Constitution, what are their privacy rights with respect to searches of their belongings? As the use of illicit drugs has become a major problem among our youths, this issue has become a serious concern.

CASE 7-21: In March 1979, the school authorities of Highland, Indiana, were concerned about the growing problem of marijuana smoking in their public schools. There had been more than 20 incidents involving the drug in the past 6 months and 13 in the past 3 weeks. In an dramatic effort to stop the problem, an unannounced 2½ hour search of the junior and senior high schools using drug-sniffing dogs was planned. March 23 was the day of the big sniff. In one junior high school class, the dog "alerted" in front of a girl. She was asked to empty her purse, and no contraband was found. She was then subjected to a strip search in the school nurse's office. Still, nothing was found. Later it was discovered that before coming to school that day the girl had been playing with the family dog who was in heat.

CASE 7-22: The high school girl caught smoking in the girls' room in Piscataway, New Jersey, was not so innocent. When brought to the vice principal's office, she claimed that she did not smoke. No fool he, the vice principal noticed cigarettes in the young woman's purse. He inspected further and discovered not only tobacco products but also marijuana, a substantial roll of dollar bills, and a note soliciting a classmate to join her in dealing the "joints."

In both these cases, appeals were lodged asserting the children's rights to freedom from unreasonable searches and seizures. The dog-sniffing case (*Dow v. Renfrow*, 1979) was decided in favor of the girl. The court determined that it was important to consider the student's age, history, and record in school, the seriousness and prevalence of the drug problem, and the exigency requiring warrantless searches. Although the dog sniffing was not deemed unreasonable per se, the nude search based only on the dog's "alert" was deemed unreasonable. The psychological distress suffered as a result of the embarrassing strip search was cited by the court as a factor in their ruling. The youngster from New Jersey was not so lucky; the search was ruled proper in this case (*New Jersey v. T.L.O.*, 1985), given the clear reasonable cause the vice principal had and relative noninvasiveness of the search.

Corporal Punishment

Although many states ban corporal punishment in public schools, this is not universal. Many states still permit school administrators or teachers to administer physical punishments as a means to promote discipline. While it is our view that this practice is little more than officially sanctioned abuse of children, the United States Supreme Court has refused to consider school administered corporal punishments as "cruel and unusual," even when the result is significant physical injury to the child.

CASE 7-23: James Ingraham and Roosevelt Andrews had the misfortune to run afoul of an assistant principal at Drew Junior High School in Dade County, Florida, during October 1970. Because they were slow to respond to a teacher's instructions, James was subjected to 20 "licks" with a half-inch thick wooden paddle across his buttocks. He suffered a hematoma and was out of school for several days. Roosevelt was paddled several times and on one occasion was without the full use of his arm for a week.

Although a federal appeals court found the punishment "so severe and oppressive as to violate the Eighth and Fourteenth Amendments," the Supreme Court opinion expressed the belief that common law remedies rather than constitutional ones were sufficient in this case. That is to say, the routine local oversight of the schools by the school board and local court action should have resolved the matter (*Ingraham v. Wright*, 1977). The reasoning in the opinion reflected no awareness of or interest in the significant body of psychological literature in both social psychology and learning theory that shows that aggression tends to breed aggressive behavior. A common rationale cited by supporters of official corporal punishment tends to be the same as that used by Mary Bergamasco (see case 1-3, chap. 1): "It taught me a lesson when I was their age." Of course, all that is truly taught with such techniques is how to pass on the tradition of abuse.

The Constitutional Right to Play Video Games

We have addressed issues of life and liberty for children in this chapter. How about the pursuit of happiness, as guaranteed by our Constitution? Is government entitled to regulate the exercise of recreational choice?

> CASE 7-24: The city of Mesquite passed an ordinance that prohibited certain amusement facilities from allowing children under age 17 to play coin-operated games unless accompanied by a parent or guardian. The operator of one video arcade challenged the ordinance as unconstitutionally vague.

The U.S. Court of Appeals for the Fifth Circuit and the U.S. Supreme Court agreed and also ruled in part that the age restriction was unconstitutional (*Aladdin's Castle v. City of Mesquite*, 1980, 1982). We know that the judge in this case did not rely on advice from mental health professionals. Perhaps because of his own prior recreational history, the judge needed no psychological testimony to resolve the case.

CLOSING COMMENTS

The range of issues that bring children to the attention of the courts is quite broad, and the potential involvement of mental health professionals in forensic matters involving children is growing. Some of the cases will deal with grave matters, including control over parenting, quality of life, incarceration, and even the potential for sentencing children to die for the commission of violent crimes. Other issues such as those involving less dramatic civil rights and social needs of children will also be the subject of important legislative and judicial decisions in the coming years. All too often, the men and women cast as decision makers in these cases are left to rely on their personal knowledge without input from qualified mental health professionals. We hope that our colleagues will increasingly be willing to accept this fact as a challenge. We hope our colleagues will step forward as ethical professionals, as thoughtful experts, and as wise advocates in cases in which their knowledge and expertise can legitimately inform decision makers and advance the well-being of children.

GUIDELINES

1. Before agreeing to become involved in a forensic case involving children, be certain that you understand the legal principles, criteria, and process bearing on the particular case at hand.

2. Carefully clarify your professional role, including such factors as, Who is the client? What am I being asked to undertake (e.g., an investigation, a mediation, a hypothetical analysis)? What potential dual relationships or conflicts of interest must I be aware of?

3. Be certain that your clients and the attorneys involved have a clear understanding of your role in the case, including the limits of your areas of competence and the extent of your participation.

4. Limit your testimony to your legitimate areas of expertise and resist the temptation (or invitation) to speculate beyond the state of current accepted professional and scientific knowledge.

5. If you become aware of important situations in which psychological knowledge would be relevant and constructive in resolving a social, legal, or ethical problem, resist the temptations of inertia and offer your knowledge and support to advance the welfare of the child.

•

Rambo Meets
Bambi Revisited

While working on this volume, we tried very hard to remain relatively dispassionate in presenting and analyzing all sides of both issues and case material. We resisted polemic calls for child advocacy, focusing instead on basic ethical principles and court rulings. Although such a stand is highly desirable for purposes of even-handed scholarship, it is not sufficient to meet the needs of children who interact with mental health professionals and the legal system.

At the opening of the book, we used the cinematic analogy of Rambo and Bambi to contrast the power and authority of the legal system with the weaker constraints self-imposed by the professions in terms of ethical codes and standards. As we close, it seems appropriate to revisit the analogy again from the perspective of thoughtful child advocacy. Rambo generally shoots first and asks questions later. The law, like Rambo, knows only firm resolutions to controversy: guilt or innocence, negligence or adequate care, competence or incompetence, right or wrong.

The legal system does not tolerate ambiguities well and is not much concerned with the human aftermath of justice in action. Bambi, on the other hand, is sensitive, hesitant, and often takes a very long time to make decisions. Ethical codes, like Bambi, reflect thoughtful concern for human welfare, but often in a halting, reflective, and occasionally obsessive manner that seldom leads to satisfying solutions for either offenders or victims.

We urge our readers to consider the limitations of both systems and to strive for fostering the optimal development of children in both arenas. This means adopting a position of thoughtful, reasoned child advocacy within appropriate limits of scientific knowledge and granting the benefit of any doubt to the outcome best serving the child's needs. This means reporting suspicions of abuse or neglect as the law requires, placing the well-being of the child ahead of that of adults in multiple-client situations, and being willing to take necessary risks to "blow the whistle" on inappropriate or illegal actions by colleagues and agencies. The cases of Sylvia Sharp (case 3-10) and Muriel Forrest (case 3-11) provide excellent examples of child advocacy at considerable personal cost. Sharp and Forrest are genuine heroines in our eyes.

At the other end of the continuum is the cowardice or small-mindedness of otherwise well-intentioned agencies and organizations. The case of *Palmore v. Sidoti* (see full discussion in case 7-9) presents an excellent example. The abortive efforts to involve the APA in entering the case by filing an *amicus* (i.e., friend of the court) brief illustrate the worst reasoning of professional bureaucracies. At the state court level, a psychologist testified without benefit of any scientific foundation that a young girl would be harmed emotionally by living with her mother in a bi-racial family. As the case reached the Supreme Court, the APA's Division of Child, Youth, and Family Services and many individual colleagues urged the APA to enter the case as an *amicus*. The goal was to inform the courts that no data existed to support the unrefuted opinion of the psychologist who testified at the initial trial. Although those in authority at the APA agreed fully with the lack of scientific foundation for the psychologist's testimony, which had contributed to removing the child from the custody of her mother, participation as an *amicus* was refused. No public rationale was provided, but the private feedback was simple and direct. The APA did not want to go to the Supreme Court and tell the world about things that psychologists do not know. Were it possible to make a positive statement regarding psychological knowledge, the organization would have been willing to file an *amicus* brief. This case, however, was not deemed to be the right kind of vehicle. Making a public admission that the local psychologist was not testifying from any sound knowledge base would have been an embarrassment to the profession, from the perspective of those in charge of making such decisions.

Keeping one's mouth closed is often quite easy and safe by comparison with speaking out firmly on controversial issues. This is especially true when strong arguments exist to contradict the prevailing public viewpoint. We would argue, however, that the best interests of children are far better served by giving credible voice to informed criticism of conventional wisdom. At times, this may take the form of providing better data. At other times it may require an open acknowledgment that we do not have a scientifically sound answer on which to base a particular public policy. In the words of Jane Addams, "Social advance depends as much upon the process through which it is secured as upon the result itself."

•

Major Case Law
Decisions Cited

Aladdin's Castle v. City of Mesquite, 630 F.2d 1029 (5th Cir. 1980), *reversed in part and remanded*, 455 U.S. 283, 102 S. Ct. (1982).

The facts of this case are discussed in chapter 7 as case 7-24.

Bartley v. Kremens, 402 F. Supp. 1039 (E.D. Pa. 1975).

Case 2-5 is a detailed account of this legal case. See also *Parham v. J.R.* and *J.L. v. Parham*. These cases all address the issue of "voluntary" psychiatric hospital commitment of minors by their parents and are discussed in chapter 2 under case 2-5.

Bellotti v. Baird, 443 U.S. 646, 99 S. Ct. (1979).

This decision affirmed the right of a minor to make her own decision regarding an abortion. The Supreme Court noted that an unwanted pregnancy is probably more of a crisis for a minor than for an adult because the decision cannot be postponed until she reaches the age of majority. The formal decision noted, "There are few situations in which denying a minor the right to make an important decision will have consequences so grave and indelible."

Cairl v. Minnesota 323 N.W.2d 20 (Minn., 1982).

The facts of this case are discussed in chapter 4 as case 4-15.

Commonwealth v. Bergstrom, 402 Mass. 534 (1988).

The facts of this case are discussed in chapter 7 as case 7-3.

Coy v. Iowa, 487 U.S. 857, 108 S. Ct. (1988).

In this case, the U.S. Supreme Court made a ruling similar to that of the Massachusetts Supreme Judicial Court in *Commonwealth v. Bergstrom*. The case involved testimony by an adolescent sexual assault victim while the defendant sat behind a one-way viewing screen in the courtroom. The rationale for the screen was to increase the comfort of the victim, who was afraid of the alleged perpetrator. The Supreme Court, however, noted the constitutional right of a defendant to meet his accuser face to face.

Custody of a Minor, 385 Mass. 697, 434 N.E.2d 601 (1982).

In this case, the Supreme Judicial Court of Massachusetts upheld the ruling of a juvenile court judge who had permitted a hospital administrator to enter a "no code" (i.e., do not resuscitate order) for a newborn child with severe cardiac problems. The child had been abandoned at birth and was in the custody of the Massachusetts Department of Social Services. As a matter of policy, the department would not consent to the order directing hospital staff "not to apply extraordinary intrusive resuscitative measures in the event of cardiac or respiratory failure." A guardian *ad litem* had also refused to consent. The court ruled that the juvenile court had proper jurisdiction and was correct in applying the substituted judgment rule to enter the "no code" order.

Doe v. Doe, 222 Va. 736, 284 S.E.2d 799 (1981).

This case involved an attempt by the stepmother legally to adopt the son of her husband over the objections of the child's biological mother. A trial court approved the adoption despite the mother's refusal to consent because she was living in what the court described as a lesbian relationship. The appeals court reversed the trial court ruling that no evidence that Jane Doe was unfit had been presented aside from her sexual orientation. Her sexual lifestyle had no clear effect on her parenting skills and was not detrimental to the child's welfare. While not condoning Jane Doe's "unorthodox" and "unnatural life-style," the court decision noted, "We decline to hold that every lesbian mother or homosexual father is *per se* an unfit parent."

Dow v. Renfrow, 475 F. Supp. 1012 N.D. Ind. (1979).

The facts of this case are discussed in chapter 7 as case 7-21.

Fare v. Michael C. 442 U.S. 707 (1979).

The facts of this case are discussed in chapter 7 as case 7-8.

Feldman v. Feldman 45 A.D.2d 320, 358 N.Y.S.2d 507 (1974).

The facts of this case are presented in chapter 7 as case 7-10.

Forrest v. Ansbach, 436 N.Y.S.2d 119 (S. Ct. 1980).

The facts of this case are summarized and discussed in chapter 3 under case 3-11.

Globe Newspaper Company v. Superior Court, 102 S. Ct. 2613 (1982).

The facts of this case are discussed in chapter 7 as case 7-6.

Goldstein v. Goldstein 115 R.I. 152, 341 A.2d 51 (1975).

Ann Robin Goldstein, age 9½, was left in her father's custody after her parents divorced in 1970. Her father immediately moved to Israel and took her along. With the help of the Supreme Court of Israel, Mrs. Goldstein forced both to return to Rhode Island in July 1973 for a hearing to press for reestablishing a mother/daughter relationship. The judge met with Ann in chambers and engaged her in conversation. She reportedly told the judge that, while she did not want to say so in open court, she loved her father more than her mother and wanted to live with him in Israel. At the judge's urging, Ann agreed that it would be a "fair bargain" to spend 4 weeks visiting her mother in the United States each summer. The judge entered such an order, which was appealed. The appelate court found that the factors bearing on the fitness of each parent for custody were "in a state of equipose." Under those circumstances, giving significant weight to the child's preferences was not inappropriate.

Guardianship of Phillip B. 139 Cal. App. 3d 407, 188 Cal. Rptr. 781 (1983).

Phillip B. was born on October 16, 1966, with Down syndrome. His parents, Warren and Patricia B., placed him in institutional care shortly thereafter and initially visited him frequently. As time went on, their visits became less frequent, and they appeared to become more detached from him. When Phillip was 3 years old, a pediatrician advised his parents that he suffered from a congenital heart problem (i.e., a ventricular septal defect) that affects significant numbers of children with Down syndrome. The defect affecting Phillip consisted of an opening between the lower chambers of the heart resulting in progressive vascular dysfunction and ultimately his death by age 30. Corrective open-heart surgery was suggested when Phillip was 6; however, his family took no action to investigate or remedy the problem. In 1972, Patsy and Herbert H. began working with Phillip as volunteers through the licensed residential facility where he lived. Phillip was visited and tutored by them frequently and was ultimately able to attend a school for the trainable mentally retarded. As his parents became less frequent visitors, Phillip became increasingly attached to Patsy and Herbert H., visiting in their home with his parents' consent. Phillip began to refer to Patsy and Herbert as "Mama Pat" and "Dada Bert." Faced with the need for medical and surgical treatment of the cardiac defect in mid-1977, Mr. and Mrs. B. decided against it. They expressed the belief that they would be unable to care for Phillip in his later years and did not wish him to outlive them. This began a series of legal actions, including an unsuccessful effort to prosecute them for neglect by virtue of withholding surgery (*In re Phillip B.*, 1979). Ultimately, the 1983 decision granted limited guardianship to Patsy and Herbert H., who authorized medical care for Phillip.

H.L. v. Matheson, 450 U.S. 398 (1981).

The question in this case was whether a state law requiring a physician to "notify, if possible," the parents of an unmarried 15-year-old prior to performing an abortion on that girl violated her constitutional rights. The Supreme Court of Utah had upheld the statute, noting that it represented a legitimate interest of the state, and the U.S. Supreme Court agreed in a split decision.

Illinois v. Berry, 463 N.E.2d 1044 (Ill. App. 1984).

The facts of this case are discussed in chapter 7 as case 7-2.

In re Phillip B., 94 Cal. App. 3d 796, 156 Cal. Rptr. 48, *cert. den. sub nom.* Bothman v. Warren B. 445 U.S. 949, 100 S. Ct. 1597, 63 L. Ed.2d 784 (1980).

See *Guardianship of Phillip B.* (above).

In re Gault, 387 U.S. 1 (1967).

Gerald Francis Gault had been in trouble before he was arrested in June 1964 for allegedly making lewd and indecent telephone calls to his neighbor, Mrs. Cook. He was already on probation in Gila County Arizona as a result of having been in the company of another boy who had possession of a wallet stolen from a lady's purse 4 months earlier. In the days and weeks that followed, he was not given adequate notice of the charges against him, the right to counsel, the right to confront and cross-examine witnesses, the right not to incriminate himself, the right to a transcript of the proceedings, or the right to appellate review. In a landmark ruling, the Supreme Court secured these rights for minors in delinquency proceedings.

In re Green 448 Pa. 338, 292 A.2d 387 (1972).

Rickey Ricardo Green had polio, causing problems with obesity and paralytic scoliosis (94% curvature of the spine). Without medical intervention, Ricky would soon become bed-bound with a collapsed spine. His physician recommended spinal fusion surgery. His parents were separated, and his mother at first approved the surgery. She later revoked her consent when she learned that blood transfusions would be necessary. As a member of the Jehovah's Witness faith, such transfusions were not acceptable to her. While the operation had the potential to prove beneficial, it was not without risk and was not needed on an emergency basis. Still, the director of the State Hospital for Crippled Children at Elizabethtown, Pennsylvania, sought a court declaration that Rickey was a neglected child because his mother had declined surgical consent. The courts ruled that Rickey, who was 17-years-old at the time, ought to be heard on the matter of his preferences. Ultimately, he was permitted to decline surgery, and the hospital director's petition was dismissed.

In re Guardianship of Barry, 445 So.2d 365 (Fla. App. 1984).

The details of this case are discussed in chapter 2 as case 2-22.

Ingraham v. Wright, 430 U.S. 651, 97 S. Ct. 1401, 51 L. Ed.2d 711 (1977).

The facts of this case are discussed in chapter 7 as case 7-23.

J.L. v. Parham, 412 F. Supp. 112 (M.D. Ga. 1976).

See also *Parham v. J.R.* and *Bartley v. Kremmens*. These cases all address the issue of "voluntary" psychiatric hospital commitment of minors by their parents and are discussed in chapter 2 under case 2-5.

Larry P. v. Riles, 343 F. Supp. 1306 N.D. Cal. 1972 (preliminary injunction), *affirmed*, 502 F.2d 963 (9th Cir. 1974), *opinion issued* No. C-71-2270 RFP (N.D. Cal. October 16, 1979).

In this case, the court found that certain standard IQ tests, including the WISC-R and the Standord-Binet, had been used inappropriately to assign black children to classes for the educable mentally retarded (EMR). The judge permanently enjoined the California school district in question "from utilizing, permitting the use of, or approving the use of any standardized tests . . . for the identification of black E.M.R. children or their placement into E.M.R. classes, without first securing approval by this court" (p. 989). (See also *PASE v. Hannon*.)

McIntosh v. Milano, 403 A.2d 500 (N.J. Super. Ct. 1979).

The facts of this case are discussed in chapter 4 as case 4-13.

Merriken v. Cressman, 364 F. Supp. 913 E.D. Pa (1973).

The consent-seeking aspect of this case is presented, in part, in chapter 5 as case 5-13. The major finding by the federal district court was that the school's questionnaire contained sensitive and personal items and, as such, interfered with family relations and violated the parents' constitutional right to privacy by utilizing a consent technique that did not allow them to protect invasion of their personal lives adequately. The court did not deal with the issue of children's rights to consent or protect their own privacy.

Meyer v. Nebraska, 262 U.S. 390 (1923).

Mr. Meyer, an instructor at the Zion Parochial School, was erroneously tried and convicted in Hamilton County, Nebraska, for having unlawfully taught the subject of reading in the German language to 10-year-old Raymond Parpat. Meyer had violated a law relating to the teaching of foreign languages in the state of Nebraska, approved in April 1919. The law prohibited teaching any subject to any person in a language other than English and forbade the teaching of foreign languages earlier than the eighth grade. In reversing the conviction, the Supreme Court noted that the mere knowledge of the German language cannot reasonably be regarded as harmful and that teaching of the language in this Lutheran school was within the rights of the teacher and the parents who had engaged him to instruct their children.

Miranda v. Arizona, 348 U.S. 436 (1966).

This landmark case led to the arrest warning well known to all watchers of crime dramas and those who have been arrested in the United States since late 1966: "You are under arrest. You have the right to remain silent. You have the right to have an attorney present during questioning. If you cannot afford an attorney, one will be appointed for you by the court. Anything you say can and will be held against you in a court of law."

Morris v. Florida, 456 So.2d 925 (Fla. Dist. Ct. App. 1984).

The facts of this case are discussed in chapter 7 as case 7-1.

New Jersey v. T.L.O., 105 S. Ct. 733 (1985).

The facts of this case are discussed in chapter 7 as case 7-22.

Nielsen v. Regents of the University of California et al. Case No. 655-049, Superior Court of California, County of San Francisco, as amended December 20, 1973.

James Neilson, a member of the Committee on Human Subjects at the University of California, San Francisco, took exception to a longitudinal study of allergic children. The study was to use healthy children as a control group and proposed to subject these children to invasive medical procedures. He contended that this would constitute violation of the healthy children's constitutional rights. He sought a judgment declaring that parents may not consent to have their children participate in research that is not intended to benefit them directly. The case received wide attention even though his application was denied on the grounds that he failed to show sufficient standing and irreparable injury to warrant issuance of injunctive relief. Another minor aspect of this case, allegations of monetary coercion, is illustrated in chapter 5 as case 5-24.

PASE v. Hannon, 506 F. Supp. 831, N.D. Ill. (1980).

Parents in Action on Special Education (PASE) involved an Illinois version of the *Larry P.* case, but in this case the judge ruled, "The WISC, WISC-R, and Stanford-Binet Tests, when used in conjunction with the statutorily mandated [other criteria specified by Public Law 94-142] . . . do not discriminate against black children" (p.883) when used in determining appropriate educational placement. (See also *Larry P. v Riles* in chap.3.)

Palmore v. Sidoti, 466 U.S. 429. (1984).

The facts of this case are discussed in chapter 7 as case 7-9.

Parham v. J.R. 442 U.S. 584 (1979).

This case is described in chapter 7 as case 7-7. See also *Bartley v. Kremmens* and *J.L. v. Parham*. These cases all address the issue of "voluntary" psychiatric hospital commitment of minors by their parents and are discussed in chapter 2 under case 2-5.

Pierce v. Society of Sisters, 268 U.S. 510 (1925).

The Society of Sisters is an Oregon corporation organized in 1880 to care for orphans, educate and instruct youths, and maintain schools. The society objected to the Compulsory Education Act of 1922, under which every parent or guardian having custody of a child between 8 and 16 years of age would be required to send the child to public school. The court ruled that the act was deemed an unreasonable interference with the rights of parents and guardians to direct the upbringing and education of children under their control.

Prince v. Massachusetts, 321 U.S. 158, 170 (1944).

Sarah Prince unsuccessfully appealed a conviction for violating Massachusetts's child labor laws on the grounds that she was rightfully exercising her religious convictions as a member of the Jehovah's Witness faith. She was the aunt and legal guardian of 9-year-old Betty M. Simmons. Both aunt and child were ordained ministers and would distribute or sell copies of *Watchtower* and *Consolation* on the streets of Brockton both day and night. The court noted that, while parents may be free to become martyrs themselves, it does not follow that they are free to make martyrs of their children. Any infringement of freedom of the press or freedom of religion in this case was deemed slight, incidental, and appropriate given the child welfare issues at hand.

Quiner v. Quiner (1967), Court of Appeals of California, Second District.

The facts of this case are discussed in chapter 7 as case 7-11.

Thompson v. County of Alameda, 614 P.2d 728 (Cal. Super. Ct. 1980).

The facts of this case are discussed in chapter 4 as case 4-14.

Tinker v. Des Moines Independent Community School District 393 U.S. 503, 89 S. Ct. 733, 21 L. Ed. 2d 731 (1969).

The facts of this case are discussed in chapter 7 as case 7-20.

References

Ackerman, T. F. (1979). Fooling ourselves with child autonomy and assent in non-therapeutic clinical research. *Clinical Research*, 27, 345–348.

Adair, J. G., Dushenko, T. W., & Lindsay, R. C. L. (1985). Ethical regulations and their impact on research practice. *American Psychologist*, 40, 59–72.

Aladdin's Castle v. City of Mesquite, 630 F.2d 1029 (5th Cir. 1980), *reversed in part and remanded*, 455 U.S. 283, 1025 S. Ct. (1982).

Alexander, L. (1970). Psychiatry: Methods and processes for investigation of drugs. *Annals of the New York Academy of Sciences*, 169, 347–351.

American Educational Research Association, American Psychological Association, and National Council on Measurement in Education. (1985). *Standards for educational and psychological testing*. Washington, DC: American Psychological Association.

American Psychological Association. (1981). Ethical principles of psychologists. *American Psychologist*, 36, 633–638.

American Psychological Association. (1982). *Ethical principles in the conduct of research with human participants*. Washington, DC: American Psychological Association.

Angell, M. (1984). Patients' preferences in randomized clinical trials. *New England Journal of Medicine*, 310, 1385–1387.

Appelbaum, P. S., & Roth, L. H. (1982). Competency to consent to research: A psychiatric overview. *Archives of General Psychiatry, 39,* 951–958.

Areen, J. (1985). *Cases and materials on family law.* Mineola, NY: Foundation Press.

Bajt, T. R., & Pope, K. S. (1989). Therapist-patient sexual intimacy involving children and adolescents. *American Psychologist, 44,* 455.

Bartley v. Kremens, 402 F. Supp. 1039 (E.D. Pa. 1975).

Baumrind, D. (1976). *Nature and definition of informed consent in research involving deception* (Report prepared for the National Commission for the Protection of Human Subjects of Biomedical and Behavioral Research). Washington DC: Department of Health, Education, and Welfare.

Baumrind, D. (1977). *Informed consent and deceit in research with children and their parents.* Paper presented at the biennial meeting of the Society for Research in Child Development.

Baumrind, D. (1985). Research using intentional deception: Ethical issues revisited. *American Psychologist, 40,* 165–174.

Beauchamp, T. L., & Childress, J. F. (1983). *Principles of biomedical ethics* (2d ed.). New York: Oxford University Press.

Bellotti v. Baird, 443 U.S. 622 (1979).

Belter, R. W., & Grisso, T. (1984). Children's recognition of rights violations in counseling. *Professional Psychology: Research and Practice, 15,* 899–910.

Bersoff, D. N. (1980). *Brief for amici curiae in the matter of Muriel Forrest v. Gordon M. Ansbach.* Washington, DC: American Psychological Association.

Bersoff, D. N. (1983). Children as participants in psychoeducational assessment. In G. B. Melton, G. P. Koocher, & M. J. Saks (Eds.), *Children's competence to consent* (pp. 149–178). New York: Plenum.

Beyer, H. A., & Wilson, J. P. (1976). The reluctant volunteer: A child's right to resist commitment. In G. P. Koocher (Ed.), *Children's rights and the mental health professions* (pp. 133–148). New York: Wiley-Interscience.

Blau, T. H. (1987). *Psychotherapy tradecraft.* New York: Brunner-Mazel.

Blum, G. (1950). *The Blacky pictures.* New York: Psychological Corp.

Boruch, R. F., & Cecil, J. S. (1982). Statistical strategies for preserving privacy in direct inquiry. In J. E. Sieber (Ed.), *The ethics of social research: Surveys and experiments* (pp. 207–232). New York: Springer.

Boruch, R. F., & Cecil, J. S. (Eds.). (1983). *Solutions to ethical and legal problems in social research.* New York: Academic.

Botkin, D., & Nietzel, M. (1987). How therapists manage potentially dangerous clients. *Professional Psychology: Research and Practice, 18,* 84–86.

Bower, R. T., & de Gasparis, P. (1978). *Ethics in social research*. New York: Praeger.

Boy, A. V., & Pine, G. J. (1980). Avoiding counselor burnout through role renewal. *Personnel and Guidance Journal, 59*, 161–163.

Burbach, D. J., Farha, J. G., & Thorpe, J. S. (1986). Assessing depression in community samples of children using self-report inventories: Ethical considerations. *Journal of Abnormal Child Psychology, 14*, 579–589.

Cairl v. Minnesota 323 N.W.2d 20 (Minn., 1982).

Campbell, A. G. M. (1974). Infants, children, and informed consent. *British Medical Journal, 3*, 334–338.

Carroll, J. D. (1973). Confidentiality of social science research sources and data: The Popkin case. *PS* (American Political Science Association), *6*, 268–280.

Caron, R. F., Caron, A. J., & Caldwell, R. C. (1971). Satiation of visual reinforcement in young infants. *Developmental Psychology, 5*, 279–289.

Cavanaugh, J., & Rhode, S. (1976). The unauthorized practice of law and pro se divorce. *Yale Law Journal, 86*, 104–184.

City of Akron v. Akron Center for Reproductive Health, 462 U.S. 416 (1983).

Clingempeel, W. G., & Reppucci, N. D. (1982). Joint custody after divorce: Major issues and goals for research. *Psychological Bulletin, 91*, 102–127.

Clouser, K. D. (1973). Some things medical ethics is not. *Journal of the American Medical Association, 223*, 787–789.

Cole, N. S. (1981). Bias in testing. *American Psychologist, 36*, 1067–1077.

Comiskey, R. J. (1978). The use of children for medical research: Opposite views examined. *Child Welfare, 57*, 321–324.

Committee on Professional Standards and Committee on Psychological Tests and Assessment. (1986). *Guidelines for computer-based tests and interpretations*. Washington, DC: American Psychological Association.

Commonwealth v. Bergstrom, 402 Mass. 534, N.E.2d (1988).

Conner, R. F. (1982). Random assignment of clients in social experimentation. In J. E. Sieber (Ed.), *The ethics of social research: Surveys and experiments* (pp. 57–78). New York: Springer.

Cooke, R. E. (1977). An ethical and procedural basis for research on children. *Journal of Pediatrics, 90*, 681–682.

Cowen, E. (1982). Primary prevention research: Barriers, needs, and opportunities. *Journal of Primary Prevention, 2*, 131–137.

Coy v. Iowa, 487 U.S. 857, 108 S. Ct. (1988).

Cupples, B., & Gochnauer, M. (1985). The investigator's duty not to deceive. *IRB: A Review of Human Subjects Research, 7*, 1–6.

Custody of a Minor, 385 Mass. 697, N.E.2d (1982).

Daley, M. R. (1979). Preventing worker burnout in child welfare. *Child Welfare, 58,* 443–450.

Davidson, G. C., & Stuart, R. B. (1975). Behavior therapy and civil liberties. *American Psychologist, 30,* 755–763.

de Chesnay, M. (1984). Father-daughter incest: Issues in treatment and research. *Journal of Psychosocial Nursing and Mental Health Services,* 22, 9–16.

Department of Health and Human Services. (1983, March 8). *Protection of human subjects.* (45 C.F.R. 46). Washington, DC: Department of Health and Human Services.

Dickens, B. M. (1984). Interests of parents in pediatric laboratory medicine—ethical and legal. *Clinical Biochemistry, 17,* 60–63.

Diener, E., & Crandall, R. (1978). *Ethics in social and behavioral research.* Chicago: University of Chicago Press.

DiTomasso, R. A., & McDermott, P. A. (1981). Dilemma of the untreated control group in applied research: A proposed solution. *Psychological Reports,* 49, 823–828.

Doe v. Doe, 119 N.H. 773, 408 A.2d 785 (1979).

Dow v. Renfrow, 475 F. Supp. 1012 N.D. Ind. (1979).

Drane, J. F. (1984). Competency to give an informed consent. *Journal of the American Medical Association,* 252, 925–927.

Dubanoski, R. A. (1978). The catch-22 of ethical research. *Society for Research in Child Development Newsletter,* 3, 8.

Dubanoski, R. A., & Tokioka, A. B. (1981). The effects of verbal pain stimuli on the behavior of children. *Social Behavior and Personality,* 9, 159–162.

Dupont, W. D. (1985). Randomized vs. historical clinical trials. *American Journal of Epidemiology,* 122, 940–946.

Edsall, G. A. (1969). A positive approach to the problem of human experimentation. *Daedalus,* 98(4), 463–479.

Emery, R. E., & Wyer, M. M. (1987). Divorce mediation. *American Psychologist,* 42, 472–480.

Ethics Committee of the American Psychological Association. (1988). Trends in ethics cases, common pitfalls, and published resources. *American Psychologist,* 43, 564–572.

Eysenck, H. J. (1965). The effects of psychotherapy. *International Journal of Psychiatry,* 1, 97–178.

Eysenck, H. J. (1966). *The effects of psychotherapy.* New York: International Science Press.

Fagan, J., & Deschenes, E. P. (1988) The juvenile court and violent youths: Determinants of the judicial transfer decision. Unpublished manuscript, John Jay College of Criminal Justice.

Fare v. Michael C., 442 U.S. 707 (1979).

Feldman v. Feldman, 45 A.D.2d 320, 358 N.Y.S.2d 507 (1974).

Ferguson, L. R. (1978). The competence and freedom of children to make choices regarding participation in research: A statement. *Journal of Social Issues, 34,* 114–121.

Fetterman, D. M. (1982). Ibsen's baths: Reactivity and insensitivity—a misapplication of the treatment-control design in a national evaluation. *Educational Evaluation and Policy Analysis, 4,* 261–279.

Fisher, C. B., & Tryon, W. W. (1988). Ethical issues in the research and practice of applied developmental psychology. *Journal of Applied Developmental Psychology, 9,* 27–39.

Folberg, J., & Taylor, A. (1984). *Mediation: A comprehensive guide to resolving conflicts without litigation.* San Francisco: Jossey-Bass.

Forrest v. Ansbach, 436 N.Y.S.2d 119 (1980).

Foster, R. E. (1980). Burnout among teachers of severely handicapped, autistic children. *Pointer, 24,* 24–28.

Freedman, J. L., & Fraser, S. C. (1966). Compliance without pressure: The foot-in-the-door techniques. *Journal of Personality and Social Psychology, 2,* 195–202.

Freudenberger, H. J. (1974). Staff burn-out. *Journal of Social Issues, 30,* 159–165.

Freudenberger, H. J. (1977). Burn-out: Occupational hazard of the child care worker. *Child Care Quarterly, 56,* 90–99.

Furlow, T. G. (1980). Consent for minors to participate in nontherapeutic research. *Legal Medicine Annual,* 261–273.

Garbarino, J., & Gilliam, G. (1980). *Understanding abusive families.* Lexington, MA: Lexington.

Garfield, S. L. (1987). Ethical issues in research on psychotherapy. *Counseling and Values, 31,* 115–125.

Gaylin, W. (1982). The "competence" of children: No longer all or none. *Journal of the American Academy of Child Psychiatry, 21,* 153–162.

Gaylin, W., & Macklin, R. (Eds.). (1982). *Who speaks for the child: The problems of proxy consent.* New York: Plenum.

Geller, D. M. (1982). Alternatives to deception: Why, what, and how? In J. E. Sieber (Ed.), *The ethics of social research: Surveys and experiments* (pp. 39–56). New York: Springer.

Glantz, L. H., Annas, G. J., & Katz, B. F. (1977). Scientific research with children: Legal incapacity and proxy consent. *Family Law Quarterly, 9,* 253–295.

Globe Newspaper Company v. Superior Court, 102 S. Ct. 2613 (1982).

Goldstein v. Goldstein, 115 R.I. 152, 341 A.2d 51 (1975).

Goodman, G. S. (1984a). The child victim witness [Special issue]. *Journal of Social Issues, 40*(2).

Goodman, G. S. (1984b). Children's testimony in historical perspective. *Journal of Social Issues, 40*(2), 9–31.

Gray, J. N., & Melton, G. B. (1985). The law and ethics of psychosocial research on AIDS. *Nebraska Law Review, 64,* 637–688.

Gray, S. W. (1971). Ethical issues in research in early childhood intervention. *Children, 18,* 83–89.

Green, B. F. (1981). A primer of testing. *American Psychologist, 36,* 1001–1011.

Greenberg, E. F. (1983). Predictors of children's competence to participate in child-custody decision making. Unpublished doctoral dissertation, University of Illinois, Urbana-Champaign.

Grisso, T. (1981). *Juveniles' waiver of rights: Legal and psychological competence.* New York: Plenum.

Grisso, T. (1983). Juveniles' consent in delinquency proceedings. In G. B. Melton, G. P. Koocher, & M. J. Saks (Eds.), *Children's competence to consent* (pp. 131–148). New York: Plenum.

Grisso, T. (1989). Minors' assent to behavioral research without parental permission. In the proceedings of the symposium on *Ethical issues in sensitive behavioral research involving minors.* San Mateo, CA, Feb. 14–15. Workshop sponsored by Office for Protection from Research Risks, National Institutes of Health.

Grisso, T., & Vierling, L. (1978). Minors' consent to treatment: A developmental perspective. *Professional Psychology, 9,* 412–427.

Guardianship of Phillip B., 139 Cal. App. 3d 407, 188 Cal. Rptr. 781 (1983).

Guion, R. M. (1974). Open a new window: Validities and values in psychological measurement. *American Psychologist, 28,* 287–296.

Guyer, M. J., Harrison, S. I., & Rieveschl, J. L. (1982). Child psychiatry and the law. *Journal of the American Academy of Child Psychiatry, 21,* 298–302.

H. L. v. Matheson, 450 U.S. 398 (1981).

Hare-Mustin, R. T., Marecek, J., Kaplan, A. G., & Liss-Levenson, N. (1979). Rights of clients, responsibilities of therapists. *American Psychologist, 34,* 3–16.

Harper, G. P., & Irvin, E. (1985). Alliance formation with parents: Limit-setting and the effect of mandated reporting. *American Journal of Orthopsychiatry, 55,* 550–560.

Hayvren, M., & Hymel, S. (1984). Ethical issues in sociometric testing: Impact of sociometric measures on interaction behavior. *Developmental Psychology, 20*, 844–849.

Hobbs, N. (Ed.). (1975). *Issues in the classification of children* (2 vols.). San Francisco: Jossey-Bass.

Holmes, D. S. (1976a). Debriefing after psychological experiments: 1. Effectiveness of post-deception dehoaxing. *American Psychologist, 31*, 858–867.

Holmes, D. S. (1976b). Debriefing after psychological experiments: 2. Effectiveness of post-experimental desensitizing. *American Psychologist, 31*, 868–875.

Hyers, T. M., & Scoggin, C. H. (1979). Ethical and practical problems of a high risk to benefit ratio study in children. *Clinical Research, 24*, 293–296.

Ilfeld, F. W., Ilfeld, H. Z., & Alexander, J. R. (1982). Does joint custody work? A first look at outcome data of relitigation. *American Journal of Psychiatry, 139*, 62–66.

Illinois v. Berry, 463 N.E.2d 1044 (Ill. App. 1984).

Imber, S. D., Glanz, L. M., Elkin, I., Sotsky, S. M., Boyer, J. L., & Leber, W. R. (1986). Ethical issues in psychotherapy research. *American Psychologist, 41*, 137–146.

Ingraham v. Wright, 430 U.S. 651 (1977).

In re C.M.S., 609 P.2d 240 Mont. (1979).

In re Gault, 387 U.S. 1 (1967).

In re Green 448 Pa. 338, 292 A.2d 387 (1972).

In re Guardianship of Barry, 445 So. 2d 365 (Fla. App. 1984).

In re Pernishek, 268 Pa. Super. 447, 408 A.2d 872 (1979).

In re Phillip B., 94 Cal. App. 3d 796, 156 Cal. Rptr. 48, *cert. den. sub nom.* Bothman v. Warren B. 445 U.S. 949, 100 S. Ct. 1597, 63 L. Ed. 2d 784 (1980).

J.L. v. Parham, 412 F. Supp. 112 (M.D. Ga. 1976).

Janofsky, J., & Starfield, B. (1981). Assessment of risk in research on children. *Journal of Pediatrics, 98*, 842–846.

Jessor, R. (1984). Adolescent development and behavioral health. In J. D. Matarazzo, S. M. Weiss, A. J. Herd, N. E. Miller, & S. M. Weiss (Eds.), *Behavioral health: A handbook of health enhancement and disease prevention* (pp. 69–90). New York: Wiley.

Jewish Child Care Association v. Elaine S.Y., 73 A.D.2d 154, 425 N.Y.S.2d 336 (1979).

Keith-Spiegel, P. C. (1976). Children's rights as participants in research. In G. P. Koocher (Ed.), *Children's rights and the mental health professions* (pp. 53–82). New York: Wiley.

Keith-Spiegel, P. C. (1983). Children and consent to participate in research. In G. B. Melton, G. P. Koocher, & M. J. Saks (Eds.), *Children's competence to consent* (pp. 179–214). New York: Plenum.

Keith-Spiegel, P. C., & Maas, T. (1981, August). *Consent to research: Are there developmental differences?* Paper presented at the meeting of the American Psychological Association, Los Angeles.

Kelly, Joan B. (1988a). Longer-term adjustment in children of divorce: Converging findings and implications for practice. *Journal of Family Psychology*, 2, 119–140.

Kelly, Joan B. (1988b). The mediation process and role: Comparisons to psychotherapy. *Group Analysis*, 21, 21–35.

Kelman, H. C. (1967). Human use of human subjects: The problem of deception in social psychological experiments. *Psychological Bulletin*, 67, 1–11.

Kessler, M., & Albee, G. W. (1975). Primary prevention. *Annual Review of Psychology*, 26, 557–591.

Kinard, E. M. (1985). Ethical issues in research with abused children. *Child Abuse and Neglect*, 9, 301–311.

Knerr, C. R. (1982). What to do before and after a subpoena of data arrives. In J. E. Sieber (Ed.), *The ethics of social research: Surveys and experiments* (pp. 191–206). New York: Springer.

Koch, M. A. P., & Lowery, C. P. (1984). Evaluation of mediation as an alternative to divorce litigation. *Professional Psychology: Research and Practice*, 15, 109–120.

Koocher, G. P. (1976a). A bill of rights for children in psychotherapy. In G. P. Koocher (Ed.), *Children's rights and the mental health professions*. New York: Wiley-Interscience.

Koocher, G. P. (1976b). Civil liberties and aversive conditioning for children. *American Psychologist*, 31, 94–95.

Koocher, G. P. (1980). Pediatric cancer: Psychosocial problems and the high cost of helping. *Journal of Clinical Child Psychology*, 9, 2–5.

Koocher, G. P. (1983). Competence to consent: Psychotherapy. In G. B. Melton, G. P. Koocher, & M. J. Saks (Eds.), *Children's competence to consent* (pp. 111–127). New York: Plenum.

Lacher, M. J. (1981). Patients and physicians as obstacles to a randomized trial. *Seminars in Oncology*, 8, 424–429.

Lambert, N. M. (1981). Psychological evidence in Larry P. versus Wilson Riles. *American Psychologist*, 36, 937–952.

Langer, D. H. (1985). Child psychiatry and the law. *Journal of the American Academy of Child Psychiatry*, 24, 653–662.

Lapin, C. L., & Donnellan-Walsh, A. (1977). Advocacy and research: A parent's perspective. *Journal of Pediatric Psychology*, 2, 191–196.

Larry P. v. Riles, 343 F. Supp. 1306 N.D. Cal. 1972 (preliminary injunction), *affirmed*, 502 F.2d 963 (9th Cir. 1974), opinion issued No. C-71-2270 RFP (N.D. Cal. October 16, 1979).

Lea, S. E. G. (1979). Alternatives to the use of painful stimuli in physiological psychology and the study of animal behavior. *Alternatives to Laboratory Animals*, 7, 20–21.

Leikin, S. L. (1983). Minors' assent or dissent to medical treatment. *Journal of Pediatrics*, 102, 169–176.

Leikin, S. L. (1985). Beyond pro forma consent for childhood cancer research. *Journal of Clinical Oncology*, 3, 420–428.

Levine, R. J. (1978). Research involving children: The National Commission's report. *Clinical Research*, 26, 61–66.

Lewis, C. C. (1981). How adolescents approach decisions: Changes over grades seven to twelve and policy implications. *Child Development*, 52, 538–544.

Lewis, C. E. (1983). Decision making related to health: When could/should children act responsibly? In G. B. Melton, G. P. Koocher, & M. J. Saks (Eds.), *Children's competence to consent* (pp. 75–92). New York: Plenum.

Lewis, C. E., Lewis, M. A., & Ifekwunigue, M. (1978). Informed consent by children and participation in an influenza vaccine trial. *American Journal of Public Health*, 68, 1079–1082.

Lewis, M. (1981). Comments on some ethical, legal, and clinical issues affecting consent in treatment, organ transplants, and research in children. *Journal of the American Academy of Child Psychiatry*, 20, 581–596.

Lidz, C. W., Meisel, A., Zerubavel, E., Carter, E., Sestak, R. M., & Roth, L. (1984). *Informed consent: A study of decisionmaking in psychiatry*. New York: Guilford.

Lippman, W. (1922, November 15). The abuse of tests. *New Republic*, pp. 297–298.

Liss-Levenson, N., Hare-Mustin, R. T., Marecek, J., & Kaplan, A. G. (1980, March). The therapist's role in assuring client rights. *Advocacy Now*, pp. 16–20.

Loftus, E. (1987, June 29). My turn: Trials of an expert witness. *Newsweek*, pp. 10–11.

Lovaas, O. I., & Simmons, J. Q. (1969). Manipulation of self-destruction in three retarded children. *Journal of Applied Behavior Analysis*, 2, 143–157.

Lowe, C. U., Alexander, D., & Mishkin, B. (1974). Nontherapeutic research on children: An ethical dilemma. *Journal of Pediatrics*, 84, 468–472.

Maslach, C. (1982). *Burnout—the cost of caring*. Englewood Cliffs, NJ: Prentice-Hall.

Maslach, C., & Pines, A. (1977). The burnout syndrome in the day care setting. *Child Care Quarterly*, 6, 100–113.

Massachusetts General Laws Annotated, 278, 16A (1971).

Matter of Male R., 102 Misc. 2d 1, 422 N.Y.S. 819 (Kings Co. Fam. Ct. 1979).

McCartney, J. J., & Beauchamp, T. L. (1981). Ethical issues in pediatric treatment and research. *Journal of Pediatric Psychology, 6,* 131–143.

McCormick, R. (1974). Proxy consent in the experimentation situation. *Perspectives in Biology and Medicine, 18,* 1–20.

McCormick, R. A. (1976). Experimentation in children: Sharing in sociality. *Hastings Center Report, 6,* 41–46.

McIntosh v. Milano, 403 A.2d 500 (N.J. Super. Ct. 1979).

Melton, G. B. (1980). Children's concepts of their rights. *Journal of Clinical Child Psychology, 9,* 186–190.

Melton, G. B. (1982). Children's rights: Where are the children? *American Journal of Orthopsychiatry, 52,* 530–538.

Melton, G. B. (1983a). *Child advocacy: Psychological issues and interventions.* New York: Plenum.

Melton, G. B. (1983b). Decision making by children: Psychological risks and benefits. In G. B. Melton, G. P. Koocher, & M. J. Saks (Eds.), *Children's competence to consent* (pp. 21–40). New York: Plenum.

Melton, G. B. (1983c). A problem in law and social science. In G. B. Melton, G. P. Koocher, & M. J. Saks (Eds.), *Children's competence to consent* (pp. 1–20). New York: Plenum.

Melton, G. B. (1984a). Developmental psychology and the law: The state of the art. *Journal of Family Law, 22,* 445–482.

Melton, G. B. (1984b). Child witnesses and the First Amendment: A psycholegal dilemma. *Journal of Social Issues, 40*(2), 109–123.

Melton, G. B. (Ed.). (1986). *Adolescent abortion: Psychological and legal issues.* Lincoln: University of Nebraska Press.

Melton, G. B. (1987). The clashing of symbols: Prelude to child and family policy. *American Psychologist, 42,* 345–354.

Melton, G. B. (1988a). Ethical and legal issues in research and intervention. Paper presented at National Institute of Mental Health, workshop, Washington, DC.

Melton, G. B. (1988b). When scientists are adversaries do participants lose? *Law and Human Behavior, 12,* 191–198.

Melton, G. B., & Gray, J. (1988). Ethical dilemmas in AIDS research. *American Psychologist, 43,* 60–64.

Melton, G. B., Koocher, G. P., & Saks, M. J. (Eds.). (1983). *Children's competence to consent.* New York: Plenum.

Melton, G. B., Pertrila, J., Poythress, N. G., & Slobogin, C. (1987). *Psychological evaluations for the courts*. New York: Guilford.

Merriken v. Cressman, 364 F. Supp. 913 E.D. Pa (1973).

Meyer v. Nebraska, 262 U.S. 390 (1923).

Mills, D. H. (1984). Ethics education and adjudication within psychology. *American Psychologist, 39*, 669–675.

Miranda v. Arizona, 348 U.S. 436 (1966).

Mischel, W. (1971). *Introduction to personality*. New York: Holt, Rinehart & Winston.

Mishkin, B. (1982). The report and recommendations of the National Commission for the Protection of Human Subjects: Research involving children. *Advances in Law and Child Development, 1*, 63–96.

Mitchell, R. G. (1964). The child and experimental medicine. *British Medical Journal, 1*, 721–727.

Morris v. Florida, 456 So. 2d 925 (Fla. Dist. Ct. App. 1984).

Morrissey, J. M., Hofmann, A. D., & Thrope, J. C. (1986). *Consent and confidentiality in the health care of children and adolescents: A legal guide*. New York: Free Press.

National Commission for the Protection of Human Subjects of Biomedical and Behavioral Research. (1977). *Report and recommendations: Research involving children*. (Department of Health, Education, and Welfare Publication No. [05] 77-0004). Washington, DC: U.S. Government Printing Office.

Nebraska v. Wedige, 205 Neb. 687, 289 N.W.2d 538 (1980).

New Jersey v. T.L.O., 105 S. Ct. 733 (1985).

New York City Bar Association Committee on Professional and Judicial Ethics. (1981, February). *Opinion No. 80–23*. New York: New York City Bar Association.

Nielsen v. Regents of the University of California et al. Case No. 655–049, Superior Court of California, County of San Francisco, as amended December 20, 1973.

Noonan, M. J., & Bickel, W. K. (1981). The ethics of experimental design. *Mental Retardation, 19*, 271–274.

Northern Health Region in Current Medicine/Ethical Problems, Working Group. (1986). Consent to treatment by parents and children. *Child Care, Health and Development, 12*, 5–12.

Nuremberg Code. (1946). *Journal of the American Medical Association, 132*, 1090.

Palmore v. Sidoti, 466 U.S. 429 (1984).

Parham v. J.R. 442 U.S. 584 (1979).

PASE v. Hannon, 506 F. Supp. 831, N.D. Ill. (1980).

Pearn, J. H. (1981). The child and clinical research. *Lancet, 2*, 510–512.

Pence, G. E. (1980). Children's dissent to research—a minor matter? *IRB: A Review of Human Subjects Research, 10*, 1–4.

Phillips, J. L. (1975). *The origins of intellect: Piaget's theory.* San Francisco: Freeman.

Pierce v. Society of Sisters, 268 U.S. 510 (1925).

Plotkin, R. (1981). When rights collide: Parents, children, and consent to treatment. *Journal of Pediatric Psychology, 6,* 121–130.

Pope, K. S., Keith-Spiegel, P. C., & Tabachnik, B. G. (1986). Sexual attraction to clients: The human therapist and the (sometimes) inhuman training system. *American Psychologist, 41,* 147–158.

Porter, J. P. (1985). Regulatory considerations when children are involved as subjects in research. *Journal of School Health, 55,* 175–178.

Prince v. Massachusetts, 321 U.S. 158, 170 (1944).

Protecting confidentiality in mediation. (1984). *Harvard Law Review, 98,* 441–459.

Quiner v. Quiner (1967), Court of Appeals of California, Second District.

Ramsey, P. (1976). The enforcement of morals: Nontherapeutic research on children. *Hastings Center Report, 6,* 21–30.

Rae, W. A., & Fournier, C. J. (1986). Ethical issues in pediatric research: Preserving psychosocial care in scientific inquiry. *Children's Health Care, 14,* 242–248.

Reatig, N. (1979). Confidentiality certificates: A measure of privacy protection. IRB, *1*(3), 1–4, 12.

Reatig, N. (1981). DHHS internal policies for reviewing research involving children. *IRB: A Review of Human Subjects Research, 3,* 1–4.

Richardson, G. A., & McCluskey, K. A. (1983). Subject loss in infancy research: How biasing is it? *Infant Behavior and Development, 6,* 235–239.

Roberts, M. C., Maddux, J. E., & Wright, L. (1984). Developmental perspectives in behavioral health. In J. D. Matarazzo, S. M. Weiss, A. J. Herd, N. E. Miller, & S. M. Weiss (Eds.). *Behavioral health: A handbook of health enhancement and disease prevention* (pp. 56–68). New York: Wiley.

Robertson, J. A. (1983). *The rights of the critically ill.* Cambridge, MA: Ballinger.

Rosen, C. E. (1977). Why clients relinquish their rights to privacy under sign-away pressures. *Professional Psychology, 9,* 17–24.

Roth, L. H., Meisel, A., & Lidz, C. W. (1977). Tests of competency to consent to treatment. *American Journal of Psychiatry, 134,* 279–284.

Rothman, D. J., & Rothman, S. M. (1980). The conflict over children's rights. *Hastings Center Report, 10,* 7–10.

Rubenstein, C. (1982). Psychology's fruit flies. *Psychology Today, 16*(7), 83–84.

Rutstein, D. R. (1969). The ethical design of human experiments. *Daedalus, 98*(4), 523–541.

Schafer, A. (1982). The ethics of the randomized clinical trial. *New England Journal of Medicine, 307*(12), 719–724.

Schafer, A. (1984). The randomized clinical trial: For whose benefit? *IRB: A Review of Human Subjects Research, 7*, 4–6.

Schwartz, L. L. (1983). Contested adoption cases: Grounds for conflict between psychology and the law. *Professional Psychology: Research and Practice, 14*, 444–456.

Seeman, J. (1969). Deception in psychological research. *American Psychologist, 24*, 1025–1028.

Shapiro v. Shapiro (1983). 54 Md. App. 477, 458 A.2d 1257.

Sieber, J. E. (1982a). Deception in social research: 1. Kinds of deception and the wrongs they may involve. *IRB: A Review of Human Subjects Research, 4*, 1–6.

Sieber, J. E. (1982b). Deception in social research: 2. Evaluating the potential for harm or wrong. *IRB: A Review of Human Subjects Research, 5*, 1–6.

Sieber, J. E. (1982c). Deception in social research: 3. The nature and limits of debriefing. *IRB: A Review of Human Subjects Research, 6*, 1–6.

Sieber, J. E. (1989). Community intervention research on minors. In the proceedings of the symposium on *Ethical issues in sensitive behavioral research involving minors*. San Mateo, CA, Feb. 14–15. Workshop sponsored by Office for Protection from Research Risks, National Institutes of Health.

Society for Research in Child Development. (1973, Winter). Ethical standards for research with children. *Society for Research in Child Development Newsletter*, pp. 2–3.

Society for Research in Child Development. (1976, Spring). Research ethics: A report by the SRCD Ethics Survey Committee. *Society for Research in Child Development Newsletter*, pp.4–8.

Striker, L. J. (1967). The true deceiver. *Psychological Bulletin, 68*, 13–20.

Swoboda, J. S., Elwork, A., Sales, B. D., and Levine, D. (1978). Knowledge and compliance with privileged communication and child abuse reporting laws. *Professional Psychology, 9*, 448–457.

Tarasoff v. Regents of University of California, 17 Cal. 3d 425, 551 P.2d 334, 131 Cal. Rptr. 14 (1976).

Taub, H. A. (1986). Comprehension of informed consent for research: Issues and directions for future study. *IRB: A Review of Human Subjects Research, 8*, 7–10.

Taylor, L., Adelman, H. S., & Kaser-Boyd, N. (1984). Attitudes toward involving minors in decisions. *Professional Psychology, 15*, 436–449.

Thomasma, D. C., & Mauer, A. M. (1982). Ethical complications of clinical therapeutic research on children. *Social Science and Medicine, 16*, 913–919.

Thompson, R. A. (1989). Vulnerability in research: A developmental perspective on research risk. In the proceedings of the symposium on *Ethical issues in sensitive behavioral research involving minors*. San Mateo, CA, Feb. 14–15. Workshop sponsored by Office for Protection from Research Risks, National Institutes of Health.

Thompson, T. L. (1984). A comparison of methods of increasing parental consent rates in social research. *Public Opinion Quarterly, 48*, 779–787.

Thompson v. County of Alameda, 614 P.2d 728 (Cal. Super. Ct. 1980).

Thompson v. Oklahoma, 487 U.S. ——, 101 L. Ed. 2d 702, 108 S. Ct. (1988).

Thornburgh v. American College of Obstetricians and Gynecologists, No. 84-495 (U.S. pending).

TIMI Study Group. (1985). Thrombolysis in myocardial infarction (TIMI) trial: Phase I findings. *New England Journal of Medicine, 312*, 932–936.

Tinker v. Des Moines Independent Community School District 393 U.S. 503, 89 S. Ct. 733, 21 L. Ed. 2d 731 (1969).

van Eys, J. (1982). Clinical research and clinical care: Ethical problems in the "War on Cancer." *American Journal of Pediatric Hematology/Oncology, 4*, 419–423.

Veatch, R. M. (1987). *The patient as partner*. Bloomington: Indiana University Press.

Wadlington, W. J. (1983). Consent to medical care for minors: The legal framework. In G. B. Melton, G. P. Koocher, & M. J. Saks (Eds.), *Children's competence to consent* (pp.57–73). New York: Plenum.

Wadlington, W. J., Whitebread, C. H., & Davis, S. M. (1983). *Children in the legal system*. Mineola, NY: Foundation Press.

Weinrach, S. G., & Ivey, A. E. (1975). Science, psychology, and deception. *Bulletin of the British Psychological Society, 28*, 263–267.

Weithorn, L. A. (1983a). Children's capacities to decide about participation in research. *IRB: A Review of Human Subjects Research, 5*, 1–5.

Weithorn, L. A. (1983b). Involving children in decisions affecting their own welfare: Guidelines for professionals. In G. B. Melton, G. P. Koocher, & M. J. Saks (Eds.), *Children's competence to consent* (pp. 235–260). New York: Plenum.

Weithorn, L. A. (1984). Children's capacities in legal contexts. In N. D. Reppucci, L. A. Weithorn, E. P. Mulvey, & J. Monahan (Eds.), *Children, mental health and the law* (pp.88–125). Beverly Hills, CA: Sage.

Weithorn, L. A. (1987). *Psychology and child custody determinations: Knowledge, roles, and expertise*. Lincoln: University of Nebraska Press.

Weithorn, L. A., & Campbell, S. B. (1982). The competency of children and adolescents to make informed treatment decisions. *Child Development, 53*, 1589–1598.

Weithorn, L. A., & McCabe, M. A. (1987). Legal and ethical problems in pediatric psychology. In D. K. Routh (Ed.), *The handbook of pediatric psychology* (pp. 567–606). New York: Guilford.

Wells, K., & Sametz, L. (1985). Involvement of institutionalized children in social science research: Some issues and proposed guidelines. *Journal of Clinical Child Psychology, 14*, 245–251.

Wikler, D. (1981). Ethical consideration in randomized clinical trials. *Seminars in Oncology, 8*, 437–441.

Wilson, L. S. (1982). Regulation of research involving children: Origins, costs, and benefits. *Advances in Law and Child Development, 1*, 153–179.

Table of Cases

Subject Index

Author Index